A LITTLE HISTORY OF ECONOMICS

NIALL KISHTAINY

A LITTLE
HISTORY
of
ECONOMICS

YALE UNIVERSITY PRESS
NEW HAVEN AND LONDON

For information about this and other Yale University Press publications, please contact:

U.S. Office: sales.press@yale.edu   yalebooks.com
Europe Office: sales@yaleup.co.uk   yalebooks.co.uk

Typeset in Minion Pro by IDSUK (DataConnection) Ltd
Printed in the United States of America

Library of Congress Cataloging-in-Publication Data

Names: Kishtainy, Niall, author.
Title: A little history of economics / Niall Kishtainy.
Description: First Edition. | New Haven : Yale University Press, 2017. |
    Includes bibliographical references and index.
Identifiers: LCCN 2016042806 | ISBN 9780300206364 (c1 : alk. paper)
Subjects: LCSH: Economics. | Economic history. | Economists.
Classification: LCC HB71 .K527 2017 | DDC 330.09—dc23
LC record available at https://lccn.loc.gov/2016042806

A catalogue record for this book is available from the British Library.

10 9 8 7 6 5 4 3 2 1

Contents

CHAPTER 1

Cool Heads and Warm Hearts

The fact that you're holding this book in your hands puts you in a special position. For a start, you (or whoever gave you this book) had the money to buy it. If you were from a poor country, your family would probably be scraping by on a few dollars a day. Most of your money would go on food and there wouldn't be any left to buy a book. Even if you did get hold of a copy, chances are that it would be useless to you because you wouldn't be able to read it. In Burkina Faso, a poor country in West Africa, less then half of young people can read; only a third of girls can. Instead of learning algebra or languages, a 12-year-old girl there might have spent the day heaving buckets of water to her family's hut. You might not think of you and your family as being especially rich, but to many people around the world spending money on a book and being able to read it would seem as likely as a trip to the moon.

People who burn with curiosity – and perhaps with anger – about this vast difference often turn to economics. Economics is the study of how societies use their resources – the land, coal, people and machines that are involved in making useful goods like bread and shoes. Economics shows why it's quite wrong to say that people in Burkina Faso are poor because they're lazy, as some do. Many of them work very hard, but they were born into an economy which as a whole isn't very good at producing things. Why does Britain have the buildings, books and teachers needed to educate its children when Burkina Faso doesn't? This is an incredibly difficult question and no one has quite got to the bottom of it. Economics tries to.

Here's a stronger reason to be fascinated by economics, and perhaps to come up with your own ideas about it. Economics is a matter of life and death. A baby born today in a rich country has a tiny chance of dying before the age of five. The death of a young child is a rare and shocking event when it happens. In the poorest countries of the world, though, more than 10 per cent of children never make it to the age of five because of a lack of food and medicine. Teenagers in those countries could count themselves lucky to have survived.

The word 'economics' might sound a bit dry, and make you think of a load of boring statistics. But all it's really about is how to help people to survive and to be healthy and educated. It's about how people get what they need to live full, happy lives – and why some people don't. If we can solve basic economic questions, maybe we can help everyone to live better lives.

Economists have a particular way of thinking about resources – that is, the bricks to build a school, the drugs to cure diseases and the books people want. They talk about these things being 'scarce'. The British economist Lionel Robbins once defined economics as the study of scarcity. Rare things like diamonds and white peacocks are scarce, but to economists pens and books are scarce too, even though you can easily find them at home or in your local shop. By scarcity they mean that there's a limited amount, and people's desires are potentially unlimited. If we could, we might go on buying new pens and books forever – but we can't have it all because everything has a cost. This means that we have to make choices.

Let's think a bit more about the idea of cost. Cost isn't just pounds or dollars, though they're important. Imagine a student choosing which subject to study next year. The options are history or geography, but not both. The student chooses history. What's the cost of that choice? It's what you give up: the chance to learn about deserts, glaciers and capital cities. What about the cost of a new hospital? You could add up the prices of the bricks and steel that went into it. But if we think in terms of what we give up, then the cost is the train station that we could have built instead. Economists call this 'opportunity cost', and it's easy to overlook. Scarcity and opportunity cost show a basic economic principle: there are always choices to be made, between hospitals and train stations, shopping malls and football pitches.

Economics, then, is about how we use scarce resources to satisfy needs. But it's more than this. How do the choices facing people change? Those in poor societies face stark ones: a meal for the children or antibiotics for a sick grandmother. In rich countries like America or Sweden they rarely do. They might have to choose between a new watch and the latest iPad. Rich countries face serious economic problems – sometimes firms go bust, workers lose their jobs and struggle to buy clothes for their children – but they're less often matters of life and death. A central question of economics, then, is how societies overcome the worst effects of scarcity – and why some don't do it nearly as rapidly. An attempt at a good answer needs more than a mastery of opportunity cost – being good at working out whether we should have a new hospital or football pitch or whether to buy an iPad or a watch. Your answer would need to draw on all sorts of theories of economics, and a deep knowledge of how different economies actually work in the real world. Meeting history's economic thinkers in this book is a great starting point; their ideas show how wonderfully varied economists' attempts have been.

Economists study 'the economy', obviously. The economy is where resources are used up, new things are made and it's decided who gets what. For example, a manufacturer buys cloth and hires workers to produce T-shirts. Consumers – you and I – go to the shops, and if we have money in our pockets can buy goods like T-shirts (we 'consume' them). We also consume 'services', things that aren't physical objects – haircuts, for example. Most consumers are also workers because they earn money from a job. Firms, workers and consumers are the key elements of an economy. But banks and stock markets – the 'financial system' – also influence how resources are used. Banks lend money to firms – they 'finance' them. When one lends money to a clothes manufacturer to build a new factory, the loan allows the manufacturer to buy cement, which ends up as part of the factory rather than in a new bridge. To raise money, companies sometimes sell 'shares' (or 'stock') in the stock market. When you own a share in Toshiba you own a tiny bit of the company and if Toshiba does well the price of its shares rise and you get richer. Governments are part of the economy, too. They affect how resources are used when they spend money on a new motorway or power station.

In the next chapter we'll meet some of the first people to think about economic questions: the ancient Greeks. The word 'economics' comes from the Greek *oeconomicus* (*oikos*, house, and *nomos*, law or rule). So for the Greeks economics was about how households manage their resources. Today, economics also includes the study of firms and industries. But households and the people who live in them are still fundamental. After all, it's individuals who buy things and who make up the workforce. So economics is the study of humans' behaviour in the economy. If you're given £20 for your birthday how do you decide what to spend it on? What makes a worker accept a new job at a certain wage? Why do some people carefully save their money and others splurge it on a pet palace for their dog?

Economists try to approach these sorts of questions in a scientific way. Perhaps the word 'science' makes you think of bubbling test tubes and equations scribbled on blackboards – rather removed from the question of whether people have enough food. In fact, economists try to explain the economy as scientists do the flight of rockets. Scientists look for physical 'laws' – how one thing causes another – such as one that relates a rocket's weight to how high it will go. Economists look for economic laws, like how the size of the population affects the amount of food available. This is called 'positive economics'. The laws aren't good or bad. They just describe what's there.

If you're thinking that there must be more to economics than this, you're absolutely right. Think of the African children who don't survive their infancy. Is it enough to describe the situation and leave it at that? Surely not! If economists didn't make a judgement, they'd be rather heartless. Another branch of economics is 'normative economics', which says whether an economic situation is good or bad. When you see a supermarket throwing away good food you might judge it bad because it's wasteful. And when you think of the difference between the rich and the poor, you might judge it bad because it's unfair.

When accurate observation and wise judgement come together, economics can be a force for change, for creating richer, fairer societies in which more of us are able to live well. As the British economist Alfred Marshall once said, economists need 'cool heads, but warm hearts'. Yes, describe the world like a scientist, but make sure that you do it with compassion for the human suffering around you – then try to change things.

Today's economics, the kind people study at university, emerged only relatively recently in the thousands of years of human civilisation. It appeared a few centuries ago, when capitalism, the type of economy now found in most countries, was born. Under capitalism, most resources – food, land and people's labour – are bought and sold for money. This buying and selling is called 'the market'. Also, there's a group of people, the capitalists, who own the capital: the money, machines and factories needed to make goods. Another group, the workers, are employed in the capitalists' firms. It's hard now to imagine it any other way. But before capitalism, things were different. People grew their own food instead of buying it. Ordinary people didn't work for firms, but for the lord who controlled the land that they lived on.

Compared with mathematics or literature, then, economics is new. Much of it is about things that concern capitalists: buying, selling and prices. A lot of this book is about this kind of economics. But we'll also look at economic ideas that go back much earlier.

After all, every society, capitalist or not, has to deal with the problem of scarcity. We'll examine changing ideas about the economy, and see how the economy itself changed – how people over time tried to overcome scarcity as they worked in the fields and factories and gathered round their cooking pots.

Do economists always describe the economy and make judgements about it like careful scientists and wise philosophers? They've sometimes been accused of overlooking the hardships faced by disadvantaged groups of people who get left behind as the economy moves forward, women and black people especially. Is that because over history economic thinkers have often come from societies' most advantaged groups? At the beginning of the twenty-first century there was a big economic crisis caused by the reckless activities of banks. Many people blamed economists for not foreseeing it. Some suspected that this was because a lot of them were influenced by those who benefited from an economy dominated by finance and big banks.

Perhaps, then, economists need something else to go with their cool heads and warm hearts: self-critical eyes, the ability to see beyond their own concerns and habitual ways of looking at the world. Studying the history of economics helps us do this because by learning about how the ideas of earlier thinkers came out of their unique concerns and circumstances, we might see more clearly how ours do. That's why bringing history together with ideas is so fascinating – and so vital to creating a world in which more of us live well.

CHAPTER 2

The Soaring Swans

Like all people, the first humans faced the basic economic problem of scarcity, which for them was about finding enough to eat. But there was no 'economy' in the sense of a collection of farms, workshops and factories. Early people survived in the forest by gathering berries and killing animals. It was only when more complex kinds of economies appeared, such as those in ancient Greece and Rome, that people began thinking about questions of economics.

The first economic thinkers were the Greek philosophers, who began the tradition of Western thought of which economics is a part. Their ideas flowered after thousands of years of human struggle to create the first civilisations. Long before them, humans sowed the seeds of economic life by learning to bend nature to their needs. When people first lit fires, for example, they could make new things out of what they found: they fashioned pots from clay, and cooked meals using plants and animals. Then, over 10,000 years ago, came the first economic revolution: bands of humans invented agriculture when they discovered how to grow plants and tame animals. More of them could survive on an area of land, and they clustered together in villages.

From these beginnings, civilisations with complex economies appeared in Mesopotamia, the site of present-day Iraq. An important meaning of 'complex' here is that people don't have to produce their own food. Today, you probably get your food not by growing it yourself but by buying it from those who do. Mesopotamia contained new kinds of people who never harvested barley or milked a goat: the kings who ruled the cities and the priests in charge of the temples.

Economic complexity was possible because people had become so good at growing crops and raising animals that farmers could produce more than they needed for their own survival. The surplus fed the priests and kings. Getting food from the growers to the eaters required organisation. Today it happens through buying and selling with money, but ancient societies fell back on old traditions. Crops were brought to the temples as offerings and shared out by the priests. To organise the distribution of food, the early civilisations invented writing; some of the first examples we have are lists of deliveries of crops by farmers. Once officials could write things down they could take a share of what people produced (in other words, 'tax' them), then use the resources to dig channels to get water to the crops and build tombs to honour the kings.

A few centuries before the birth of Christ, human civilisations had existed in Mesopotamia and in Egypt, India and China, for thousands of years, and the ingredients were present for the new civilisation that appeared in Greece. There, people began to think more deeply about what it means to be a human living in a society. Hesiod, one of the first Greek poets, stated the starting point of economics: 'Gods keep men's food concealed.' This comes back to the idea of scarcity: bread doesn't rain down on us from the sky. To eat we have to grow wheat, harvest it, grind it into flour and then bake it into loaves. Humans must work to stay alive.

A forefather of all thinkers is the Greek philosopher Socrates, whose words we know only through the writings of his disciples. It's said that one night he dreamt of a swan spreading its wings and flying away while hooting loudly. The next day he met Plato, the man who would become his star pupil. Socrates saw in Plato the swan of his dream. The pupil became a teacher of humanity, his thought soaring high and wide for centuries to come.

Plato (428/427–348/347 BC) imagined an ideal society. Its economy would be different from the kind that we now take for granted. And the society in which he actually lived was different from our own. For one thing there was no nation in the way that we understand it. Ancient Greece was a collection of city-states such as Athens, Sparta and Thebes. The Greeks called the city-state the *polis*, which is where our word 'politics' comes from. Plato's ideal society, then, was a compact city rather than a big country. It would be closely organised by its rulers and there'd be little room for markets in which food and labour is bought and sold for a price. Take labour, for example. Today we think of how we use our labour as a choice: perhaps you decide to become a plumber because you like fixing things and the job pays well. In Plato's ideal state, everyone has their place determined at birth. Most people, including slaves, work the land. They're the lowest class, with bronze in their souls, said Plato. Above the farmers Plato put the class of silver-souled warriors. At the top were the rulers, a group of 'philosopher-kings', men with souls of gold. Near Athens, Plato set up his famous Academy to create the wise men fit to rule over the rest of society.

Plato thoroughly distrusted the pursuit of wealth, so much so that in the ideal state soldiers and kings wouldn't be allowed to own private property in case gold and palaces corrupted them. Instead they'd live together and share everything, even their children, who'd be raised in common rather than by their parents. Plato feared that if wealth became too important people would start to compete for it. Eventually the state would be ruled by the rich who'd be envied by the poor. People would end up quarrelling and fighting.

Plato was joined in the Academy by Aristotle, the next soaring swan. Aristotle (384–322 BC) was the first to try to organise knowledge into different fields: science, mathematics, politics and so on. His curiosity ranged over deep questions of logic and all the way to the design of the gills of fish. Some things he said might sound bizarre to us, such as the claim that people with big ears like to gossip, but this is unsurprising for a man who tried to gulp in the whole of the world around him with his mind. For centuries, thinkers considered him to be the ultimate authority and he became known simply as 'The Philosopher'.

Aristotle criticised Plato's plan for society. Instead of imagining the ideal society, he thought about what worked given people's imperfections. He believed that it would be impractical to ban private property as Plato had recommended. It was true, he said, that when people own things they envy each other's possessions and fight over them. If they share everything, though, they'd probably end up fighting even more. Better to let people own their goods because then they'll take better care of them and there'll be fewer disputes about who contributed the most to the common pot.

If people create wealth using the seeds and tools that they own, then how would someone get a new pair of shoes when they don't make shoes? They get them from a shoemaker in exchange for some of their olives. Here Aristotle shines a light on the fundamental particle of the economic universe: the exchange of one good for another. Money helps this, he said. Without it you'd have to lug around olives to swap for the shoes you need, and you'd have to be lucky enough to bump into someone offering shoes and in need of olives. To make it easier, people agree to designate an object, often silver or gold, as the money with which to buy and sell – to trade – useful things. Money creates a measuring rod of economic value – what something is worth – and allows value to be passed from person to person. With money you don't need to find someone who can give you shoes right now in exchange for your olives; you can sell your olives for coins and the next day use the coins to buy a pair of shoes. Coins are standardised nuggets of the metal designated as money. The first were made of electrum, a natural mixture of silver and gold, in the sixth century BC in the kingdom of Lydia, today a part of Turkey. Money really took off in ancient Greece, though. Even Olympic champions were honoured with money, receiving 500 drachmas each. By the fifth century BC there were nearly 100 mints making coins. Their river of silver coins helped keep the wheels of trade turning.

Aristotle realised that once people exchange goods using money, there's a difference between what something is used for (olives for food) and what something can be exchanged for (olives for a price). It's perfectly natural for households to grow and eat olives, and to sell them for money so that they can obtain the other goods that they need, he said. When households see that they can make money from selling olives they might start to grow them purely for profit (the difference between how much they sell the olives for and what it cost to grow them). This is commerce: buying and selling things to make money. Aristotle was suspicious of it, and thought that trade that goes beyond obtaining what's needed for the household was 'unnatural'. By selling olives to make a profit, households make money at others' expense. As we'll see later in our story, to modern economists this is hard to understand because when buyers and sellers compete with each other to trade things, society gains. In Aristotle's time, though, there simply weren't all the competing buyers and sellers that seem so normal today.

Aristotle pointed out that wealth that came from 'natural' economic activities has a limit because once there's enough to satisfy the needs of the household there's no need for any more. On the other hand, there's no limit to the unnatural accumulation of wealth. You can go on selling more olives, and find all sorts of new things to sell. What's to stop you accumulating riches as high as the sky? Absolutely nothing – except the risk to your wisdom and virtue. 'The type of character which results from wealth is that of a prosperous fool,' said Aristotle.

There was one thing worse than growing olives to create an ever-larger pile of coins, and that was using money itself to earn more money. Just as the natural use of olives is to eat them (or to exchange them for something that the household needs), then the natural use of money is as a means of exchange. Making money out of money by lending it to someone for a price (for an 'interest rate') is the most unnatural economic activity possible; as we'll see in the next chapter, Aristotle's attack on moneylending influenced economic thinking for centuries to come. To Aristotle, then, it was clear that virtue lay with the honest farmers, not the clever bankers.

As Plato and Aristotle were writing, Greece was moving away from their visions for the economy. The city-states were in crisis. Athens and Sparta had fought a long war. The philosophers' economic designs were ways of hanging on to past glory. Plato's solution was a disciplined state, Aristotle's a practical guide to saving society from too much commerce. Greeks were becoming money-minded, even as Aristotle and Plato condemned the love of money. It's said that a ruler of Sparta discouraged moneymaking by having the city's currency in the form of iron bars that were so heavy they had to be pulled around by oxen. But across much of the Greek world commerce flourished. Cities traded olive oil, grains and many other goods across the waters of the Mediterranean. After Aristotle and Plato, the currents of trade flowed wider still, pulled in the wake of Aristotle's most famous pupil, Alexander the Great, whose armies swept across the Mediterranean world and beyond, spreading Greek culture throughout a vast new empire.

Like all empires, the great Greek civilisation and that of the Romans which followed it eventually died out, and new thinkers emerged. After the fall of the Roman Empire in the fifth century AD, economic thought was taken forward by Christian monks around Europe who kept learning alive in their remote monasteries.

CHAPTER 3

God's Economy

In the Bible, people have to work to survive as a result of sin. When they were in the Garden of Eden, life was easy for Adam and Eve. They drank from a river and ate fruit from the trees. They sat around all day and didn't have to do very much. But one day they disobeyed God and he sent them out of the garden – and from a life of plenty they fell into one of scarcity. 'By the sweat of your brow will you eat your food,' God told Adam. From then on, people had to work to survive. However, Jesus warned that when they worked, people were in danger of committing sins that might shut them out of heaven. They might only care about getting rich. They might get jealous of other people's wealth. They could end up loving clothes, jewels and money more than God.

At either end of the long medieval age sat two Christian thinkers, intellectual giants of their time. They thought long and hard about what Christ's teaching meant. What did it say about how Christians should participate in the economy? At the beginning was St Augustine of Hippo (354–430), a restless young teacher who matured into a wise holy man. Towards the end came St Thomas

Aquinas (1224/25–1274), an Italian monk who lived when a new commercial civilisation was emerging in Italy. His writings gave guidance to Christians about how to live in this changing society.

Augustine was born into the dying Roman Empire and he had one foot in the ancient world, the other in the emerging medieval one. After long wanderings and soul-searching, he converted to Christianity. The Greeks had thought about the society and economy of cities of kings, small states with wise rulers. Augustine transformed this into the City of God, at the top of which sits Christ, the saviour of humanity. The City of God was governed by human laws as well as God's laws. That was because people had to take part in the ordinary, everyday activity of making money. Wealth was a gift from God to sinful people who needed it to survive. The best life would be had by giving up possessions, which some Christians did by living without money as hermits or in communities of monks. But in an imperfect world, people have to own property, and then it was important not to love one's possessions, to understand that they were simply the means to live a good and holy life.

Augustine's ideas helped to shape the medieval society which replaced that of the Romans. The Romans had created a vast empire. Their cities were marvels of elegance and engineering. Rome alone had 1,000 public baths fed with water by aqueducts. After Augustine died, the empire was overrun by invaders, and for the next few centuries trade collapsed. Communities turned inwards, growing food for themselves rather than buying and selling it. Towns shrank and the Romans' bridges and roads crumbled. From the single cloth of the empire came a jumbled patchwork of local rulers. The common thread was the new Christian faith and the teachings of men such as Augustine.

Another part of medieval society was an economic system that became known as feudalism. Rulers needed warriors to hold back hordes of horseback invaders. It was expensive to maintain warriors, so kings gave them land in return for their loyalty. The warriors promised to fight for the king when he needed them. From here a whole system of production developed which was based not on money, but on promises made between the rulers and the ruled. God's economy on earth was arranged as a 'chain of being'. This was the medieval view of the universe as organised in a strict pecking order. At the top was God and Christ; their representatives on earth were first the pope and then the kings who gave land to the great lords, and at the bottom were the peasants who worked the land. The peasants would hand over crops to the lord, keeping some for themselves. The economy was governed by religion rather than by the profits and prices that rule today; its authorities were men like Augustine and those who came after him, the learned monks and church preachers.

Thomas Aquinas was one of them. He was born into a rich family, but as a young man joined the Dominicans, an order of monks who lived without money or possessions. His parents hated this and had him kidnapped and locked up in one of their castles. They even put a prostitute in his room to try to make him forget about becoming a monk, but he refused to give in to temptation. Instead he prayed and wrote books about the methods of logic. Eventually his parents gave up and released him, and he moved to Paris where he continued his religious and intellectual quest.

Aquinas pictured the chain of being as a beehive, with the bees' roles given by God: some gather honey, some build the walls of the hive, others serve the queen bee. The human economy was like this. Some people work the land, some people pray and others fight for the king. The important thing was not to be greedy and not to envy other people's money.

Just as Augustine had realised, in a world of sin people need to own things in order to make a living for themselves and their families. It was fine to sell something for profit as long as the money was put to good use, said Aquinas; if someone had more money than they needed then they had to give some to the poor. Suppose that someone was making their living by selling meat. The question that Aquinas tried to answer was what was a 'just price' for the meat? What was the fair, morally correct amount to charge customers? Aquinas said that it wasn't the highest price that a seller would be able to get, perhaps by lying about the quality of the meat.

Cheating was a constant worry in medieval times: one Englishman complained that butchers in London had taken to painting blood onto the eyes of rotting sheep to make them look fresh. Aquinas said that a price agreed under such conditions would be unjust; a just one was that normally charged in a community without any tricks or powerful sellers who dominated trade.

Like thinkers before him, Aquinas believed that the worst economic sin was 'usury': the lending out of money for a price (in other words, at a rate of interest). Usury was condemned by the medieval church. Priests who buried moneylenders in holy ground could be expelled from the church, and moneylenders would go to hell along with the thieves and murderers. One preacher told the story of a moneylender who asked to be buried with his treasure. After he died, his wife dug up his grave to retrieve the money. She saw demons shoving coins – now turned into burning coals – down her husband's throat.

The medieval churchmen said that lending money for interest was stealing because money was 'barren': it was infertile, and so couldn't reproduce. Leave it in a pile and it doesn't breed like a flock of sheep does. If you took twenty-five coins back from a man you'd lent twenty-two coins to, you were taking back three coins too many. The three coins rightly belonged to the man. Aquinas, like the thinkers of ancient Greece, said that the proper use of money was for buying and selling. It was wrong to try to make it breed through the trick of charging interest on it so that the amount owed to you gets bigger. When money is used to buy and sell things, the buying and selling 'uses up' the money. It's just like when you use bread for its purpose of eating – you use up the bread. (It's different with a house because you can live in a house without using it up.) It's wrong to make someone pay for bread and to pay for the use of the bread. That's making them pay twice. In the same way it's wrong to make someone pay back the money you lent them and make them pay you interest on top of that. Even worse, usury is a sin that never stops. At least murderers stop murdering when they're asleep. The sins of moneylenders go on and on as they lie in bed and the debts owed to them grow ever larger.

Aquinas was writing at a time when Europe was rediscovering trade and commerce. A few centuries before he was born the population began to grow and towns came back to life. Inventions such as heavy ploughs and new kinds of horse harnesses helped farmers get more out of the land. Waterwheels began to turn on the rivers, powering mills for grinding corn. Communities broke out of their isolation and started trading with each other, and money once more helped to stimulate the buying and selling of goods.

In the great cities of Venice and Florence the medieval chain of being was stretched and strained by new kinds of people: the merchants who bought and sold goods for profit and the bankers who dealt in money. No longer was society just made up of those who prayed, those who farmed and those who fought. The town dwellers put sparks under the embers of commerce and now they burst into flame. Ships took glass and wool to Asia and brought back silks, spices and precious stones. Venice created the first commercial empire since ancient times.

As trade flourished, so did finance. In Venice and Genoa, merchants stored their coins in the secure vaults of money-changers. Merchants could then settle debts by having the money-changers transfer money between their accounts. They also obtained loans from them. In this way, the money-changers had turned themselves into the first bankers – but also into sinful moneylenders. Another development was to help deal with the risks involved in sending expensive cargoes across dangerous seas. Merchants developed insurance: paying someone an amount of money in return for them promising to compensate you for losses caused by bad luck, such as your ship sinking after a storm.

The buzzing towns weakened feudalism because peasants left the land and moved to the cities to work for money. The buzz started to drown out traditional church teachings, too. The patron saint of Milan was Ambrose, who'd commanded death to the moneylenders, but it did little to discourage Milan's townsfolk from getting rich by lending money. Economic life came to be governed more by money and profit, less by tradition. Even the monks began to see that moneylending was essential to the economy and that it wouldn't happen unless lenders were paid for it. Aquinas said that interest on loans was in fact sometimes acceptable. It was fine for lenders to charge it to make up for the profits they had to give up when they lent out their money. Gradually the churchmen came to see that there was a difference between usury – high interest rates that ruin the borrower – and reasonable rates that were needed for banks to work.

At the beginning of the eleventh century the pope said that merchants could never enter heaven. At the end of the following century the pope made a merchant called Homobonus a saint. The idea that to be close to God you had to be poor started to die out. Jesus told his disciples that they couldn't serve both God and money, but by the time of Aquinas the merchants believed that they could. In 1253 an Italian firm began its handwritten accounts with the words 'In the name of God and of profit'. God's economy was merging with the new world of commerce.

CHAPTER 4

Going for Gold

In the spring of 1581 the English merchant and explorer Francis Drake held a banquet on-board his ship, the *Golden Hind*. The *Hind* had just taken Drake and his crew around the world and survived a dangerous three-year voyage. Now docked on the River Thames, the ship had been scrubbed and decorated with banners in preparation for the arrival of the guest of honour and Drake's patron, Queen Elizabeth I. As soon as the queen stepped aboard she ordered Drake to kneel in front of her. An attendant touched him on both shoulders with a gilded sword, making common Francis Drake – born poor and brought up by pirates – into Sir Francis, thereby securing his position as a symbol of England's great military power at sea.

Elizabeth had sent Drake off on his expedition instructing him to seek revenge on her enemy, King Philip of Spain. Cunning Drake had done his best, attacking Spanish ships around the globe. He returned home with a huge haul of booty including gold, silver and pearls – now under royal safekeeping in the Tower of London.

At that time, the monarchs of Europe were creating modern nations out of the medieval patchwork of lands under the control of different princes and dukes. The nations competed with each other to be the strongest. Spain was Europe's leading power and now the Dutch and the English were coming up behind. At that time, too, merchants like Drake were gaining power and influence like never before. Merchants helped to enrich their monarchs, and monarchs paid for the merchants' voyages. Elizabeth's knighting of Drake on the deck of his ship symbolises the alliance between the rulers and the merchants.

The alliance came to be called 'mercantilism' (from the Latin word for merchant). It emerged when thinkers began to turn away from medieval religion towards reason and science. In earlier times, writers on economic questions had been monks who were rather removed from the hurly-burly of commerce, but now new economic thinkers appeared who were less interested in religion. They were practical people, often merchants or royal officials, who wrote about how kings and queens could best look after the wealth of their nations. One of them was a merchant named Gerard de Malynes (c.1586–1641) to whom Drake once sold pearls looted during a battle with the Spanish. The most famous was the Englishman Thomas Mun (1571–1641) who as a young man carried out trade around the Mediterranean. Once, near Corfu, he was captured by the Spanish and his colleagues feared that he was going to be burnt at the stake. Luckily they managed to get him released and Mun went on to become a wealthy, influential man.

The mercantilists held a hodgepodge of beliefs rather than a fully developed economic theory. Economists nowadays often ridicule them for not understanding the most basic economic truths. For example, what do you actually mean when you say that a country is rich? A basic version of mercantilism says that wealth is gold and silver, so a rich country is one with a lot of it. Here the criticism is that the mercantilists commit the 'Midas fallacy'. In Greek legend, the god Dionysus granted King Midas a wish. Midas asked that everything he touched would turn to gold; when he tried to eat, his food did exactly that, and hunger threatened. The story tells us that it's foolish to see wealth in the glitter of gold rather than in loaves and meat. You could end up starving, or like Smaug, the dragon in J.R.R. Tolkien's *The Hobbit*, dazzled into sitting on a pile of gold, doing nothing all day except counting coins and breathing fire at treasure hunters.

Even so, for centuries explorers looked for gold and monarchs tried to build up their stocks of it. Europe's original explorers, a century before Drake, were the Portuguese and Spanish, and one of them, Hernán Cortés, knew a thing or two about the attraction of gold when he said, 'We Spaniards suffer a sickness of the heart that only gold can cure.' They opened Europe's gates to a golden flood from the late 1400s when their explorers sailed across the Atlantic and discovered the New World of the Americas. There they found ancient civilisations chock-full of gold and silver. The explorers attacked the cities, murdered their inhabitants and brought the treasure back to Spain. They ruled over the new lands to keep the gold flowing. Spain built up a mountain of treasure and became the mightiest nation in Europe. To the English, Spain became something like Smaug: a fierce hoarder of riches, with an apparently invincible skin but with weak points that could be attacked. Men like Drake made a living out of trying to pierce Spain's hide. Eventually it turned into all-out war.

Modern economists criticise the mercantilists for being obsessed with gold instead of the goods that we need to live. Today we measure how rich a nation is in terms of the amount of food, clothes and other goods that its businesses produce. We no longer pay for things using gold. Instead we use 'paper money': pound notes and dollar bills which in themselves are worthless. Our coins, too, are made out of cheap metals worth much less than the actual value of the coins. Notes and coins are valuable simply because we all agree that they are. But in the days of the mercantilists gold was the only way of buying things, and as commerce expanded more of the useful things that people needed, whether food, land or labour, had to be bought with it. Nowadays governments can create money by printing more of it; back then kings and queens had to find actual gold to pay for the armies and castles needed to defend their borders. So in their love of gold the mercantilists weren't as misguided as they're sometimes made out to be. Economic ideas are to do with the circumstances that societies find themselves in, and long ago those circumstances were quite different from our own – something that's easy to forget when we look back into the past.

Malynes wrote a book entitled *A Treatise of the Canker of England's Common Wealth* which followed the mercantilist line that the nation needed a healthy stock of gold. To Malynes, England's economic disease (its 'canker') was too many purchases of foreign goods and too few sales of English goods to foreigners. People in England buy wine from winemakers in France using gold; they earn gold when they sell their wool to the French. When England buys many foreign goods and doesn't sell many of its own goods to foreigners, the country's stock of gold shrinks. Malynes's cure was to put restrictions on the outflow of gold to preserve the nation's stock. They were common policies at the time; some governments, like that of Spain, made the taking of gold and silver out of the country punishable by death.

But in his most famous book, *England's Treasure by Forraign Trade*, Mun said that the best way for England to get gold was not by restricting the flow of treasure or, indeed, by Drake's method of stealing from foreign ships, but rather by selling to foreigners as many goods as possible. Countries do well at this when they get good at making things. The aim was to achieve a favourable 'balance of trade' in which the value of exports (goods going out) exceeded that of imports (goods coming in). From the sixteenth century, with sturdier, faster ships, the Spanish, Portuguese, English, Dutch and French competed for dominance in foreign trading to improve their balance of trade. Their crafts travelled back and forth along new routes, transporting sugar, cloth and gold across the Atlantic Ocean, and capturing millions of Africans to be sold as slaves to plantation owners in the Americas.

Governments took steps, supported by the mercantilists, to encourage exports and to discourage imports. Imported goods were subject to taxes, making them more expensive, which made people buy more locally produced goods. There were 'sumptuary' laws, too, which banned expensive (sumptuous) products. In England, show-offs could be put in the stocks for wearing silks and satins; many of the illegal luxuries were foreign imports.

As explorers and armies conquered new lands, rulers gave merchants the right to trade with the territories. Sea voyages were risky, so a single person wouldn't want to finance them alone. Rulers allowed the merchants to set up special companies in which a group of investors each contributed money and each received a share of the profits. The companies led the push into the foreign lands, earning wealth and fame for themselves and their rulers. The English East India Company, founded in 1600, of which Mun was an official, was one of them. The company turned into a powerful organisation and helped England to establish an empire in India.

By protecting them from imported goods and helping them to export their own goods, governments helped the merchants get rich. The mercantilist writers argued that what was good for the merchants was good for the nation. Here we see how economic ideas sometimes end up favouring certain groups in society. By restricting imports, mercantilism favoured businesspeople over workers. When imports are taxed, the country's businesses make more money, but ordinary people end up paying more for the food and clothes that they need. This is another reason why later thinkers thought the mercantilists were wrong. In a few chapters we'll meet Adam Smith, who is often considered to be the father of modern economics. He thought that the task of economists was to uncover objective laws about how the economy worked and he said that the mercantilists failed to do this because they mainly argued for their own interests. What was good for merchants wasn't always good for the nation, said Smith.

The mercantilists thought that imports were bad, though economists today think that's nonsense. Back then, the view was that if England sells nails to the Dutch then England's gain (payment for the nails) is Holland's loss. But imports aren't bad if what Dutch people want is English nails – or Russian caviar and French cheese. Often imports are essential to economic progress, for example if strong foreign nails are used to build the carriages needed to transport food from the countryside to the towns. So if England sells nails to the Dutch then both England and Holland gain: England earns money and Holland obtains good cheap nails.

Smith attacked mercantilism at the end of the eighteenth century. At the same time it suffered another blow when Britain's American colonies broke away. Britain's control of the colonies had given its merchants a guaranteed market in which to sell their goods, but this came to an end when the colonies rebelled against British rule and declared themselves independent.

Thinkers like Mun straddled two ages. At one end was the medieval era in which economic life was local and shaped more by religion and personal ties than by money. At the other was the coming of an industrial age in which money ruled and economic life expanded across regions and the globe. The mercantilists linked the two. They were some of the first to emphasise concerns about resources and money over moral ones, the hallmark of much economic thought after them. They didn't worry about whether the pursuit of wealth was allowed by biblical teaching. To them, money was the new god. As the men of commerce became more powerful, others mourned the passing of old ways of life in which what was valued wasn't trading and making money, but chivalry: the honour and bravery of knights and kings. 'The age of chivalry is gone,' said the Irish statesman and writer Edmund Burke in 1790. 'That of . . . economists and calculators has succeeded; and the glory of Europe is extinguished for ever.'

CHAPTER 5

Nature's Bounty

At the Palace of Versailles one afternoon in 1760, François Quesnay (1694–1774) was in a state of despair. His friend and intellectual collaborator, the Marquis de Mirabeau, had just published a book which had annoyed a lot of people. Called *The Theory of Taxation*, it sounded really rather dull. But it had got Mirabeau thrown into prison. Quesnay was the doctor of Madame de Pompadour, King Louis XV's favourite mistress. A few years earlier, at the age of 60, he'd become (with Mirabeau's help) the leading figure in a group of thinkers who gathered in Mirabeau's palace every Tuesday to talk ideas. They were the world's first 'school' of economists. Quesnay was a well-known figure in the royal court and he made his powerful criticisms of the French economy in a respectful way. But Mirabeau was a hothead: in his book he trumpeted Quesnay's proposal that taxes on France's peasant farmers be done away with and the aristocrats taxed instead. The king was furious and had Mirabeau locked up. Madame de Pompadour tried to soothe her worried doctor, telling him that she'd tried to calm the king and that it would all blow over. Quesnay gloomily remarked to her that whenever he was in the presence of the king all he could remember was that 'this is a man who can have my head cut off'.

As Mirabeau had discovered, taxes are a delicate matter. Rulers have to tax their subjects. How else to pay for their court and for soldiers to defend the realm? France in those days spent lots of money fighting wars and needed even more to pay for the king and noblemen's splendid castles, banquets and jewellery. First, though, there's the problem of who to tax, then of how much to tax them. The ruler has to keep the powerful aristocrats on side, so taxing them isn't easy. If taxes on the peasants become too heavy, they might stop working – or worse, they might rebel. Jean-Baptiste Colbert, the previous king's finance minister a century earlier, had this balancing act in mind when he said: 'The art of taxation consists in so plucking the goose as to obtain the largest amount of feathers with the least possible amount of hissing.' Quesnay believed that the French goose – French society and its economy – had been plucked so hard that it was practically bald. A few decades later the goose hissed loudly and rose up in revolution. For now, though, it wasn't so much hissing as dying. Compared to Britain, France's agriculture was backward and unproductive. The peasant farmers were living a wretched existence. Life in the countryside was a long, hard grind full of poverty and famine. Quesnay blamed the high taxes imposed on the farmers which went to the royal court and the aristocrats. In contrast, the aristocrats and the wealthy clergy didn't have to pay any taxes at all.

Quesnay said that agriculture was special. Nature, harnessed in the fields, rivers and hunting grounds, was the ultimate source of a nation's wealth. This is why the ideas of his circle of thinkers, the first to call themselves economists, came to be known as 'physio-cracy', meaning 'rule by nature'. The physiocrats said that wealth was the wheat and pigs produced by the land. Farmers use their crops, or the earnings from selling them, to feed themselves. In addition they sometimes produce a surplus that can be sold to other people. Quesnay believed that the surplus was the life-force of the economy. He called it the 'net product': it was what was left over from farming production (the total product) after the farmers had taken what they needed. He said that the net product could only be produced by people alongside nature: by the fisherman making a catch in the river, by the shepherd grazing sheep in the grasslands.

The physiocrats believed that the net product sprang forth from the economy according to laws of nature which were unchanging and God-given. It was unwise for a ruler to try to tamper with them, but that was exactly what the French monarchy had done, they said. It had bled the peasants dry and hobbled the country's agriculture. Even worse, while the farmers were exploited, the state showered the craftsmen and merchants in the towns with privileges. France had a maze of laws designed to build up its industry, in large part by protecting manufacturers from competition at home and from abroad. Much of it was along the lines suggested by the mercantilist thinkers whom we met in the last chapter.

Merchants and craftsmen defended their privileges through their 'guilds'. Guilds were organisations going back to medieval times, and they were often very powerful. A look at Paris some decades earlier shows how far the guilds would go to protect their members' position. In June 1696 the city's button-makers had been in uproar. They were barging into tailors' shops searching for illegal buttons that threatened their domination of the trade in silk buttons. The problem was that some enterprising tailors had begun to make buttons out of wool. The guild of button-makers complained and the authorities issued a ban on woollen buttons. The shopkeepers of Paris ignored the ban, and now the wardens of the guild were hunting down rebellious tailors, and even trying to arrest anyone in the street found wearing woollen buttons. Today it's amazing to think that a manufacturers' association had such power over what people were allowed to buy. The privileges enjoyed by the button-makers helped them make money. The physiocrats believed that manufacturers' profits were possible only because of the privileges given to them, not because they'd created any real surplus.

Manufacturing industries were in fact completely incapable of creating a surplus, said Quesnay. Button makers earn a profit from selling buttons only because of the labour and silk they use up in making them. All they do is transform what nature has already created. Quesnay therefore called manufacturing a 'sterile' activity. What was worse was that the French state's promotion of industry had taken resources away from productive farms and put them into many sterile industries. He was even more critical of the bankers and merchants, who in his view were economic parasites who shuffled around the value created by other people without contributing any of their own.

Quesnay, doctor as he was, saw the economy as a giant organism, with the precious economic surplus acting as its vital blood supply. To explain the idea he made the first economic 'model', a simplified picture of the economy. Quesnay created it in his ingenious *Tableau Economique* (economic table). He drew a series of zigzags to represent the circulation of resources around the economy. Farmers produced the surplus, and paid it in the form of rent to the aristocrats who owned the land and who then bought silk buttons and silver candlesticks from the craftsmen. The craftsmen in turn bought food from the farmers, so completing the cycle. The economy was a circular flow of surplus between farmers, landowners and craftsmen. When the surplus increases, more resources flow between them and the economy grows. When the surplus falls the economy shrinks, just what the physiocrats believed had happened in France.

Quesnay's zigzags impressed and baffled people. Once Mirabeau had worked out what they meant he declared Quesnay to be the wisest man in Europe, as clever as Socrates. The table was certainly influential: later economists including Adam Smith praised it, and to this day the idea of a circulation of resources between workers, companies and consumers is fundamental to our understanding of the economy.

The doctor had a cure for France's illness. The main thing was to increase the surplus produced in the economy. Mirabeau had landed himself in hot water trying to explain just how to do it. Quesnay's zigzags showed the problem with taxing the farmers. Higher taxes left them with fewer seeds to sow the following year and less money to spend on improving their tools. If the landowning aristocrats alone were taxed then the farmers would be left with more resources with which to cultivate the land. This would help to increase the overall surplus in the economy. In the end, even the aristocrats would benefit because the economy would get bigger, an argument that had fallen on deaf ears when the unlucky Mirabeau was imprisoned.

As well as being oppressed by heavy taxes, the farmers weren't allowed to export corn and had to follow rules on how they could sell it to their own countrymen. The restrictions lowered the price they earned, reducing the surplus still further. Quesnay urged the state to release agriculture from all the stifling controls, and to abolish the privileges enjoyed by the merchants. He was arguing for a policy of *laissez-faire*, literally meaning 'allow to do'; we still use the French phrase today to describe a hands-off economic policy by the government. The physiocrats had some influence on policy, for example when the French government in the 1760s made it easier for farmers to sell their corn. Later, Quesnay's school of thought went into decline, and he retreated from practical questions of economics to the abstract delights of geometry.

Quesnay was thoroughly modern in trying to find laws to describe the behaviour of the economy and in depicting them in models; today this is the method of economics. Before him, the economy was seen through the lens of religion and tradition or, when religion was left out (as by the mercantilists), through a fog of conflicting ideas – hardly a clear set of principles. In arguing that the economy was often best left alone, he anticipated a belief of many of today's economists: that it's often best for the government not to meddle in the economy, for example, by imposing lots of heavy taxes. He was revolutionary in locating the source of economic value firmly in real things – wheat, pigs and fish – rather than in money alone. But by restricting the source of value to agriculture the physiocrats were stuck in the past. They were writing just before an economic revolution that was to transform Europe, in which manufacturers would create value by making goods more cheaply, and by inventing new ones. Nature's bounty would soon bear fruit in the factories, not just in the rivers and fields.

In the end Quesnay was both a critic and a defender of France's economic system. He was bold to argue for taxes on France's aristocrats: not having to pay taxes was a privilege that they held dear and an important symbol of their status in society. He was bold, too, for criticising France's kings for smothering their economy. (In the end, Quesnay's worries about annoying the king didn't come to much. After Mirabeau had disgraced himself with his book, Madame de Pompadour helped get him released, and Quesnay made it to a ripe old age, outliving his king by a few months.) Although Quesnay risked upsetting the rich and powerful, he was loyal to them. He spent his days padding along palace corridors to audiences with the king and Madame de Pompadour. He was very much a part of Europe's 'old regime' of kings and queens, and believed in the division of society into classes of aristocrats and peasants. So even though he urged the king to alter his approach to the economy, he still wanted an all-powerful monarch to rule over everything. Even bold economists like him often have to think within the terms of the most powerful people in their societies.

After Quesnay died, France's aristocrats got swept away in streams of blood when the mighty revolution of 1789 shattered the old regime of kings, dukes and peasants. Economists discarded Quesnay's faith in the absolute authority of monarchs, but he'd cleared a path for them towards today's modern form of economics.

CHAPTER 6

The Invisible Hand

The Scottish philosopher Adam Smith (1723–90) was known for getting so lost in thought that he'd sometimes forget where he was. His friends would notice him talking to himself, his lips moving and his head nodding, as if he was testing out some new idea. One morning he woke up and started walking around the garden of his house in the small Scottish town of Kirkcaldy, deep in concentration. Wearing only his dressing gown, he wandered onto the road, and walked on until he reached the next town 12 miles away. He was only brought back to his senses by the sound of church bells ringing for the Sunday service.

He had good reason to be caught up in his thoughts. He'd moved away from the buzz of the cities where he'd made his name as a philosopher to write what would become arguably the most celebrated book in the history of economics. It led some to call him the father of modern economics. Fuelled by bracing walks and sleepless nights, the hefty book was published in 1776 and called *The Wealth of Nations*.

In it Smith posed one of the fundamental questions of economics. Is self-interest compatible with a good society? To understand what this means, let's compare the workings of society with those of a football team. A good football team needs good players, obviously. Good players do more than simply dribble and shoot well. They know how to play as a team. If you're a defender you stay back and protect the goal; if you're an attacker you move forward and try to score, and so on. In a bad team players only care about personal glory: they only want to score goals themselves so they all rush after the ball rather than spreading out and helping each other score. The result is chaos on the pitch and very few goals.

Society is a team of millions of people who work together and trade together. What does it take to make that team work well? If economics is like football, then what society needs is for people to work for the team, in the interest of society as a whole. What it doesn't need is people caring mainly for themselves – for their self-interest – like footballers obsessed with personal glory. For example, instead of trying to make as much money as possible, bakers would ensure that their neighbours had enough bread for their dinner. Butchers would take on new assistants not because they really needed them, but because their friends needed jobs. Everyone would be nice to each other and society would be a place of harmony.

Smith turned this upside down. He argued that society does well when people act in their own self-interest. Instead of trying to be nice all the time, do what's best for you and in the end more people will benefit. 'It is not from the benevolence of the butcher, the brewer, or the baker, that we expect our dinner, but from their regard to their own interest,' he said. You get your dinner from the baker not because bakers are nice, kind people. Some are, some aren't. It doesn't really matter either way. What matters is that you get bread because bakers pursue their own self-interest by selling it in order to earn money. In turn, bakers make a living because you pursue your own self-interest by buying bread. You don't care about the baker and the baker doesn't care about you. You probably don't even know each other. People benefit each other not because they're like the Good Samaritan who wants to helps strangers but because they're doing what's best for themselves. In the end, self-interest leads to social harmony rather than chaos.

There's another important difference between a football team and an economy. A football team needs a manager to organise its players. Think of the manager as taking the players by the hand, as it were, and leading them to different areas of the pitch, defenders at the back, strikers at the front and so on. The manager's guiding hand ensures that the team plays well. But no one does the same in the economy. No one tells bakers how many loaves to bake, brewers what kind of beer to brew. They decide for themselves on the basis of what they think will make them money. Society functions just fine like that. It seems as if there must be the hand of a manager organising things, but when you try to find it, it isn't there. To describe the situation Smith came up with one of the most famous phrases in economics. He said it's as if society is guided by an 'invisible hand'.

At this point you might be thinking: what about the government? Doesn't it guide the economy? It's true, it does to some extent. Wherever you're from, there's likely to be a government that does all sorts of things. A later part of our story will be about just what, exactly, it does. (As we'll also see, in a few societies – 'communist' ones – the government took over completely and told everyone what to do all the time.) Even so, the economy of your country probably has a lot in common with what Smith talked about. Next time you're in your local shop, look around at the crates of tomatoes, cartons of milk and piles of newspapers. How did they get there? Because the shopkeeper decided to buy them in order to sell them to people like you who want them. No one – not the government, not anyone – told the shopkeeper what to do.

It's tempting to think of Smith's idea of the invisible hand as 'greed is good'. This would be a distortion of it, though. Smith saw that commercial society involved a range of good human qualities. Bakers and butchers are often nice to other people. They feel sad when their friends get ill or lose money. That's how people develop a sense of right and wrong. Commerce wouldn't work very well if people were totally selfish all the time: bakers would lie about the weight of their loaves and brewers would water down their beer.

Lying and cheating would become normal, and chaos would result. It's when people are honest and reliable that their acting in their own self-interest benefits society.

Smith's invisible hand works, then, when decent people have the freedom to exchange goods with each other – to buy and sell things. The urge to exchange things sets humans apart from other animals. You never see dogs swapping bones, but humans do that sort of thing all the time. I give you bread in exchange for some of your beer (or more likely I sell my bread for money and then go and buy some beer). One result of all this exchange is that people specialise in particular jobs: a 'division of labour' emerges. In a small village, everyone might have started off baking their own bread and brewing their own beer. Then some people became good at baking bread, had more than they needed and sold the extra for beer. Eventually they stopped brewing beer for themselves entirely and just baked bread to sell, buying all the beer they needed from those good at brewing beer, to the benefit of all.

The division of labour was taking on a new form when Smith was writing. In Britain, businessmen set up factories powered by massive waterwheels. Some were several storeys high and employed hundreds of people. Each room contained tools and workers to carry out a particular stage of production. Smith explained how specialised labour improves the efficiency of the economy. Imagine trying to make a pin, he said. First you'd have to draw out the wire, then file the end into a point. Then you'd have to make the head and attach it to the body of the pin. At the end you'd have to package the finished pins. Smith observed eighteen separate stages to making a pin. On your own you'd probably struggle to make more than one or two pins in a day. If a group of you made pins together, however, each could work on a separate task and get really good at it, particularly if you had special machines for the various tasks. Together you'd be able to produce many pins each day. When the system of specialised work spreads through the economy, many kinds of goods can be made at a lower cost.

Specialisation deepens when markets do. In a settlement of only ten people with no links to the outside world, the market is small and there'd be little point in having some people spending all day filing the ends of pins, others just making the heads. There'd be no need for a separate baker, brewer and butcher either. When markets spread, the village gets connected with others and specialised work becomes profitable. A large town allows a really complicated division of labour in which architects and piano tuners, rope makers and gravediggers are all able to make a living. All of this happens through the invisible hand when people buy and sell things to each other.

It helps everyone, even the poorest in society, said Smith. The production of a labourer's cheap shirt depends on the efforts of many people and machines doing specialised tasks: wool spinners to make the thread, weavers to create the cloth and tailors to sew on the buttons. Then think of the people who chopped the wood to make the loom on which the fabric was woven and the miners who dug the iron to make the nails of the ship on which the finished shirt was transported. The work of thousands went into the shirt. Together their actions form a vast social mechanism, each piece moving with the others like those of a clock to deliver the shirt onto the body of the labourer exactly when he wants it.

Smith also brought a new understanding of what wealth itself was. The physiocrats thought that it was what grows in the ground, the mercantilists that it was gold. To Smith, the wealth of a nation was the entire amount of useful goods – wheat, beer, shirts, books – that a country's economy produces for the people. This is how today's economists think of it. A nation's income (its 'national income') is the total value of all the goods that a country's businesses make. Smith realised that the point of the economy was to provide goods for people to consume. The mercantilists, in contrast, weren't so concerned with the benefits to people from having access to goods. What mattered to them was producing goods to sell to foreigners for gold; the availability of many goods, including imported ones, could even be a bad thing if spending on them led to an outflow of gold from the country.

Smith had a vision of a new economy that was then being born, one based on the division of labour and self-interest. He has been acclaimed as a sage, often by those who believe that markets should rule above all else, that governments should do as little as possible and businesses do what they like. Two hundred years after *The Wealth of Nations* was published, American President Ronald Reagan championed these principles, taking Smith as his inspiration. Some of his White House officials even took to wearing ties with Smith's portrait on them.

But Smith might not have felt flattered by this. For one thing, he championed the role of markets as an attack on the mercantilist system which then ruled Europe with its many restrictions on buying and selling. He wanted the system to be dismantled, but he still believed that governments had important roles to play in the economy. Also, behind the harmony of decent people pursuing their self-interest, Smith heard clashing chords. The division of labour makes each worker's task simple. Although it increases production, it makes workers 'stupid and ignorant'. Also, how was all the new wealth to be divided up between the workers and their employers? The new economy had the potential for both conflict and harmony; economists after Smith each came to emphasise one of these over the other.

CHAPTER 7

Corn Meets Iron

The French historian and traveller Alexis de Tocqueville was amazed by the signs of a new society that he found when he visited Manchester in the 1830s. Tall factories pumped out smoke and soot over the streets and houses. All around he heard the sounds of industry: the 'crunching wheels of machinery, the shriek of steam from boilers' and 'the regular beat of the looms'. Factories like the ones in Manchester transformed Britain's economy over the nineteenth century. Factory owners bought the tools and the machines needed to make goods – cloth, glass and cutlery – and paid wages to the workers who streamed in every day from the surrounding cottages. Goods were made more cheaply and new ones invented. Men, women and children left the farms and moved to the expanding towns. There they toiled alongside steam-powered machinery and were ruled no longer by the rising and setting of the sun over fields but by the clocks and schedules of their employers. The changes were so profound that they later came to be called the Industrial Revolution.

Beyond the town was the countryside, where the wheat needed to feed the factory workers was grown. Agriculture had long been the backbone of the economy, and landowners were rich and powerful as a result. In the past, the land had been shared out according to old customs of the village. Bit by bit, though, landowners enclosed areas of land to create large farms, and the village farmers and shepherds became labourers hired to work on them for a wage. Capitalist farmers employed the labourers and produced crops to sell for a profit, not to eat themselves. New farming methods made it possible to produce a greater amount of food to feed the growing population in the cities. Then, as Manchester and towns like it filled with warehouses and factories, the basis of the country's wealth shifted away from agriculture towards industry. People started to build up fortunes by investing in the industrial economy. One of them was David Ricardo (1772–1823), a leading British stockbroker (someone who trades in the stock market). After making himself a rich man, he turned to economics, displaying powers of logic never before seen in an economist.

In the eighteenth century, boys from well-to-do families were tutored in Greek and Latin before going to university. Not so the young Ricardo. His father, a successful Jewish businessman, believed that a practical education was more important, so at the age of 14 Ricardo was sent to work in the stock market. He was brilliant at it and earned himself lots of money. Later, he helped lend money to the British government to fight Napoleon. One of his deals was effectively a bet on the outcome of the Battle of Waterloo in 1815. By lending to the government Ricardo was taking a huge risk: if the British were defeated, he'd lose a lot of money. His friend and fellow economist, Thomas Malthus, who we'll meet properly soon, had a small stake in the loan. Malthus panicked, and wrote to Ricardo to ask him to get rid of his share. Ricardo held his nerve, though, and held onto his own stake. When news came of the British victory, he became one of the wealthiest men in Britain overnight.

Ricardo stumbled upon economics in a library where he discovered Adam Smith's *The Wealth of Nations*. It turned out to be the most important book he ever read, and inspired him to apply his formidable mind to the analysis of the economy at a time when the new capitalists were competing for power with the old land-owning aristocrats. The question was how the country's growing wealth was to be divided between the landowners, the capitalists and the mass of workers. Although Smith had shown how markets brought prosperity, he'd detected notes of conflict. They got louder early in the nineteenth century when the workers became angry about high food prices.

Some people thought that high food prices were caused by the high rents earned by landowners, which pushed up farmers' costs. Ricardo disagreed, claiming that it was the other way round: high food prices caused high rents. Ricardo believed that the landlords were getting the lion's share of the nation's wealth at everyone else's expense because food was so costly. Lowering rents would do nothing to correct the imbalance.

To explain his logic, Ricardo asks us to think of the economy as a giant farm producing grain. Landlords rent land to capitalist farmers. The farmers hire workers to dig the earth and sow seeds, and then sell what they produce. When the population increases, more grain is needed. Land is in short supply so to grow more, the farmers resort to growing grain in less fertile areas. Grain gets harder to produce, so its price rises. Farmers on the least fertile land need many workers to produce a bushel of grain, so have little profit left over after they've paid the workers' wages. You might think that farmers on more fertile land would end up with higher profits because they can produce a bushel with fewer workers. In fact it's the landlords who gain because farmers compete for the use of the land: if there were farmers making really high profits because they were on very fertile land then other farmers would offer to pay landlords a higher rent to use that land. Hence high grain prices boost the rents earned by landlords, not the profits earned by the capitalist farmers. What about the capitalists who own factories in the towns? Their profit falls too because the high price of grain makes bread expensive and so they have to pay higher wages to ensure the survival of their workers. As for the workers, they lose out from high grain prices because their food costs them more. Ricardo therefore concluded that 'the interest of the landlord is always opposed to the interest of every other class in the community'.

The power of the landlords dragged down the economy, Ricardo said. When capitalists build factories and hire workers to make and grow things, they increase production in the economy. But with lower profits the capitalists have less to spend and so wealth creation slows down. Landowners get rich simply by collecting rent on the land. Instead of investing their income like the capitalists, they consume it on maids and butlers, on libraries for their mansions, perhaps on expeditions to the tropics to collect plants for their gardens, none of which contributes to the long-term wealth of the nation.

In Ricardo's time, the imbalance swung further in favour of the landowners because Britain had laws that banned cheap foreign grain. They were called the Corn Laws, and they stopped Britain from importing the extra grain needed to feed its growing population. The result was even higher grain prices. Ricardo's reasoning showed that the laws helped swell the landlords' rents, shrink the capitalists' profits and impoverish the workers. In 1819 a demonstration was held in St Peter's Fields in Manchester demanding the vote for all and the end of the Corn Laws. The protest turned into a bloodbath when soldiers fired into the crowd killing several and injuring hundreds. Likened to the Battle of Waterloo, the incident came to be known as the Peterloo massacre.

That same year Ricardo became a member of parliament. There he put forward his solution to the country's problems: to do away with the Corn Laws. It would help make Britain 'the happiest country in the world', he said. His proposal fell on deaf ears. People weren't used to hearing arguments based on strict economic analysis. To many, they seemed rather removed from reality. A fellow member of parliament said that Ricardo had 'argued as if he had dropped from another planet'. (People still grumble about economists for the same thing.) Eventually he won the argument and Britain scrapped the Corn Laws – but not until the middle of the nineteenth century, decades after his death.

According to Ricardo, what would happen if the Corn Laws were removed? Cheap foreign grain would flood in. Workers wouldn't have to struggle with high food prices. Capitalists would have a lower wage bill, because their workers wouldn't need to spend so much on food. Capitalists' profits would increase and they'd start investing again. Wealth creation would speed up.

Without the Corn Laws, the country would buy in cheap foreign grain and produce less of its own grain. Growing all your own grain didn't always make sense, said Ricardo. A country can make other things – cloth and iron in factories – to sell to foreigners for their grain. If Russia can produce grain more cheaply than Britain and Britain can produce iron more cheaply than Russia, then it's easy to see that both countries gain when Britain just makes iron, Russia just grows grain and the two countries then trade iron for grain.

Ricardo's clever reasoning took this a step further. Both countries could gain from trade, even if one of them was better at producing both grain and iron. To understand his logic, imagine that you and a friend are given a chore to do: to move some heavy boxes from the garage and to sweep the floor. You can shift boxes faster than your friend. You're also faster at sweeping up. Should you sweep up and shift boxes? Not necessarily. By sweeping up you'd give up making fast progress on moving the boxes. Your friend, however, in sweeping a metre of floor might not give up as much in terms of the number of boxes moved. Perhaps in the time your friend takes to sweep a metre of floor she could move two boxes. In the time that you take to sweep a metre of floor you could move five. Relatively speaking, your friend has an advantage over you in sweeping. She has a 'comparative advantage' in sweeping even if in absolute terms she's worse at it. Together you'd finish the chore quickest if you stick to moving boxes, your friend to sweeping.

The same logic implies that if Britain has a comparative advantage in iron and Russia in grain, then Britain should just make iron and import its grain from Russia, and Russia should just grow grain and import its iron from Britain. The idea is profound because every country has a comparative advantage in something and so every nation has the potential to gain by specialising and trading. It's better for countries to open their borders to foreign trade than to try to be self-sufficient. Although a few economists have challenged it (see Chapter 12), Ricardo's idea of comparative advantage became one of the most cherished principles of economists.

Ricardo was praised for bringing a new standard of reasoning into economics. The nineteenth-century British writer Thomas de Quincey turned to economics after finding that his consumption of opium had made him unable to tackle his usual reading of mathematics and philosophy. He was totally unimpressed by the writings of the economists. He said that anyone with a bit of sense would throttle the daft economists and 'bray their fungus-heads to powder with a lady's fan'. Then someone lent him a book by Ricardo and before he'd finished the first chapter he exclaimed 'Thou art the man!' Ricardo's style of thinking was to begin from a simple starting point – pieces of land are of varying fertility, for example – and to see where it led, never leaving the path of strict logic. De Quincey praised him for using logic to find economic laws, rays of light in the chaos of facts and history. Many of Ricardo's starting points were discarded by later economists, but his method of building up a long chain of cause and effect became that of economics. His friends often said that he didn't care much for winning arguments, only for using reason to find the truth, even when the truth went against his own interests. In 1814 he bought a 5,000 acre estate, from which he earned a tidy income. Ricardo had become a landlord. But his position didn't stop him from arguing tirelessly for free trade – something that would threaten the wealth he had earned from his own land, but which his principles of economics had shown to be right.

CHAPTER 8

An Ideal World

People sometimes say that the poor deserve it: they're poor simply because they're lazy or wicked. But in the nineteenth century the writer Victor Hugo, in his most famous book, *Les Misérables*, tells us about Fantine, who after being sacked from her factory job resorts to selling her front teeth to support her daughter. Fantine wasn't lazy or wicked. She was the victim of a cruel economy that cared more for profit than for human beings. At that time people had begun to question the view that the poor were to blame for their own misfortunes, and some said they shouldn't have to put up with being poor any longer.

The Industrial Revolution made some people rich, but many continued to live in deep poverty. People crowded into cities where living conditions were grim. There were thousands upon thousands of Fantines. Children were crippled by long hours of factory work and disease was everywhere. In Britain the poorest people could go to the 'workhouse' where they were given food and a bed, if they could stand the harsh conditions.

Earlier we met Adam Smith and David Ricardo, who said that trade and competition led to prosperity. They knew that moneymaking wasn't all good, but overall they believed that capitalism meant progress. A different group of thinkers completely despaired of the society around them. They looked at the squalor of the cities – the skinny, illiterate children and the workers spending their last pennies on drink to drown their sorrows – and thought that capitalism couldn't be repaired. Only a totally new society would save humanity.

One of these thinkers was Charles Fourier (1772–1837), a Frenchman who led a lonely and unexciting life working as a clerk. He made up for it by pouring out eccentric writings with strange titles like *The Theory of the Four Movements and of the General Destinies*. Fourier condemned the entire civilisation of Europe. He thought that its society of factories and moneymaking was brutal and inhuman. Think back to Adam Smith's pin factory, where each person performs one small task. Many pins get made, but how dull to spend your days filing the point of a pin! Commercial society makes people hostile towards each other, too. Sellers of glass hope for a hailstorm to smash everyone's windows so that they can sell more glass. And in commercial society, the rich and powerful do everything they can to protect their position and end up trampling on the poor.

Fourier proposed a new society. He called it a system of harmony. He imagined people living in small communities called 'phalansteries'. The phalanstery would be a rectangular building containing workshops, libraries, even an opera house. It would be a place where you'd be able to follow your passions to the full. Fourier talked about familiar passions like friendship, ambition and the love of food and music. There was also the passion of the 'butterfly', the love of flitting between lots of different activities, and even that of the 'cabalist', a fondness for plots and intrigue. The passions could combine to create 810 human character types, said Fourier.

In the phalanstery the passions would be carefully organised. Each day people would set off for work in groups of people with different passions helpful to the tasks they had to carry out. There'd be groups that grow roses, some that look after the chickens, others that produce operas. What's more, each person could belong to dozens of different groups. Instead of spending every day getting bored stiff grinding the end of a pin, you'd be able to do whatever took your fancy and fulfil all your passions. How would people earn their money, though? Instead of being paid wages, as under capitalism, people would be given a share of the profits that the phalanstery made.

Fourier waited at home at noon each day for someone to call and give him the money to set up his phalansteries. No one ever came. His new world remained only an amazing picture in his mind. He wrote that after the establishment of the phalansteries people would grow tails with eyes on the end of them, six moons would appear and the seas would turn into lemonade. Wild animals would make friends with humans: friendly 'anti-tigers' would carry us from place to place on their backs. All this is great material for those who say that Fourier was a madman. Still, he raises questions about work which conventional economics has hardly touched. Once we have food and shelter, how can we find work that makes use of all parts of our personalities? Perhaps today's trend of careers advisers in schools who help students to choose jobs that match their skills and interests is one attempt at answering that question.

Like Fourier, the Welshman Robert Owen (1771–1858) thought that the creation of new communities would save humanity. Owen couldn't have been a more different man, though. He got lucky in Britain's young industrial economy, using the newfangled steam engine to power the machinery in his cotton-spinning factories. He'd risen from shop assistant to famous industrialist and had dealt with everyone from factory workers to dukes. He was proud of mixing with all kinds of people. This inspired the main idea in his essays, *A New View of Society*. Owen believed that people's characters were the product of their environments. People were bad because they came from bad conditions. If you wanted a good society you had to establish the right conditions. In an environment free of the cut-throat competition of capitalism, the poor could become good, happy people. Owen had a plan for creating the perfect environment.

He'd made enough money to set up a 'model' village, an experiment in creating an alternative to the dangerous, dirty factories in the big cities. He did this at a cotton mill he bought at New Lanark in Scotland. Owen imagined a world full of places like it. In the end, that didn't happen – but even so, Owen did things that were remarkable for the time and a stream of important people came to look at his little community. He opened an infant school, one of the earliest in Britain, and called it the Institute for the Formation of Character. He shortened working hours and encouraged his workers to keep themselves and their houses clean and to avoid drinking too much. To promote good working habits, Owen hung in front of each worker a 'silent monitor': a wooden cube with its sides painted in different colours. Each colour represented the worker's conduct: white for excellent, yellow for good, blue for so-so, black for bad. A supervisor would turn the cube according to how well the worker was doing that day and the colours for each worker would be written down in a 'book of character'. When a worker was being lazy, instead of shouting at them the supervisor would simply turn the cube to black. At first most of the cubes showed black and blue. Over time there was less black, and more yellow and white.

Later, Owen founded a community at New Harmony in Indiana. It was even more ambitious than New Lanark, a town of farms, workshops and schools, which Owen believed would offer a complete alternative to capitalism. Scientists, teachers and artists who believed in a better life flocked to it from all over America and Europe (and quite a few rascals and oddballs did too). Unfortunately the writers and thinkers who went there, while good at writing and thinking, weren't so good at digging ditches and chopping wood. The rascals avoided work altogether. Soon the people began to squabble and the experiment failed. As an old man, Owen turned to 'spiritualism', the Victorian craze for communicating with the dead. He'd talk to William Shakespeare and the Duke of Wellington and he thought that the new society would come into being with the help of the ghosts of the great men of the past. Ultimately, men like Owen and Fourier hoped for an economy that would raise up the spiritual, not just the material, condition of the people, even if they didn't quite know how to bring it all into being.

An ambitious French aristocrat called Henri de Saint-Simon felt these yearnings with a particular intensity. Saint-Simon (1760–1825) had huge ambitions from a young age, and believed himself to be the reincarnation of none other than Socrates. As a boy, he was woken each morning by his servant with the cry: 'Arise, Monsieur le Comte, you have great things to do today!' His first work was addressed 'to humanity'. He fought in the American War of Independence, and spent a year in prison during the French Revolution. Upon his release he managed to get rich by buying up church land, but in a few years he had spent all his money. Later on, he tried to kill himself, deeply upset about what he felt was a lack of recognition of his ideas.

Saint-Simon thought that society should be ruled by talented people, not by princes and dukes. Everyone should allow their fellow humans to flourish and to develop as best they can. There'd be differences between people, but because of differences in abilities, not differences of birth. No longer would people exploit each other. Instead they'd exploit nature together, using scientific principles to enrich society. At the top would be the scientists and industrialists who'd direct the economy as a single national workshop. Under them, the workers would act together in a spirit of cooperation. The state would create an industrial society that was humane and free from poverty.

At the end of his life Saint-Simon published *The New Christianity*, which made his vision into a religion for the industrial age. After he died his followers set up churches. They dressed in white trousers, a red vest and a blue tunic: white for love, red for labour and blue for faith. They devised a waistcoat made in such a way that it could only be put on with the help of someone else, so symbolising humans' bonds of fellowship. Unsurprisingly, curious Parisians used to visit the Saint-Simonians' retreat to gawp at them.

Fourier, Owen and Saint-Simon believed that markets and competition weren't the route to a good society. That's why they're sometimes thought of as inventors of socialism, an alternative to capitalism which was tried out by some countries in the centuries following. Under socialism, resources aren't owned by individuals as their private property. Instead, they're shared out between people so that everyone has a similar standard of living. In fact, though, these thinkers had a mishmash of ideas, not all of which we'd today think of as part of socialism. For example, some of them thought that private property was fine as long as it didn't lead to big differences between people.

But all of them believed that a perfect world – a 'utopia' – could be created by appealing to people's reason and goodwill. They were against revolution and conflict between rich and poor. Their hopes for peaceful change were swept away by a series of revolutions that broke out across Europe in the middle of the nineteenth century. Not only that, but their plans seemed naive after the revolutionary writings of Karl Marx, who we'll meet in Chapter 10, and who was the most famous critic of capitalism in history. Although they influenced him, Marx said that Fourier, Owen and Saint-Simon were dreamers who thought up new worlds but didn't know how to get to them. A better world wouldn't come about by appealing to people's goodwill, said Marx. Conflict between workers and their bosses would have to become so fierce that capitalism would collapse in a mighty revolution. The new society wouldn't emerge harmoniously, but in a great hubbub and upheaval.

CHAPTER 9

Too Many Mouths

In Charles Dickens's story *A Christmas Carol*, we meet that most bad-tempered of misers, Ebenezer Scrooge. On Christmas Eve he's sitting in his office counting his money and grumbling at his clerk who wants to stay at home with his family on Christmas Day. Two gentlemen come in to ask for a donation of a few pennies to buy meat and drink for the poor. Scrooge scowls at the men and shoos them out of the room. Speaking about the poor, he says to the departing visitors: 'If they would rather die they had better do it, and decrease the surplus population.'

Earlier, we met a financial genius and one of the great British economists, David Ricardo and his good friend, the clergyman Thomas Malthus. Malthus (1766–1834) wasn't as good at earning money as Ricardo but turned out to be very good at coming up with economic theories that made people sit up and take notice. He was the first ever professor of economics, appointed in 1805 to the East India College, which trained officers of the East India Company, the famous British trading company. Some thinkers' ideas don't become widely known while they're alive, but Malthus's most certainly did. Shortly before Dickens wrote his tale, Malthus achieved fame for an economic doctrine that made people think of him as the Scrooge of economics, the pedlar of a truly mean and stingy theory. Malthus feared an ever-growing population: more people meant more poverty, he claimed. All that a growing population would do was to condemn more and more people to a wretched existence. And there was no point in trying to help the poor; that would only make the situation worse.

Earlier economic thinkers hadn't shared Malthus's pessimism about the effect of big populations. The mercantilists were in favour of them. They believed that large populations helped nations to win out over foreign rivals because a large labour force working for low wages allowed manufacturers to make cheap goods to sell abroad, and a large army and navy made possible the defence of the nations' trade routes.

After the mercantilists, the utopian thinkers – Charles Fourier, Robert Owen and Henri de Saint-Simon – said that people weren't doomed to poverty. They believed above all in progress. If people helped each other, poverty and squalor could be abolished, they said. Malthus's father, Daniel, admired the utopians, believing their ideas to be the keys to a better society. Malthus strongly disagreed, and father and son spent hours arguing it out. Eventually Malthus set down his ideas in a pamphlet he published in 1798, and which made his reputation. In its title he named some of the British and French prophets of progress with whom he disagreed. It was called *An Essay on the principle of population, as it affects the future improvement of society with remarks on the speculations of Mr. Godwin, M. Condorcet, and other writers.* The last named, the Marquis de Condorcet, was a leader of the French Revolution of 1789 in which the people rose up and overthrew their king in the hope of creating a better society, one in which ordinary folk had the power. The revolution was a blazing comet, but would it lead to humanity's victory over poverty? Condorcet said that it would: humanity was on a march towards perfection. Civilisation had already progressed through nine stages of improvement, and the tenth stage – equality between all peoples and nations – was just round the corner.

Malthus poured cold water on all of this. He takes some harmless-sounding starting points. First, humans need food to survive. Second, they must have sex in order to reproduce. What's more, they like having sex and will keep doing it. In a couple of decades, today's child will produce a couple of children who in turn will have a couple of children, and so on. The population expands by bigger amounts as time goes on. Malthus says that if left unchecked the population tends to double every generation, so after two generations a population of 1,000 will have grown to 4,000, after six generations to 64,000. What about the food needed to feed the extra people? You can certainly increase food production a bit, but not by anything like as fast as the doubling population. For one thing, you can't double the area of the land. Malthus said that food production grows by a fixed amount each generation, at a much slower rate than population. Population will quickly outstrip food supply. There'll soon be too many mouths gobbling up too little food.

So what happens? Brakes on population act to bring the number of people back into line with the supply of food. First, famines and disease kill people off. Second, people have fewer children. The problem is that they have fewer children by committing sins. The worst would be the murder of a newborn. But people also reduce the number of children by carrying out abortions and using contraception, both of which were widely judged as sinful in those days. The result, then, is misery and vice: more deaths as a result of illness and hunger, fewer births as a result of human beings' sins.

Suppose that the country gained a new source of wealth – perhaps land captured during a war, which allowed it to feed more people. At first there'd be more food to go around. Being richer, people would have more children, and being healthier, fewer people would die. As the population grew, there'd be more mouths gobbling up the food supply with less available for each. Eventually society would end up where it started. The people would have simply bred themselves back to the lower standard of living that they'd had before the new land was discovered. The belief that people tend to get stuck at a subsistence standard of living – just enough to survive – was shared by other nineteenth-century economists such as David Ricardo. It implied that workers' wages only ever cover their subsistence and came to be known as 'the iron law of wages'. With his ratios of food and population, Malthus showed the grim logic of the law.

Malthus's arithmetic had another gloomy implication. For centuries, local areas in Britain had supported the poor and the sick. In Malthus's time the poor were given payments to help them to buy food. Malthus criticised this. The payments simply rewarded laziness: if people weren't helped they were more likely to help themselves. According to his population principle, help to the poor is like finding new land. It boosts population but then produces more misery and sin to bring population back into line with food production. Charity doesn't help the poor or society at large but simply creates greater numbers of immoral, miserable beggars. Marriage and sex are some of life's great joys, but they'll eventually lead to wretchedness. So much for the human progress held so dear by the utopians! There was a ray of hope, though: men and women could choose to restrain their sex drive and so reduce their contribution to the burden of a higher population. Malthus encouraged people to delay getting married, following his own advice by waiting until his late thirties to do so. For some, though, it might mean never marrying.

Unsurprisingly, Malthus's writings provoked howls of disapproval. He was attacked for being a grumpy killjoy, or worse, a cold-hearted man who condemned the poor of the earth. Karl Marx branded Malthus's ideas 'a libel on the human race'. The Victorian philosopher and historian Thomas Carlyle called them mournful and dreary and he gave economics a nickname: 'the dismal science'.

Later history disproved many of Malthus's ideas. The population started to grow fast but the brakes on it from disease and famine receded. In the nineteenth century better medicine and cleaner cities helped people to live longer; they stopped getting wiped out by famines and disease. Malthus said that when people get richer they have more children. But the opposite happened over the nineteenth and twentieth centuries, when in many countries population growth slowed down. More reliable contraceptives were invented and became easier to get hold of, and most people stopped believing that it was wrong to use them. Even Malthus's miserable mass of poor people started having fewer children because new kinds of work – in factories and offices – offered better earnings than digging the fields. With fewer children to feed they could spend more on schooling them so that they could do the new jobs.

Over the nineteenth century something else happened which neither Malthus nor the prophets of progress foresaw. New technology raised living standards so that people could permanently earn more than the bare minimum needed to survive. Britain was one of the first countries to increase the productivity of its farms so that more mouths could be fed. Later on, once the effects of steam, iron and railways came together in the Industrial Revolution, other necessities of life were produced more cheaply and for a greater number of people. If you drew graphs of population and average income in Europe from the start of our story to the present you'd see the two lines bob up and down slightly for centuries but stay more or less flat most of the time. After the eighteenth century the lines zoom upwards and keep on going: there were many more people and they had ever-higher incomes. Think of what people in Britain had in the middle of the twentieth century – plentiful food, clothes, perhaps a car – compared with 1700 when they had to eat scraps and trudge through mud for hours to get anywhere. And by the mid-twentieth century there were six times as many of them! For the first time, the economies of Europe and America supported big cities and a constantly expanding population. It was one of the most extraordinary transformations in human history, certainly the most remarkable economic one. After humankind's long battle against scarcity, material progress had accelerated dramatically.

Before the take-off, however, economies were quite like how Malthus had described them. Income never grew that much; peasant farmers often struggled to survive. Sometimes relatives or the church helped out when times were hard, but a bad harvest or an outbreak of disease could mean starvation and death. Many mothers died during childbirth and many children never survived their infancy. If Malthus's ideas were mournful and dismal, then so were the conditions in which people had to live. Malthus was spelling out with grim clarity the constraints facing people living in those early societies. In our own time, this is still the fate of many of the world's poorest countries.

Today, when people talk about a 'population explosion' they're usually borrowing Malthus's ideas. Many believe that there are just too many people and that the world is getting uncomfortably crowded. However, in parts of his writings that often get forgotten Malthus said that he wasn't anti-population at all, and that he thought that having many people was a good thing as long as society had the means to feed them. Perhaps he wasn't such a Scrooge after all – his friends remembered him as a kind and friendly man, not at all mean and miserly. Many economists who today study the growth of economies over the long term think that large populations go with healthy economies. People use up resources, but they also create new ones: more people mean more brains, and so more new ideas about how to produce society's wealth.

CHAPTER 10

Workers of the World

'A spectre is haunting Europe – the spectre of communism.' This is the first line of *The Communist Manifesto*, which was written in the middle of the nineteenth century and is perhaps the most famous political pamphlet ever. The spectre – something scary and menacing – was the threat to Europe's existing system of capitalism. The threat came from an alternative system, communism, which was about to sweep capitalism away. Under communism there would be no private property and the workers, not the bosses, would have control of everything. The words were written by two Germans, Karl Marx (1818–83), the philosopher, historian, economist, and the most famous revolutionary in history, and his friend Friedrich Engels (1820–95). Marx is remembered by some as a social prophet, a great thinker who could see the future like no one else. Others think he's a villain who took economics down a dangerous alley.

Marx gave his warning about the end of capitalism in 1848, just as European nations did seem about to fall off a cliff. In France, the monarchy had been restored after the revolution of 1789 had removed it. Now the people were once more angry with their king.

As Marx published his manifesto, demonstrations erupted in Paris. Protestors built barricades and fought in the streets with soldiers. Marx rushed to join the struggle. By the time he arrived, the king had fled and a republic had been declared. Crowds of cheering revolutionaries filled the squares.

The reason for Marx's excitement comes a few sentences after the famous opening line. He says: 'The history of all hitherto existing society is the history of class struggles.' By this he meant that history is about dispute and conflict, that between rich and poor, bosses and workers. Marx believed that in Paris he'd seen the historical struggle in action. He'd predicted the overthrow of the capitalist bosses (the 'bourgeoisie') by the workers (the 'proletariat'). He hoped that the uprisings were the start of this, but a few months later Europe's revolutions fizzled out. It seemed that the death of capitalism was going to be a long and drawn-out one.

Marx retreated to Britain, one of the last remaining European powers not to have expelled him for his troublesome writing. In London he became leader of a circle of foreign revolutionaries. He had a frightening stare, long beard and hairy hands, and used his phenomenal learning to expose stupidity. He often scolded his fellow revolutionaries in public, and he liked taunting famous and powerful people. He said that the British philosopher Jeremy Bentham was so dry and boring that he must have had a tongue made of leather, and he called the prime minister, Lord Russell, a 'distorted dwarf'.

Marx began an intense study of economics that resulted in a massive book in which he aimed to give a complete theory of capitalism. It took him many long years. He had incredible stamina, but also a tendency to put things off and get into a muddle. Shopkeepers were often found banging on his door demanding the payment of overdue bills. His wife and children were regularly ill and when a young daughter died he had to borrow £2 from his neighbour to buy a coffin. He'd often take refuge in the British Museum Reading Room, where he devoured difficult books on history and economics. He'd return home carrying big piles of notes and stay up all night writing, puffing away on cigar after cigar, with his children's toys and bits of broken furniture strewn all around him. Putting pen to paper was often rather painful because he suffered from carbuncles, horrible boils which he'd try to treat using arsenic. Finally, in the late 1860s – some twenty years after he began – he completed volume one of his book, moaning that he'd had to sacrifice health, happiness and family to get to the end of it. He wrote the last pages while standing up at his desk because his boils were so inflamed. When he finished he said, 'I hope the bourgeoisie will remember my carbuncles until their dying day.'

The utopian thinkers whom we met earlier said that capitalism poisoned human society. Like them, Marx believed that a new society was needed for people to truly flourish, but he thought that the utopians were fools to think that human kindness would bring it about. Instead, Marx believed that capitalism itself contained the seeds of a new society. He said that history unfolds in a series of economic systems. Before capitalism, the economy was governed by feudal traditions. There were no factory-owning capitalists, just small craftsmen, peasant farmers and noblemen. Capitalism emerges when powerful people take over the land and set up factories, and the peasant farmers and craftsmen become workers earning wages from the capitalists. Eventually capitalism itself gets replaced; this happens because of how capitalists earn their profits.

Capitalists buy raw materials (cloth, buttons, thread) to produce a good (shirts) which is then sold at a profit. Where does the profit come from? To understand this you need to see where economic value comes from. Like Adam Smith and David Ricardo, Marx said that the value of a good is the amount of labour used to make it. This is known as the 'labour theory of value'. If a shirt takes thirty minutes of labour to make, then it's worth that amount of labour. Like Smith and Ricardo, Marx also believed that workers earned what they needed to pay for their subsistence, a minimum amount of food and clothing. Suppose that after five hours of toil workers make enough shirts to earn their subsistence. This is the wage that the capitalist hires them for. If the worker's shift is twelve hours long, though, there's an extra seven hours above the five needed to earn the worker's subsistence. What happens to the 'surplus value', the money earned from selling the shirts made during the extra seven hours? It goes to the capitalist as profit. The surplus allows capitalists to buy more machines and capital and this makes the economy get bigger.

Capitalists 'exploit' the workers in the sense that they want to squeeze out as much surplus value as possible by making them work hard and long. The workers want a shorter working day and higher wages. Competition between workers keeps wages down, too, because those who have a job are always under threat of losing it to someone else. The outlook for the proletariat is bleak: capitalism turns the life of a worker into nothing but toil and 'drags his wife and child beneath the wheels of the Juggernaut of capital'.

To Marx, the conflict between the bourgeoisie and the proletariat is a deep contradiction of capitalism. Capitalists try to protect their profits by squeezing the workers harder and harder. The workers get an ever-smaller share of the economic pie. Eventually they simply don't have the money to buy all the goods churned out in the factories and so the capitalists find that they can't sell all their goods. All the while, the workers get more miserable and discontented. Eventually the whole system collapses. The workers rise up, seize the factories and fields and set up a communist society, which ends exploitation. That's because there'd be no private property: a furnace or crane wouldn't be owned by a particular capitalist, it would be owned by the community. People would be given what they needed to live rather than what a capitalist boss paid them. Communism would get rid of the division of society into different classes constantly fighting against each other.

Marx believed, then, that capitalism is all about turmoil and stress – no sign here of Adam Smith's invisible hand through which moneymaking leads to harmony. Under capitalism, the capitalists own the 'means of production': the capital needed to make the goods. The workers own nothing but their own labour. Unlike peasants in a feudal society who are tied to a lord, the workers are free to work for anyone. But all they have is their labour so their only option is to work for a capitalist and be exploited. Capitalists are able to build up their capital and get rich because the country's laws and political system allow them to own capital and to keep as profit the surplus value created by the workers. In conventional economics, which sees capitalism as largely free from conflict, capital is seen as merely a collection of things. It's the buildings, conveyor belts, saws and looms that are used to produce goods. To Marx, capital was more than these. It was about power. Capital depends on a division of society into those with property and those without, and the creation of capitalism involves those with property gaining all the power. Understanding this was vital to seeing the reality of capitalism, which is why Marx called his book simply *Capital*.

Marx's ideas later developed into a worldview, Marxism, which became one of the most influential political movements of the twentieth century. Long after he died communist systems were set up in Russia, Hungary, Poland, China and elsewhere. The state took over the economy and told the factories and farms what to produce. At first there was fast industrial development. But people in communist countries frequently suffered daily hardships – for the most unlucky of them, back-breaking work in labour camps and sometimes starvation (see Chapter 16). The state's task of managing so many factories eventually got too complicated. Producers became inefficient and were slow to develop new products and methods. In many communist countries, like those in Europe, the economy broke down completely and communism collapsed.

Later economists objected to many of Marx's ideas. As we'll see in the next chapter, they dismantled the labour theory of value and replaced it with a different theory. Critics also say that the failures of actual communist societies prove Marx was wrong. However, his theory was more to do with the tensions of capitalism than with the details of the communist future. And it's often said that the communist countries didn't establish the system that Marx had imagined: that he'd have been horrified by the cruel communist leaders who turned their people's lives into hard drudgery and didn't hesitate to kill anyone who questioned them. Also, Marx said that societies would only successfully establish communist systems once they had well-developed capitalist economies. But the first communist revolution came in the early twentieth century in

Russia, which had a poor agricultural economy, not the capitalist kind that Marx had talked about.

As the nineteenth century wore on there were many who, while concerned about the plight of the poor, didn't think the answer was the overthrow of the system. They thought that capitalism could be made kinder. In many countries the right to vote was extended from the rich to the working classes, who therefore gained a new influence in society. Governments tried to lessen the harsh consequences of capitalism on the poor. At the beginning of the twentieth century, France, Denmark and other countries introduced payments to the unemployed. The German states had led the way in providing education for the masses in the early nineteenth century, and America, France and Britain then did the same. Gradually, governments outlawed child labour, too, so illiterate, hungry children were rarely sent into mines and factories.

The living standards of the average worker eventually improved. Does this make Marx irrelevant? No, because Marxism says that capitalism hurts people even if they can afford cars and televisions. This is because of what Marx called 'alienation'. He believed that under capitalism, workers become cogs in a giant machine. They lose any real connection to the goods they make that their bosses sell for a profit. They come to see others as tools of production rather than as human beings. In the end, they become disconnected from their humanity, the very thing that unites them with other people. Higher wages don't break the heavy chain of alienation.

Alienation arises because of private property, which divides society into those who own capital and those who don't. Only by getting rid of private property through a workers' revolution will people be able to fully embrace their humanity. So *The Communist Manifesto* ends with a call to arms: 'The proletarians have nothing to lose but their chains. They have a world to win. Working men of all countries, unite!'

CHAPTER 11

A Perfect Balance

Why is a bottle of champagne so valuable? Adam Smith and Karl Marx thought that value came from the costs of producing something, especially in the labour that went into making it. But a bottle of champagne that sells for £300 didn't cost nearly that much to make. It's valuable because people like it a lot. Champagne gives them a great amount of satisfaction or happiness. So far we've heard quite a bit about rich capitalists and their weary workers toiling away in factories. But what about the people who buy the goods? They get satisfaction from them: not just from champagne, but from pots and pans, hats and coats, too. Surely this should be important for how we think about the economy?

The British economist William Jevons (1835–82) thought so. He was the first famous economist to study for a degree in economics, rather than following the traditional path of thinkers who took up economics having studied Latin and Ancient Greek. Jevons developed the idea of 'marginal utility'. Imagine eating a toffee. You love it. It gives you a lot of satisfaction, or 'utility', as economists call it. But as you eat more toffees the pleasure you get from an extra one won't be as great. The tenth toffee is nice, but not as nice as the first. After eating fifteen toffees you start to tire of them. Perhaps the twentieth toffee gives you no pleasure at all. The pleasure from an extra toffee is its marginal utility. 'Margin' means the edge of something, so the 'edge' of your utility from toffees is the utility of the very last one you ate. The tendency of marginal utility to go down as you consume more is known as the 'principle of diminishing marginal utility'.

Marginal utility is one of the most important ideas in economics. Jevons used it to explain how people spend their money. Imagine you're in a café and you have £10 to spend on hot dogs or cans of Coke. Suppose you spend it in one go. How many hot dogs and cans of Coke do you buy? You're very hungry so you pile your tray with ten hot dogs. But you quickly realise that even though you're hungry it would be silly to only buy hot dogs. If you buy ten then the marginal utility of the tenth will be very low. (This is an economist's fancy way of saying that if you eat ten hot dogs you'll be sick.) You don't have any cans of Coke on your tray, so the marginal utility from adding one is high. You should buy a can of Coke instead of the tenth hot dog because it adds more to your utility than the hot dog does. So you take a hot dog off your tray and add a can. But before you go to the till to pay, think again. Chances are that a second can would add more utility than the ninth hot dog does. Take another hot dog off and add a second can. When you increase cans of Coke and decrease hot dogs, then the marginal utility of cans goes down (because there are more of them) and the marginal utility of hot dogs goes up (because there are fewer of them). Where should you stop? When the marginal utility is the same for an extra Coke as for an extra hot dog. Because you're a hungry hot-dog lover this might be at seven hot dogs and three cans of Coke. (For me – more thirsty than hungry – it might be the other way round.) The key thing is to exactly balance those marginal utilities. Once you've figured out the right split, go to the till.

Now you might be thinking: hang on a second, I don't go through all these steps when I buy things – I didn't even know what marginal utility was until just now! If you saw someone in a café buying hot dogs and Cokes that way you'd probably think them a bit odd. But economists don't believe that people behave exactly like that. What we have here is an economic model – a picture of the world made simple. For example, we assumed that you'd spend your £10 in one go and that you'd only spend it on hot dogs and Coke. In reality there are hundreds of different things to buy. Models zero in on the key thing we want to explain. Here it's the basic problem of scarcity. In real life you know that you have a limited amount of money to spend and that there are lots of things to buy. You can't have all of them. It's true that you don't stand there calculating like a robot, but somehow you make sure that you spread your limited amount of money in a way that you're happy with. Marginal utility is a way of making this into a model that's precise enough to explain your behaviour.

In the late nineteenth century this way of reasoning using the marginal principle became the foundation of a whole new approach to economics. Today it's one of the basic methods that economists use all the time. Jevons died before he'd fully worked out his ideas, but the British economist Alfred Marshall (1842–1924) took the thinking forward. He came up with his theories during Alpine walks, trekking for days with a rucksack full of books. While resting next to glaciers, book in hand, he developed many of the ideas that are now taught to economics students in their very first lesson.

One is the law of demand. In the hot dog example we didn't really consider prices; the law is about how prices influence decisions. A high price leads to low demand for a good, a low price to high demand, and diminishing marginal utility shows where the law comes from. You see it all the time. Suppose, for example, that a shop has a closing-down sale and slashes prices to encourage shoppers to buy up its spoons. If you had no spoons, you'd get a lot of utility from one. You might be willing to pay £4 for it. A second spoon gives you less utility than the first, so you might only be willing to pay £3. What about the tenth spoon? You might pay just £1. You'll buy a lot of spoons when they cost little, but when they cost a lot you'll only buy one or two. You compare your marginal utility with the price you have to pay.

The marginal principle isn't only used to describe how people spend. It's also used to explain what firms do. A firm produces another spoon if the extra revenue from selling it (marginal revenue) is higher than the cost of making it (marginal cost). As it produces more spoons it gets costlier to produce an extra one. This is because when a factory employs more workers, each extra worker adds less to production than the last. (Imagine a factory with only one worker in it. Hiring an extra pair of hands would boost production a lot. But when the factory already employs 1,000 workers, hiring one more would boost production by much less.) The firm produces many spoons if their price is high enough to cover the high costs. A high price brings high supply from firms, a low price low supply.

Marshall combined the consumer and the firm in the theory of supply and demand, one of the most famous ideas in economics. A 'demand curve' links price with the quantity that people want. Think of it as a line on a graph. Picture the number of spoons running along the bottom and their price running up the side. The demand curve slopes downwards: as the price decreases people want more. A 'supply curve' links price with the quantity that firms produce. The supply curve slopes upwards: as the price rises firms become willing to make more spoons because the higher price covers the increased cost of production. Which determines the price of spoons – supply or demand? That's like asking which blade of a pair of scissors cuts a piece of paper. Together they determine the price. The market is balanced (in 'equilibrium') when the demand for spoons is exactly equal to the supply – where the demand and supply curves cross. Equilibrium is where the market tends to end up. It happens when the price is at a particular level: that at which firms want to produce the same number of spoons that consumers want to buy.

Sometimes the equilibrium changes. Suppose that fancy engraved spoons become fashionable. Demand for them rises and so does the equilibrium price because for firms to supply more they need a higher price to cover the extra production costs. Over time, the high price might encourage businesspeople to build new spoon factories. Supply increases and the price falls back. Supply and demand has been applied to pretty much every market, from wheat to diamonds to houses. It's one of the most basic tools of economics.

Competition is another idea that economists use all the time. Adam Smith was fascinated by it. Marshall and his colleagues made it into a model. Picture dozens of mackerel fishermen selling their fish at the harbour. The price of a mackerel – suppose it's £2 – comes from demand and supply. The crucial feature of competition is that no buyer or seller has any power in the market. If a fisherman offered you an identical mackerel for £3 you'd simply buy one from someone else. If you offered to buy it for only £1, the seller would find another buyer. No single buyer or seller can alter the price. Economists call it 'perfect competition'. No one makes huge profits because competition keeps prices down. Consumers get what they want at low prices.

Before Jevons and Marshall, economists imagined people as rather colourful characters. In Adam Smith's version of competition, merchants haggle and hustle to make the best deals, and Malthus's poor liked to breed like rabbits. Now economists placed a new character at centre stage: 'rational economic man', a person who decides what to do by weighing up marginal costs and marginal benefits, for example by comparing the price of a spoon with its utility. The economy was seen as being full of cool-headed people who do all these calculations perfectly.

This kind of economy looks calm and harmonious, quite different from how earlier economists saw it. To Marx capitalism was all about the exploitation of workers by capitalists. Workers create the economic value, but capitalists take most of it as profit. In the world of 'rational economic man' there are simply lots of people buying and selling things. There's no such thing as exploitation. You even decide how much to work using the marginal principle. You look at your marginal utility from an extra hour of leisure (playing football or going to the cinema) and then compare it with the wage on offer. If you'd get a lot of utility from playing football for an hour then you'd choose not to work, unless the wage on offer was really high. No longer does a ruthless capitalist dictate your hours.

Marshall's economics became known as 'neoclassical' economics: it was an updated version of the 'classical' economics of Smith and Ricardo. Classical economics was about how markets power the economy and make it prosper. Neoclassical economics was about how rational individuals power those markets. It abandoned the search for an ultimate measure of value like labour or gold. Value was simply the price of something that came from supply and demand. A rare bottle of wine costs a lot because there is limited supply and lots of demand.

The new way of thinking emerged as the stresses of the nineteenth century eased. The Industrial Revolution brought lace bonnets and china cups within reach of ordinary people, and the tensions that lay under the surface of the economy – those that Marx had been so concerned about – were put to one side. And so 'rational economic man', who perfectly balances marginal this with marginal that, became economists' main theory of how people behaved. Some complain that it's totally unrealistic. Have economists ever met any real people, critics ask? All theories have to simplify, the question is how far to go. As we'll see later, even some economists thought that 'rational economic man' was a step too far.

CHAPTER 12

Shut Out the Sun

In the 1840s an economist sent a joke letter to the French parliament claiming to be written by candle manufacturers. In it the candle makers complain that they're being ruined by competition from a rival who's flooding the market with light at a rock-bottom price. Who's the fearsome competitor threatening to drive them out of business? It's the sun. The candle makers ask parliament to pass a law requiring the closing of all windows and curtains and the blocking up of any holes that let in sunlight. The law would save the candle factories and help to make France rich, they say.

The author of the letter was making fun of businesspeople who constantly complain about competition from foreign products. They may try to present their arguments as being about the good of the nation as a whole, but all they really care about is gaining an advantage for their own companies. Today we still hear lots of complaints about foreign competition – for example, when American and UK steel manufacturers grumble about the cheap Chinese steel on sale in their own countries.

After Adam Smith, economists realised the importance of allowing countries to trade freely with each other. Free trade means that goods are treated the same wherever they happen to be from: cheap Indian cloth isn't banned from Britain or restricted in any way. British consumers are free to buy whatever cloth they like, and if Indian cloth happens to be cheaper they'll buy it instead of British cloth. It was the British economist David Ricardo who really perfected the economic argument for free trade. Countries should specialise in the production of the goods that they can make relatively cheaply and then trade with other countries, he said. All countries then gain.

But there were economists in the nineteenth century who might have had sympathy for the candle makers, even if they wouldn't have tried to ban sunshine. To them, it wasn't always true that free trade made countries wealthy. Sometimes it could do the opposite. One of these economists was the German Friedrich List (1789–1846). He started out as a believer in free trade but in the 1820s visited the United States. Many Americans then disagreed with the British classical economists' argument for free trade. America's new society needed a new economics, different from that of the old society of Britain, they said. Thomas Jefferson, the author of America's Declaration of Independence, even tried to stop publication of Ricardo's work in America. Alexander Hamilton, another of America's Founding Fathers, put forward his own view of trade, totally different from that of the British economists. Hamilton was one of the authors of the *Federalist Papers*, a series of essays published after America gained its independence from Britain, which set out how the new nation would work. He talked of the establishment of a specifically American economic system and argued that the government should help to build up American industry. Foreign countries tried to help their own industries by making it hard for American companies to sell their goods in their lands, and Hamilton thought that America should do the same for its own industries. Ricardo's idea of free trade simply wasn't the answer for America.

In his *National System of Political Economy*, List developed Hamilton's idea, setting himself apart from Britain's economists. Smith and Ricardo, like most economists today, believed that trade between countries isn't much different from that between people: it's just the buying and selling of goods between individuals who happen to be separated by a border. When you buy some onions from your local greengrocer both you and the greengrocer gain. What could possibly be the objection to your buying onions from a foreign supplier? List said that it was wrong to think of trade between countries as the same as that between individuals because different nations are more than groups of people with different passports. Countries have their own histories, cultures and ways of governing themselves. They're all at different stages: some are advanced industrial societies, some still mainly agricultural. In List's time, Britain was taking off, going through an industrial revolution and economically pulling ahead of America, France and Germany. For the other countries to have a chance of repeating Britain's success they'd have to do something other than the adoption of free trade, said List.

He believed that economic progress was about creating an economy based on industries and factories rather than farms. But early on, new industries are like children. As a child, you're nurtured and cared for. You're not expected to compete for a job to earn money. While you're still growing up you're shielded from those pressures. You're given the time to learn skills that one day will allow you to face the world on your own as an adult. According to List, 'infant industries' need to be nurtured if they're to grow up. Suppose that Germany wants to develop new industries such as steel and chemicals, as it did in the nineteenth century. Success would be obstructed by production of steel and chemicals in more economically advanced countries such as Britain. Producers in the leading country have learned how to make goods more cheaply than anyone else because they've had lots of practice. They've ironed out glitches in production methods and their workers are highly efficient. The problem is how to establish a new industry at home when there's a more advanced competitor in a foreign country. German buyers would always want the cheaper British goods and the new industry wouldn't stand a chance.

List's proposal was to shield new industries from foreign competition. One way is to put a tax or 'tariff' on foreign goods. A German tariff on British steel makes British steel costlier for Germans. If the tariff is high enough then it makes British steel more expensive than German steel. People would then buy German steel and so Germany's infant steel industry would survive. Economists call this policy 'protection'. A child learns carpentry not by knowing in theory how wooden boxes and shelves are made but by practising sawing and hammering over and over. By being helped to stay in business, the new industry gets to practise until it masters its line of products and has a chance of competing with foreign manufacturers. At this point the tariff can be removed and free trade established. A new industrial sector has been created, and by repeating the same thing in other sectors, the whole economy can be industrialised. Putting tariffs on foreign goods is costly because people end up paying more for what they buy. But List considered the cost to be well worth it: as the infant industries mature, the economy advances. He likened it to a parent who makes an effort today to help their child learn a skill (like carpentry) that will come in useful in the future.

To List, then, the principle of free trade wasn't valid at all times and in all places. Free trade was beneficial between countries or regions that were at the same stage of development – the various regions of Germany in the nineteenth century, for example. But it wasn't a good idea between countries at very different stages: industries in more advanced countries would simply wipe out those in other countries. He criticised the British economists for their 'cosmopolitanism'. What he meant was that they believed that whatever theory applied to the economy of Britain also applied to that of France, Germany or Russia, so if free trade was good for Britain, then it must be good for the others. What free trade really meant was freedom for Britain to dominate other countries' economies.

The nineteenth century is often called the century of free trade, the era that proved the classical economists correct. In the 1840s

Britain got rid of its Corn Laws, which had stopped the import of foreign grain to Britain and so protected British agriculture from foreign competition. Abolishing them was a step towards free trade. Over the century, connections between nations multiplied, creating a global economy in which people routinely bought and sold across borders all sorts of things such as wheat, cotton and tea. Sometimes, though, free trade was hardly 'free' because it was established by force. In the middle of the nineteenth century Britain and France went to war with China, in part because the Chinese tried to prevent British traders from selling opium into China. China was defeated and Britain forced it to open up its markets to British goods. This was a world away from how Ricardo viewed free trade, as a completely voluntary exchange of goods between nations. And despite the steps towards free trade in the nineteenth century, quite a lot of protection remained. List argued that protection had been essential to the development of Europe's leading economies, even to Britain's.

Even so, most economists nowadays are on Smith and Ricardo's side and distrust List's argument for protecting young industries. They believe that protection rewards incompetence and waste. Competition between firms is useful because businesses that make low-quality products go bust. Their workforces and buildings can then be used by other people to make better products. Protection, economists fear, stops that from happening because it helps inefficient firms to stay in business. In the twentieth century many countries in Africa and Asia protected their industries from foreign competition. The result in many places was lots of inefficient and unprofitable firms.

List also had a different view from the classical economists about the basic method of economics: what kinds of questions economists should ask and how they should answer them. Economists make all sorts of claims – trade makes countries rich, more people mean less food to go round, and so on – and they often disagree. How do they come up with their ideas about how the economy works? It's important because this is to do with how economists convince each other of the truth. List said that economics had to start with facts and history. What industries existed in a country? How many workers did they have and what kinds of technologies did they use to produce things? Armed with this sort of information you might be able to draw conclusions about how an economy worked and what policies should be used to develop it. The other way of doing economics was to use abstract reasoning as David Ricardo did. He started with basic principles and reasoned towards a conclusion. His arguments seemed to depend more on logic than on history and facts. List rejected the idea that you could produce broad economic principles from logic alone. How would you know whether they really worked in different places, in backwards Russia just as well as in advanced Britain?

In the 1880s the debate turned into a fight for the soul of economics among German-speaking economists. It was remembered as the 'battle of the methods'. On one side was a group of economists who, like List, thought that economics should be based first and foremost on history and concrete facts, and on the other side those who thought that it should be a search for abstract theories. In the end it became clear that both sides had a point. Theories need to be tested against historical experience. On the other hand, a mass of facts quickly becomes meaningless without theories to sort through them. From then on, economics embraced both the world of facts and the world of theory. Even so, as economics developed, the economists who invented new theories, rather than those who trawled through historical records and statistics, gained the greatest renown. Economists fell in love with mathematics, and they used it to create all sorts of elaborate theories that were based on general concepts rather than specific facts about the economy. Not everyone agreed with this emphasis, though. To this day, critics of economics complain that the subject has become rather removed from reality, that it's turned into a mathematical game rather than the study of actual facts about the economy, facts that affect real people's lives.

CHAPTER 13

The Profits of War

When the First World War broke out in 1914, the Russian revolutionary Vladimir Ilyich Lenin (1870–1924) was tucked away in a remote lodge in the Tatra mountains in Poland. It was the latest in a series of exiles from his native country which took him across Europe, dodging police and government agents and using false names and fake passports. In Russia, he'd encouraged revolution in his paper, *The Spark*, copies of which his comrades showered down from the galleries of theatres onto the wealthy men and women below. In prison he'd written secret messages using inkwells made out of bread. The inkwells could be quickly eaten if a guard was spotted – on one day he swallowed six of them.

To Lenin, war meant the ruling classes of opposing nations sending working men to kill each other, men who should instead stand united against their true common enemy – the capitalist bosses of Europe. A socialist could never agree to such a thing as war and Lenin and his fellow revolutionaries around Europe had agreed to oppose it firmly.

Lenin got a nasty shock on 5 August, a few days after Germany declared war on Russia. A local activist who was staying with him in the lodge brought him a copy of a Polish newspaper. The newspaper reported that the socialists in the German parliament had agreed to the war. At first Lenin thought that his Polish comrade had mistranslated the story, but the news was unmistakeable: the socialists' loyalties to their own countries had won out over their political beliefs. Socialists in Britain and France did the same. Lenin was furious.

Lenin's opposition to the war wasn't just about the horror of mass killing. It came from a theory of capitalism. Lenin was a thinker as well as a practical revolutionary, a successor of Marx who'd said that capitalism involved contradictions that in time would lead to its collapse. Lenin took Marx's ideas forward. He said that the capitalist system itself caused the conflicts between nations that led eventually to war.

Lenin pointed to three big trends. Marx had mainly looked at what was going on within single nations, but by the beginning of the twentieth century countries had become ever more connected. There was a greater volume of trade between them, and investors were putting more of their money into businesses in foreign countries. Another trend was the emergence of big firms and banks, a change from the earlier era of capitalism when firms were small and usually financed by their owners. Now large banks were financing large corporations. Lenin called it 'monopoly capitalism', monopolies being large firms controlling entire markets.

Then there was the trend of imperialism: European nations taking control of foreign territories to create empires that extended around the world. This happened through military invasion, after which the invaders often set up their own governments in the foreign lands and so established colonies. Imperialism had begun hundreds of years before when in the fifteenth century the Spanish and Portuguese conquered South America. European countries fought with each other for control of the foreign lands, which contained gold and many other valuable goods as well as people who could be made into slaves. In the late nineteenth century there was a new burst of imperialist rivalry. European countries fought for areas of the world that hadn't already been invaded; much of what was left was in unexplored parts of Africa. By the start of the First World War in 1914 the European empires had taken control of a third of the land mass of the earth.

Lenin thought that the three trends of economic interconnection, monopoly capitalism and imperialism were linked. In his day the conventional view of imperialism was that it was a heroic endeavour, an outlet for the adventurous spirit and bravery of great leaders. Furthermore, imperialist nations brought civilisation to poor countries, which would drag the peoples of Africa and Asia into the modern world. Lenin's thinking couldn't have been further from this way of looking at things. To him imperialism was about making money, pure and simple. His ideas were influenced by the writings of a British economist called John Hobson (1858–1940), a modest, bookish man, far removed from Lenin's world of secret meetings and prison plots. Hobson wasn't a Marxist, but he was a heretic – a rebel against orthodox thinking. (One of the many books he wrote was called *Confessions of an Economic Heretic*.) He was prevented from giving lectures at London University after an economics professor there read one of his books. The ideas in it – which formed the basis of Lenin's argument – seemed to many to be utter nonsense.

Hobson's theory goes against an idea taken as gospel by economists of the time: that saving is a good thing. Hobson thought that sometimes a country could end up saving too much. Workers and capitalists earn incomes from the production of goods. You can spend your income today or be careful with it and save it. People on modest incomes spend most of their money on the basics of food and clothes. Rich people, however, earn so much that they might not be able to spend it all. Someone who earns fifty times the income of a modestly earning worker won't spend nearly as much as fifty times more on the basics, and although they might buy a few antique vases, they'll probably end up with a surplus of income that they'll save. Hobson and Lenin said that under monopoly capitalism more of the economy's income goes to a few rich and powerful financiers. That means that more of the country's income is saved rather than consumed. The savings are spent on new machines and factories which allow more goods to be produced. Economists call this kind of spending 'investment': when business-people buy new sausage machines, they're investing, and they'll be able to produce more sausages in future. (When they eat sausages they're consuming rather than investing.)

The problem is that as more is invested there are fewer people willing or able to buy the goods that are produced. The rich don't buy them because they've bought as much as they want to with their enormous incomes – that's why they're saving the rest. The workers, on the other hand, don't have the money to buy anything. So the factories that the savings are used to build create less and less of a profit for their owners. As savings grow, therefore, there are fewer good investments to put them into. There are, however, good investments in foreign countries that aren't yet full of savings. To allow the savings to flow abroad, imperial powers invade foreign countries and set up colonies. European capitalists then build factories in the colonies and sell to the colonised people the goods that they can't sell at home. The invading country's army helps protect the foreign factories from any attempts by the local people to take them over. Hobson saw this in action when he was a journalist covering the war between Britain and South Africa at the turn of the century. Gold was discovered in South Africa in the mid-1880s, and Britain and South Africa went to war in 1899. Hobson believed that the war was about control of South Africa's gold mines by capitalists. For this, thousands of men, women and children died; many of them perished in terrible concentration camps. Imperialism is caused by greed, then, and the armies of imperial countries are used to crush local populations to help capi-talists get richer, said Hobson. As rival capitalist nations seek new markets, they get in each other's way, hence the jostling for terri-tory as the nineteenth century came to a close, and the outbreak of the First World War a few years later.

Hobson called the excess of savings the 'economic taproot' of imperialism – its fundamental economic cause. The idea helped to resolve the puzzle of why capitalism hadn't collapsed when Marx had predicted that it would. The reason was that it had been given new life by imperialist expansion. In the nineteenth century many hailed imperialism as a way of helping countries' trade. And doesn't Hobson's theory actually show that imperialism is a good thing because it provides a vital outlet for savings? Hobson said no. Too much saving was the result of income being concentrated in too few hands. The solution was to redistribute income, not to send armies to foreign countries. Under a more equal distribution of income the extra savings would get spent at home. That would remove the whole reason for imperialism. In the end, said Hobson, imperialism only benefits a small group – the financial monopolies and banks. It doesn't help the nation as a whole, which has to spend money on armies to fight to gain the new lands and then to defend them. And imperialism hurts the colonised populations who are put under the rule of foreign armies and governments.

In Lenin's view, the problem went deeper than an unequal distribution of wealth, though. In 1916, as millions of working-class men were slaughtering each other on the battlefield, he published a pamphlet, *Imperialism: The Highest Stage of Capitalism*. Marx had fumed at capitalism and private property for leading to the exploitation of the workers. Now Lenin added another complaint. Capitalism and private property had made war inevitable. His solution was radical: 'Convert the imperialist war into a civil war.' The working classes from different countries should stop fighting with each other and instead rise up and overthrow the capitalists in their own countries. Only then could war between nations come to an end.

But instead of starting a revolution, the working classes of Europe were taking part in the war with enthusiasm. The theory of imperialism explained why, said Lenin. The hefty profits earned by the firms through monopoly power and imperialism meant that they could pay high wages to their workers. The workers become an 'aristocracy of labour' who accept capitalism and war; happy with the home comforts bought with their wages, they prefer to keep their jobs rather than start a revolution.

Lenin and Hobson believed that imperialism was a sign that capitalism was dying. Looking back to their time, this was wide of the mark. At the turn of the twentieth century Europe's leading economies were growing, and capitalism was healthier than ever. The flow of British money to foreign countries wasn't because capitalists were fleeing a sinking economy in which they couldn't sell their goods – it was because the economy was doing so well. New technologies created wealth that entrepreneurs were able to invest around the world. For example, the growth of railways in Britain created profits that railway entrepreneurs invested overseas. And although wars and colonialism are surely bound up with economics – in struggles over trade and raw materials – they're also connected to other desires, such as those for power and status.

In the twentieth century, the word 'imperialism' turned into an insult, something that socialists accused the rotten capitalists of doing. Economists were often keen to defend capitalism and so to them imperialism became a dirty word, not really an accepted part of their vocabulary. Later on, a group of unconventional economists revived the idea as part of a new theory of capitalism (see Chapter 26).

A few years after the start of the war, Lenin slipped back into Russia in disguise and led a revolution that established the world's first communist state, inspired by the ideas of Karl Marx. The new country, the Soviet Union, was the biggest in the world and claimed to be the arch-enemy of imperialism. Later on in the century colonised peoples around Africa and Asia fought back against domination by imperialists. They staged uprisings and rebellions and eventually won back political control of their countries. They became known as 'developing' countries because they were still in the early stages of building up their economies (see Chapter 22). And as they took back control, they attempted to create economies that benefited their own people rather than foreign capitalists.

CHAPTER 14

The Noisy Trumpeter

One night soon after the start of the Second World War, the professors of King's College, Cambridge, were herded into an air raid shelter to protect them from German bombs. At dawn they were given the all-clear and came out of the shelter safe, but rather tired and bleary-eyed. In front of them on the grass they were surprised to see one of their colleagues sitting alone on a deckchair, unconcerned by the danger, his head buried in a newspaper. The man was the British economist Arthur Cecil Pigou (1877–1959). He was very much the eccentric professor, going round in a shabby old suit, and devoted to the art of thinking above all else. Pigou's teacher was the great Victorian economist, Alfred Marshall, who created some of the basic theories about markets that economists still use today. Marshall called his student a genius.

Pigou took forward the theories developed by his teacher. He showed in particular that markets don't always work perfectly. Most economists, even the strongest supporters of capitalism, believe that markets can fail – that sometimes they don't make the best use of the economy's resources. 'Fail' doesn't necessarily mean a big disaster or crisis in the economy. Sometimes a specific market – that for fish or petrol – can fail without the whole economy coming crashing down. Pigou pinpointed exactly what's meant by this, and in doing so he pioneered a field of economics known as 'welfare economics'. It examines the overall benefit to society that comes from all the decisions made, those that people make about buying, selling and working, and that firms make about production and employment. This is part of 'normative economics', the branch of economics that allows you to judge an economic situation, here whether a market is performing well or badly.

Pigou argued that markets often lead people to make choices that benefit them but have damaging side-effects on others. To see what he meant, imagine that your neighbour takes up the trumpet. You don't like the racket that he makes, especially after he's been playing for hours on end. Your neighbour's hobby has an unintended side-effect: his playing annoys you. How should we balance your neighbour's enjoyment with your annoyance? In making the judgement we're thinking about what's best for society as a whole, not just for one person. In our simple example, 'society as a whole' means what's best for you and your neighbour together. For a while you don't mind the noise that much. The benefit of the playing – your neighbour's enjoyment – is larger than the cost, your mild annoyance. For society as a whole it's therefore best for your neighbour to carry on playing. But after three hours the sound of the trumpet starts to drive you crazy. Suppose that the irritation caused to you by a third hour of trumpet practice is greater than the enjoyment that your neighbour gets from it. From the point of view of society as a whole it would be better for him to pack up his trumpet after two hours. The problem is that he'll often keep on going because when deciding how long to play he only balances the benefits and costs that affect him directly (his 'private' benefits and costs). He balances the fun he has playing against the ache in his lips from blowing into his trumpet for hours on end. He ignores the broader costs (the 'social' ones): the headache he gives you.

The same kind of problem crops up in markets all the time. We can be more precise because the costs and benefits can be measured in money. For example, let's think about the profits of a paint factory and a nearby fishery. The paint factory produces the amount of paint that leads to maximum profits for itself by balancing the cost of producing the paint with how much it can sell it for. Suppose that the production creates a chemical by-product. It has no effect on the factory's profits; it's simply waste that gets released into a nearby river. The fishery is located further downstream and when the chemical reaches it, some of its fish die. This reduces the fishery's profits. It's the paint factory's equivalent of the blaring of a trumpet giving someone a headache. When the paint factory produces a lot of paint it releases a lot of the chemical into the river, many fish die and the fishery loses a lot of money. At some point the loss to the fishery as a result of the production of some extra tins of paint by the factory is bigger than the gain to the factory from producing and selling those tins. Thinking about society as a whole – the factory and the fishery together – it would be better if those extra tins of paint weren't produced. But, like the trumpet player, the factory only looks at the private costs of its production, those that directly affect it, such as the price of the pigments that it needs to make paint. The broader social cost, the effect of the chemical on the fishery, gets ignored. From the point of view of society as a whole, markets lead to 'too much' paint being produced.

Sometimes unintended side-effects can be beneficial, though. If a packaging company invents a new kind of plastic that allows it to make food containers more cheaply then it gains a profit, but so do car manufacturers who use that knowledge to make cheaper dashboards. The benefit to society as a whole of the packaging company's research into new plastics might well be much greater than the extra profit earned by the company. But when deciding how much to spend on research the company doesn't take account of the broader social benefits, those positive effects on other companies. It therefore spends less on research than would be best for society as a whole. The problem here is the reverse of that caused by the paint factory. Now markets lead to 'too little' of something of benefit to society.

Economists call the paint factory's pollutant and the packaging company's research 'externalities', because they have effects on people or firms other than – or 'external to' – those who created them. Pigou showed that market failures arise when there's a difference between 'social' effects (the overall impacts on everyone) and 'private' effects (ones that affect only the person producing the externality). People pay for private costs and benefits in money: the paint factory pays for its pigments and its customers pay for the paint. Markets work well when private costs and benefits don't leave out any impacts. Then the social and the private are the same, and all social impacts are included in things that people pay for. When there are externalities then private costs and benefits don't include all the social ones. Externalities aren't counted in anything that people pay for, like the pollution produced by the factory. In these cases, the private impact differs from the social. That's why we say that the paint factory produces 'too much' paint. It doesn't pay for its pollution so ends up producing more paint than is best for society as a whole. The packaging company isn't paid for the full impact of its research and so does less research than is best.

An extreme case of goods that benefit even those who don't pay for them are those that economists call 'public goods'. One example is street lighting. My use of the light from a street lamp to see where I'm going at night doesn't stop you from seeing where you're going. There's no way of excluding you from the benefit. This is different from most goods: if I eat a sandwich, you can't eat it, and I can stop you from consuming the sandwich simply by not giving it to you. Why, then, would you bother to contribute to the cost of a streetlight? You could just say that you didn't care about it being installed and then enjoy the well-lit street once others had paid for it. When everyone reasons like this we all end up stumbling along dark streets. Economists call it free-riding, and it applies to many important goods and services. Why, for example, would you bother to contribute to the cost of setting up an army to keep your country safe? Once the army has secured the borders then no one can be excluded from the benefits. When goods allow free-riding, then the market may provide too little, or even none, of them.

So when people create externalities or desire public goods, Adam Smith's invisible hand goes wrong. Markets don't make the best use of society's resources: too much of some bad things are produced and not enough of some good things. Pigou said that the government then needs to give markets a push in the right direction. It should encourage 'positive' externalities and discourage 'negative' ones. Payments to companies by the government ('subsidies') for carrying out research, for example, would encourage the packaging company to develop more useful technologies than it otherwise would. A tax on the production of paint would encourage the factory to reduce production to the amount best for society as a whole. By the time Pigou was writing, governments were taxing all sorts of goods, including alcohol and petrol, both of which have effects that go beyond the people consuming them. (Drunks disturb the sober and motorists wear out the roads that we all share.)

For public goods, even stronger action is required. The government might have to collect taxes and then use them to supply the good itself. This is why street lighting and armies are nearly always provided by the government. One of the main economic arguments for having governments at all is that without them no public goods would be supplied.

By the time that Pigou was writing, economists also understood that a market can fail when it's dominated by just a few firms or by a single firm (a monopoly). At the start of the twentieth century, a giant company, Standard Oil, controlled most of America's oil market and the United States Steel Corporation controlled most of steel. Because a monopolist has no competitors it can choose how much to charge for its good: it has 'market power'. The monopolist tends to push up the price to increase profits; the higher price means consumers buy less and so the firm produces less. This hurts society as a whole because consumers would like more and cheaper goods; however, the monopolist decides how much to produce only on the basis of its own profits. In a competitive market with lots of firms a greater amount of goods get made and sold at a lower price. This is why most economists think that competitive markets are better for society than monopolies.

'Antitrust' policies by governments try to make markets more competitive by banning the creation of monopolies or splitting them up into smaller companies. At the beginning of the twentieth century the American government broke up Standard Oil into dozens of separate companies. Today, governments still worry about the economic impacts of monopolies. At the end of the twentieth century a court found that Microsoft had attempted to create a monopoly for itself; in order to help competition, the court put restrictions on how the company could sell its products.

Pigou's work, for a while, was overshadowed. When he was writing – in the 1920s and 1930s – a fierce debate raged about which economic system was best, capitalism or communism (see Chapter 16). Pigou dealt with narrower questions, those to do with how individual markets worked. After the Second World War, however, the big questions were largely settled, at least for economists, many of whom believed that capitalism was the best system but that it needed a strong dose of government action to stay healthy. Pigou's work showed some of the policies that could be used to improve the workings of specific markets – those for paint, fish, oil and so on. Today, economists still use his theories to think about how governments can use taxes and subsidies to help make better use of society's resources.

CHAPTER 15

Coke or Pepsi?

If you were feeling thirsty and went into a supermarket to get a drink, then you'd find a huge variety to choose from. If you fancied a fizzy drink there might be Coke or Pepsi, Fanta or 7Up and dozens of other brands lined up in front of you. The same would apply if you wanted a packet of crisps or needed a new tube of toothpaste. Earlier we met the British economist Alfred Marshall who perfected the theory of supply and demand. We looked at supply and demand for big categories of goods like hats, bread and coal. As economies advance, though, they start to produce many different kinds of these basic goods – different styles of hats, many kinds of bread, dozens of brands of washing-up liquid. By the start of the twentieth century firms were becoming more sophisticated and developing all kinds of new goods to meet the desires of consumers. Economists' theories about markets and firms needed to catch up with the new reality.

An advance came in the 1930s from an unlikely source, a Cambridge professor's wife named Joan Robinson (1903–83), who as a woman was very much an outsider in the world of economics.

When she was studying at Cambridge in the 1920s, the university wouldn't give women degrees – even if they passed the exams. To have any chance of breaking into the field, she knew she had to come up with an idea that would make people sit up and take notice. She did this with her first book, *The Economics of Imperfect Competition*, which presented a new explanation of the behaviour of firms. At a garden party, Robinson was congratulated on her book by Alfred Marshall's widow. She told Robinson that she'd have loved to have told Alfred (who had died nine years earlier) that he was wrong in his low estimation of women's abilities as economists: Robinson's work proved that women were more than capable of coming up with theories that changed the way we think about the economy.

Robinson's book came out within months of another one that covered similar ground, *The Theory of Monopolistic Competition* by the American economist Edward Chamberlin (1899–1967). The two books sparked off a rivalry between the representatives of two Cambridges, Robinson in Britain and Chamberlin in Cambridge, Massachusetts, the home of Harvard University. Chamberlin spent most of his career insisting that his theory was different from Robinson's. In fact their ideas were really rather similar. Both looked at markets in which there are many different kinds of the same basic good.

In Robinson and Chamberlin's time economists' minds were filled with the theory of perfect competition that we talked about earlier. The starting point for it is that there are many buyers and many firms. Each firm sells an identical product. They're in competition with each other, and each is tiny compared to the market as a whole. Firms want to maximise their profits, but they can't simply put up their prices. If a firm tried to, it would lose all its customers to other firms. At the beginning of the Industrial Revolution firms did tend to be small. They were often run within families, and managed by one person. But as firms became more sophisticated, the world resembled less and less the model of perfect competition.

The alternative to perfect competition was its opposite, the theory of monopoly, which examined how a market works when it's supplied by a single firm. But the theory of monopoly went too far in the other direction because it was rare to find a pure monopoly, a single firm making all the ketchup, for example, with no other firms competing with it. In practice, markets weren't black or white. Robinson and Chamberlin tried to bring the grey shades of reality into economics. How did firms behave in more lifelike settings?

Their ideas combined aspects of monopoly and competition. Just like today, if you went into a chemist in the 1930s you would have seen a range of soap brands. One brand cleaned the skin about as well as another, but each was slightly different. There was Pears transparent soap, and Cussons Imperial Leather designed to capture the fragrance of the Russian court. Proctor and Gamble's advertisement for Ivory Soap had the slogan 'It Floats!' informing consumers of the feature that distinguished it from other soaps (useful for not having to fish around in the bath for a lost bar). Proctor and Gamble is a monopolist for the floating Ivory Soap, Cussons for the sweet-smelling Imperial Leather. If Cussons raised its price it wouldn't lose all its customers as a seller in a perfectly competitive market would. Buyers of Imperial Leather like it more than other types and so if Cussons raised its price a bit, they wouldn't necessarily stop buying it.

Cussons isn't a monopolist over all types of soap, however. Suppose it raised its price a lot. Now its customers might decide to do without Imperial Leather and buy Pears soap instead. Firms selling other kinds of soaps act as competitors and so stop Cussons acting as a pure monopolist. Also, just like in a perfectly competitive market, new firms can open up and compete with existing firms, thus keeping prices down.

Chamberlin said that advertising could help firms distinguish their products from similar ones sold by competing firms. Sometimes advertisements didn't even bother to tell consumers about the actual characteristics of what was being sold. In the 1920s the American firm Whitman's ran an advertisement for its chocolates which said nothing about their tastiness; instead, a golfer and some fashionable young women were pictured enjoying a box of chocolates next to a shiny new car. The advert made Whitman's chocolates desirable by associating them with a glamorous lifestyle. The same goes for today's perfume or car adverts which rarely tell you anything about the smell of a perfume or the reliability of a car. By creating a 'brand image', adverts make the firm's product different in the eyes of buyers from those of its competitors. Through that difference, firms gain a little bit of the power of a monopoly, alongside competition from similar brands.

Robinson and Chamberlin's theory is known as 'monopolistic competition' because it's a mixture of competition and monopoly. It's an example of 'imperfect competition', 'imperfect' because although there's competition between firms it falls short of that in a perfectly competitive industry. Economists often say that competitive markets make good use of society's resources because they supply the products that people want at a low price, but that monopolies don't because they charge high prices and produce less. These cases seem to be black and white. But Robinson and Chamberlin's idea was more of a grey area, and it is trickier to assess. On the one hand, consumers value the variety of brands offered in monopolistically competitive industries: they like being able to choose between Coke, Pepsi and the many other kinds of drinks on offer by the soft drinks industry, for example. On the other hand, these industries are crowded with firms trying to lure away customers from their competitors by launching new brands. Do we really need yet another kind of perfume sold in a slightly fancier bottle than its competitors and marketed through an expensive advertising campaign? Probably not, some say, and in this sense monopolistically competitive industries don't make the best use of society's resources.

Later on, Robinson became rather critical of the conventional economics that she'd grown up with. 'The purpose of studying economics is . . . to learn how to avoid being deceived by economists,' she said. She was tough, didn't run from confrontation and could be rude to her opponents. She hated the trend, particularly among American economists, of relying on complicated mathematics to understand the logic of economic theory. 'As I never learnt mathematics, I have had to think,' she said. (She was on the losing side here: today the use of advanced mathematics is routine in economics.)

She loved to ask awkward questions, sometimes by turning well-known ideas on their heads. For example, away from the topic of monopolistic competition she wondered what would happen if you reversed the theory of monopoly, which dealt with situations in which a single firm sold to the entire market. What if you applied the theory to the buyer instead of the seller of the good? A 'monopsonist' is the name given to a monopolist in the purchase of a good. For example, a restaurant that buys up all the fish caught by local fishermen is a monopsonist in fish. Imagine a carpet warehouse next to a small town. It's the only employer in the area, so it has a monopoly in buying labour, that is, in employing workers. Because it's a monopsonist in labour, the warehouse can control the price it pays to its advantage, here by pushing down wages. An important principle in standard economics is that workers earn an amount equal to what they add to production. The factory's monopsony allows it to pay them less than this. There's an echo of Marx here, who said that workers get exploited by their employers. (Marx's reason was different, though: it was because capitalists lengthen the working day and drive their workers hard.) By using the conventional methods of economics, Robinson comes up with a finding that's rather awkward to a conventional economist. She used it to argue for measures to keep wages up, for example for the setting of a minimum wage and for strong workers' organisations (unions) that can press employers for high wages. A lot of economists are wary of such things for fear that they might upset the functioning of the market.

As she got older Robinson became even more unconventional. She praised the communist countries – an unlikely stance for an economist brought up on the theories of Alfred Marshall, which were all to do with the benefits of capitalism, markets and profit. In 1975, International Women's Year, *Business Week* magazine predicted that she'd win the Nobel Prize for economics. In the end she never did: perhaps her radical views spooked the jury. (A woman eventually did win, but not until 2009.)

After Robinson and Chamberlin, economists became occupied with the workings of 'oligopolies', markets served by a handful of big firms. By the start of the twentieth century huge firms controlled whole clusters of markets. Five companies dominated Germany's heavy industries, for example. One of them, Krupp, had coal, iron and steel works, employed thousands and armed Germany's military during the First World War. Britain's Imperial Tobacco was another such firm, created out of thirteen smaller companies. Companies like Krupp and Imperial Tobacco didn't fit the models of perfect competition or monopoly, but they didn't fit Robinson's theory either. Giant firms seek profits not just by launching closely competing product lines as monopolistically competitive firms do. Sometimes they create associations of firms and then work together to carve up markets between themselves to increase profits. Sometimes they fight each other in 'price wars', cutting prices to drive each other out of the market. Robinson's theory didn't capture these sorts of tactics.

It's easier to create theories for extreme cases like perfect competition where there are many identical firms, or for monopoly where there's only one. The cases in the middle are trickier. There's only one way for a market to be perfectly competitive or to be a monopoly. But there are many ways for it to be in between – to be imperfectly competitive – and so it's hard to find a theory that covers all the possibilities. Today, economists use the field of game theory, a method which allows them to examine the behaviour of firms in lots of different cases. As we'll see in Chapter 20, game theory is the study of situations in which what one person does affects the outcomes for someone else. It's especially useful for studying the behaviour of oligopolies: economists now use it all the time to examine the complex interactions that take place between firms as they battle it out for market domination.

CHAPTER 16

The Man With a Plan

During the days of communism in the Soviet Union, a factory that made digging equipment stopped delivering machines to the coal mines that desperately needed them. An inspector visited the plant and was puzzled to find it full of half-finished machines. The factory director explained that he'd been ordered to paint the machines with red varnish. The problem was that the factory store only had green varnish. If he delivered the machines in the wrong colour, he might be sent to prison; better to leave the machines unfinished than risk that, he'd said to himself. The inspector cabled his ministry for permission for the factory to paint the machines green. The machines were finished and delivered, and the mines were able to start operating again.

At that time, in the 1930s, the Soviet Union was carrying out the biggest economic experiment in history. It was setting up a communist society, what Karl Marx had looked forward to, one completely different from capitalism. The story of the mining machines is a glimpse into how the normal rules of economics were turned upside down. To a factory director in Britain or America the idea of having to take instructions from government officials, even down to what colour paint to use, would have seemed perverse. British factories could paint their machines with pink spots if they wanted to and they'd finish them like that if they thought their customers would buy them. If their customers turned out not to like pink spots, the punishment would be to go out of business rather than imprisonment.

The Soviet state took responsibility for economic decisions – what to make, how to make it, and who gets what's made – down to the tiniest detail. It drew up plans that told factories how many tractors to make and how many shoes and in what sizes. This way of deciding how to use resources is called 'central planning'. Instead of looking at what the market demanded, factories followed the government's orders. Ordinary people came under the plan too. If you wanted a new place to live, you had to apply to the government. To obtain bread or soap you'd go to government shops where prices were set by officials, not through the action of market demand and supply.

Another difference from capitalism was how people's incomes were determined. Under capitalism, if you work hard and are really good at your job you make lots of money. Perhaps you make more than you need and can enjoy going on a splurge. It's different under communism. Everyone receives the same from the government regardless of how productive they are; they receive what they 'need', not the proceeds from what they themselves make. It doesn't matter if you're extra strong or brainy and therefore capable of producing more than others – you still earn the same.

The Soviet leaders promised that communism would lead to extraordinary material abundance. The system would be more rational and humane than evil capitalism, which the communists hated for making the capitalist bosses rich on the backs of the workers. Russian folktales tell of a magic tablecloth which, when spread out, offers a delightful banquet. The government's five-year plans were supposed to make this tale into reality. They didn't. Targets for the production of food, electricity and oil were often missed. People had to stand all day in the freezing cold to get food.

Some graffiti scrawled on a factory wall read: 'Welcome the Five-Year Plan with empty stomachs.' At the beginning of the 1930s, towards the end of the first Five-Year Plan, millions starved.

Why did the Soviet economy have such huge problems? Perhaps there was something wrong with the system of communism itself. Under communism, people's earnings aren't tied to what they do because they're all given the same income, so who'd ever bother to clear out the pigsties? Who'd bother doing jobs that make your arms tired or your brain ache? In fact, why would anyone do anything at all? Communism can't work because it creates the wrong incentives, so the argument goes. Defenders of communism disagree, saying that communism makes people behave differently than under capitalism: in a communist society, people would be obedient and unselfish, dedicated to hard work not for their own sake, but for that of the nation.

Ludwig von Mises (1881–1973) lobbed a grenade into this debate. Mises was a leading Austrian Jewish economist who in 1940, troubled by the growing influence of the Nazis, immigrated to the United States. In 1920 he published an article called 'Economic Calculation in the Socialist Commonwealth'. By 'economic calculation' he meant the basic problem of economics: how to figure out who gets what. By 'socialist commonwealth' he was talking about a society under socialism, rather similar to the Soviet Union. Socialism can have different meanings; sometimes it's used to mean much the same as communism. The key thing is that the economy is no longer ruled by private profit as it is under capitalism, and this usually involves some kind of central planning. Communism is a purer version in which all property is owned by the community, no longer by individuals. Mises's article was about whether replacing markets with central planning could work, whether that's done under socialism or a strictly communist society. His argument implied that the question of whether people were selfish or unselfish was an irrelevance. He believed that communist economies like that of the Soviet Union were doomed to failure even if every last person would joyfully clean the nation's toilets for a pittance if ordered to by the government.

Think about the dizzying number of economic decisions that get made every day in even the smallest country: thousands of goods are sold, wages for many different jobs get decided, new businesses open and failing ones close down. Things are easy only for Robinson Crusoe on his desert island. He knows how much more he likes fish than pork and so he can work out whether the afternoon would be better spent fixing nets or sharpening spears. When another man, Friday, appears, things get trickier because a second person's desires need to be taken into account. In a country of millions, the problem is fiendish.

Under capitalism, people's desires are organised using prices. If people suddenly want more cuckoo clocks then their price shoots up. This encourages clockmakers to increase production and over time, attracted by the high price, furniture makers move into making clocks. The price falls back. Consumers' desire for clocks is better satisfied. Markets also direct raw materials to their best uses. By buying wood, clockmakers deprive other potential users of it, makers of chairs, perhaps. This is because clockmakers can make more money out of the wood so they're willing to pay more for it. Hence, prices allocate resources to their most profitable uses: the production of the goods that people most want.

Under central planning all this has to be worked out by the government. In the Soviet Union many decisions fell to the man at the top: Joseph Stalin. He was forever in meetings dishing out orders. Many of these were about the things that most leaders have to deal with, such as the setting up of new ministries and signing agreements with foreign powers. (Because Stalin was a ruthless dictator, the orders would also often be for the execution of people who'd displeased him.) But he was also asked to decide about tiny details of the economy: whether a new bridge should have one or two lanes and in which districts of Moscow vegetables should be grown. Meetings with his officials had hundreds of points for discussion. No wonder he'd crack under the strain, shouting at his staff: 'The paperwork you are throwing at me is piling up to my chest!'

The problem that Mises saw was deeper than information overload, though. In a market economy, prices signal where wood is best used. Without them there's no way of properly deciding how to use wood, or how many shoes or loaves of bread to make. There's no good way of deciding how much people should pay for bread or soap either. There's simply no yardstick. And when the government makes up its own prices they never work well. Often the prices of bread and soap were set so low that people wanted to buy much more than was being produced. That's why long queues built up outside the shops. So, according to Mises, Stalin's orders on prices and production were just 'groping in the dark'. Mises said that 'Socialism is the abolition of rational economy'. The reason for the Soviet Union's economic problems was that the system of socialism itself was irrational.

Mises's article fuelled a heated debate about whether capitalism or communism was better: if communism was irrational, then it had to be capitalism. As communism spread to cover a third of the world's population by the 1950s, the question became urgent. Despite the problems, the Soviet Union made great strides. New cities sprouted up and the country rapidly industrialised. Many thinkers – including quite a few economists – were sympathetic to the aim of communism, an equal society without exploitation of the workers. They thought that communism was an improvement on capitalism, and that it was only a matter of time before the Soviet Union's economy would surpass America's.

The supporters of communism thought that because economies were so complex, it was unwise to leave everything to the market. One was the Polish economist Oskar Lange (1904–65), who after the Second World War became communist Poland's first ambassador to Washington. Another was Abba Lerner (1903–82), a Jewish immigrant to Britain from Eastern Europe who as a teenager worked first as a tailor in the poor East End of London, then as a Hebrew teacher and typesetter. His printing shop went bust during the Great Depression of the 1930s when the economies of Europe and America got seriously sick. To find out why, he took an evening course in economics and eventually ended up studying, and then teaching, at the London School of Economics.

Lange and Lerner disagreed with Mises that socialism was irrational. They agreed with him that an economy needed the measuring stick of prices, but they thought that central planners would be able to make their own sticks and then manage the economy in a rational way. All that planners had to do was to solve a mathematical problem. You can think of supply and demand as an equation: when the price of shoes is at just the right level the supply of shoes equals the demand. An economy is thousands of interacting markets. In the nineteenth century, a French economist called Léon Walras examined all of the markets together, with each market represented by an equation that showed when it was in balance. Walras and his successors showed how the markets came into balance together. (We'll see how they did that in Chapter 25.) What's more, they discovered conditions for markets to lead to the best use of the economy's resources.

Lange and Lerner said: why not just solve Walras's equations? The solution would give the central planner the prices that bring about a rational use of resources. So in their socialism there were rational prices but they didn't have to come from markets. Central planners would then be able to improve on markets – otherwise, what was the point? They'd be able to calculate the best prices and then adjust them here and there in order to make the economy fairer than under capitalism.

To Mises, this was impossible. Like the game of Monopoly, the prices calculated by officials from the comfort of their armchairs would always be completely unrealistic. Markets work when people know their money is at stake. Prices with real meaning come from the actions of businesspeople as they try to make a profit, not from economists fiddling with equations. Therefore, Mises said, capitalism is the only rational economic system.

CHAPTER 17

Flashing Your Cash

On a small farm in Wisconsin a boy was raised who became one of the most unconventional economic thinkers America ever produced, the closest it had to a Karl Marx. Unlike Marx, Thorstein Veblen (1857–1929) didn't attract bands of revolutionaries. But like Marx, he was an outsider, a critical observer of the fast-changing society that he found himself living in, but wasn't wholly part of. Marx, a German of Jewish descent, observed from Victorian London the progress of the Industrial Revolution. His writings were flaming rocks hurled at the mansions of the rich. Veblen came from a small community of Norwegian farmers and was removed from what he saw as the gaudy American culture around him. In his work he made fun of the vanity of America's rich and powerful people.

Veblen grew up during America's industrialisation, which took off after the end of the Civil War in 1865. New railways criss-crossed the vast plains and factories spewed out steel, lumber and boots. America's economy was fuelled by abundant coal, oil and land, by a huge consumer market and by the labour of millions of immigrants who streamed in off the boats to find their fortunes. By the late nineteenth century America's economy had seized leadership from Britain's.

America was at first a nation of newcomers with small farms and businesses, quite different from the old societies of Europe, which were divided into aristocrats, rich industrialists and the mass of the poor. As American industries flourished, though, small companies grew into giant ones. So did the fortunes of their owners. The fortunes brought high living for a few, far beyond the reach of the ordinary American. The writer Mark Twain called it the 'Gilded Age': the new wealth had a golden sheen, but it was only surface deep and underneath it was a society that was wasteful and immoral.

Veblen looked at American society with a quizzical eye. From a young age he'd made a point of breaking convention and unsettling people. As a boy he once shot his neighbour's dog during an argument and scrawled insults on the neighbour's fence – in Greek. At college he shocked the respectable teachers by delivering an address entitled 'A Plea for Cannibalism'. After earning his PhD from Yale University, he returned to his parents' farm where he spent years dodging manual work, instead reading in many languages, covering everything from biology to ancient myths. This wide learning fed the unconventional writings that started to flow in his early middle age. He worked in a series of makeshift homes, one of which was the basement of a friend's house, which he entered through a window. There, at night, he wrote his books in violet ink with a homemade pen.

Conventional economic theory had little to say about the rise of America's new class of rich. After all, the economy was full of 'rational economic men', sensible people who accurately weighed the cost and benefit of any economic decision and then acted accordingly. Rational people always maximised their utility, or well-being, and if it meant using their wealth to buy gold watches and marble statues, then so be it.

In his most famous book, *The Theory of the Leisure Class*, Veblen argued against the conventional way of thinking about economic behaviour. Rational economic people go around weighing up their various desires for things and then buying what they like. But where do their desires come from? They come from a person's history and culture, areas that most theories of economics don't deal with. In Veblen's view, people don't make decisions about what to buy and how to spend their time through rational calculation. To really understand people's choices you have to look to their instincts and habits, things shaped by the societies they grew up in.

On the face of it, capitalism looks as if it has nothing at all in common with ancient societies of tribespeople with their rain dances, sacrifices of animals to the gods and gifts of shells to neighbouring villages. Rational people in capitalist societies are engaged in buying, selling and profit-making. But in fact, says Veblen, if you look closely you'll see primitive customs living on in the modern economy. We buy things not so much to satisfy our own desires as a completely rational person would, but in order to be approved of by others. Think about the last T-shirt that you bought: even if you bought it because you liked it, didn't you also think about whether your friends would like it too? Would you have chosen one that you liked but that you knew they'd laugh at?

In earlier societies people had gained approval from others by being powerful enough not to have to work. At some point in history, a surplus of goods was produced as people got better at growing food and making things. The surplus allowed priests, kings and warriors to survive without doing anything. Their precious things – silver goblets, elaborate headdresses, jewel-encrusted swords – brought them honour. Ordinary work came to be seen as demeaning. Certain Polynesian chiefs, Veblen tells us, were so used to having servants carry out every task for them that they preferred to starve than to be seen transferring food from their plates to their mouths.

Veblen saw this same instinct in the contemporary American economy. The new rich lived off the interest from shares and inherited fortunes without having to do very much. Like the Polynesian chiefs, they gained social recognition by demonstrating – through leisure activities and buying luxuries – that they didn't have to work. Veblen called their purchase of mansions and fur coats and their trips to the French Riviera 'conspicuous consumption'. It was buying things to show off with. He named the privileged few the 'leisure class'.

The men of the leisure class wore tailcoats and silk cravats to emphasise the absence of any productive work such as digging a field or driving a bus. Their clothing then came to be judged as being more beautiful than a farmer's simple linen shirt. But to Veblen there was no reason why the shine of a rich man's patent leather shoes was really any more beautiful than the shine on the worn sleeve of a poor man's jacket.

Women's clothes needed to be particularly impractical to show that they never had to scrub a potato or polish a window: 'The substantial reason for our tenacious attachment to the skirt is just this: it is expensive and it hampers the wearer at every turn and incapacitates her for all useful exertion.' The wives of rich men were there to show off their husbands' wealth. At an extreme, the desire to impress means that when the price of a silk dress rises the demand for it goes up rather than down. At a high price, because fewer people can afford it, the dress becomes an even better way of showing off your status, and so more wealthy people want to buy one.

Veblen said that conspicuous consumption filtered down to the lower classes who wanted to be like the rich. Middle-class people buy spoons with handles of ivory which don't improve the usefulness of the spoons but make the users look respectable to their friends. Even the poorest people might go without food before the last vase or necklace is sold off.

Conspicuous consumption is a waste, said Veblen. It diverts economic energy from the production of what people really need into what they can show off with. The result is a treadmill of dissatisfaction: people copy the rich by consuming more, the rich buy even more expensive things to keep themselves ahead and everyone has to run harder to keep up. Veblen certainly seemed to live out his criticism in his own rather modest consumption. His clothes were too big and often looked as if he'd slept in them, and he kept his watch crudely attached to his vest with a safety pin. He suggested doing away with silks and tweeds altogether and making clothes out of paper instead.

Modern America's tribal chiefs were men like Cornelius Vanderbilt, who over the nineteenth century rose from being an uneducated ferry boy to a fabulously wealthy railway owner, leaving an estate worth billions in today's money. The Vanderbilt family built giant mansions and summer estates. One of them gave his wife for her birthday the Marble House in Rhode Island, a lavish palace made from 500,000 cubic feet of white marble.

Underneath the conspicuous consumption of men like Vanderbilt was an instinct that Veblen called 'predation'. Where barbarian kings attacked each other with spears, the modern leisure class defeated their rivals with financial trickery. Take the battle between Cornelius Vanderbilt and another businessman, Daniel Drew, for control of the railway line that ran between Chicago and New York City. Drew cooked up a scheme to outwit Vanderbilt by influencing the price of the railway company's shares. To pull it off he needed the price to go sky high. He visited a New York bar frequented by stockbrokers, and while chatting to some of them pulled out a handkerchief to wipe his brow. A slip of paper fell out onto the floor, but he pretended not to notice. After he left, the brokers snatched up the scrap. It contained a 'tip': information designed to make them believe that the price of the company's shares was about to go up. The brokers rushed out to buy the shares in the hope of making a profit after the price went up; the rush did just that, and the share price rocketed. Drew's trick was just like a winning move in a game (actually, Veblen traced the popularity of sports among the rich to the same predatory instinct). It won Drew control of the railway.

Vanderbilt, Drew and others like them helped build the new American economy, but theirs was a cut-throat capitalism. They'd cheat and scheme if it made them money. For their ruthlessness they became known as the 'robber barons'. Vanderbilt once said: 'What do I care about the law? Ain't I got the power?'

The predatory instinct had little to do with real human needs, said Veblen. There was another instinct, however – that of 'workmanship'. It was the instinct to do productive work in a way that served the needs of the whole community: repairing the railway line and making sure that the trains ran on time, for example. Veblen didn't call for a revolution as Marx did. He thought that the waste caused by conspicuous consumption would be done away with when society was ruled by the instinct of workmanship rather than predation. Then society would cast off the last residue of barbarian society. It would mean an end to the merry-go-round of more and more shopping just to keep up with the neighbours. The people with the instinct of workmanship were the engineers and technicians who invented and improved machines. A better society would be one in which they helped guide the economy towards the satisfaction of real human needs.

Although his unconventional economics never really caught on, the eccentric Norwegian was given some recognition by his colleagues when in 1925, at the age of nearly 70, he was offered the presidency of the American Economic Association. Veblen refused and retreated to a hilltop cabin surrounded by weeds outside Palo Alto in California. There he lived in a simple room with furniture that he made for himself. In October 1929, far away among the skyscrapers of New York City, the stock market crashed and gales of economic depression blew the glitter off America's economic carousel. Veblen didn't quite live to see it, dying a few months before the storm hit, living to the last as the hermit that he really was, among the rats and skunks that kept him company in his hut.

CHAPTER 18

Down the Plughole

An American hit song of 1932 had the line: 'Once I built a railroad; now it's done. Brother, can you spare a dime?' The song tells of one of the sources of America's wealth: the thousands of miles of railways that moved goods and people between ports, factories and cities. At the end of the 1920s food was plentiful, many people owned their own homes, and products such as washing machines that did away with domestic drudgery were within reach of ordinary Americans. But as the song said, only a few years later many workers who'd helped build the wealth were reduced to begging.

By 1933, 13 million Americans were unemployed, a quarter of all the workers. In some cities half were out of work. The railways carried a new cargo: millions of people stowed away in the freight cars, criss-crossing the country looking for work. John Steinbeck's novel *The Grapes of Wrath* tells of the Joad family, poor farmers from Oklahoma who make a gruelling journey to California in the hope of a better life. In the cities, newly homeless people cobbled together shacks out of wood and tin cans. How was the richest nation the world had ever known reduced to such a state?

While America struggled, the British economist John Maynard Keynes (1883–1946) tried to answer the question. He was already a world-famous economist. He was also known for being part of the Bloomsbury Group, a band of unconventional writers and artists based in Bloomsbury in central London. One of them, the novelist Virginia Woolf, described him as like 'a gorged seal' with a 'double chin, ledge of red lip' and 'little eyes' – but praised his brilliant intellect. Confident in his own abilities, he'd learnt economics in his spare time, but when he took the civil service entrance exam was annoyed when his lowest mark came in that subject. 'I evidently knew more about economics than my examiners,' he said.

Keynes believed that the conventional economics of the day, which had grown out of the work of the nineteenth-century economists, couldn't explain the crisis of the 1930s. It couldn't explain why rich countries go bust. Usually, countries like America get richer every year, producing more goods and services than the last. Over time, this is how people enjoy higher standards of living. Sometimes the economy slows and produces less than the previous year. Economists call it a recession, and America had begun to move into one at the end of the 1920s. During recessions firms produce less and sack workers; many go out of business. What unfolded in America was a recession that became known as the Great Depression, so called because it was so very long and deep. It rippled through the world's economies. Canada, Germany, Britain, France and other countries caught the wave. Some believed that the depression could spell the end of capitalism itself.

Keynes said that recessions didn't happen because of bungling governments. They didn't happen because businesspeople ill-treated the workers and wanted to throw them on the streets, either. No one was doing anything 'wrong', but for some reason the economy as a whole could go wrong. It could stutter and then completely stall, all by itself. Keynes explained why.

Conventional economics was about how to use scarce resources. Boots are scarce because there are only so many of them, while society's desire for them is unlimited. If society wants more of them then it has to make do with less of something else, perhaps hats. Economics, then, is about how markets adjust to encourage more boots, fewer hats. In the conventional economic universe the income of a nation is simply how much can be produced by its factories and workers. It's assumed that factories run at full capacity and that every worker is employed. It's because the economy produces as much as it's able to that resources are scarce: to make more boots you'd have to shift workers from making hats.

Keynes saw that in the 1930s the world had moved into a parallel universe. By 1933 the amount produced by America's industries had halved since the end of the 1920s, hence the millions who found themselves out of work. With so many hands idle, the economy could have used them to make more boots without having to take any away from hat production. But it didn't. Over the decade, all the lost production was worth the equivalent of a new house for every family of four. So the problem wasn't so much one of scarcity, but of how to make use of the resources that were already there. People wanted boots, hats and cars and the workers and factories to make them were available. Somehow the connection had got broken between what people wanted and what the economy made.

In Keynes's theory, the income of a country isn't what the economy is able to produce. How can it be, when so many factories and workers lie idle that the economy is producing much less than it's able to? Instead, income is the amount that people spend, what they 'demand'. When I buy your hats, I give you an income. When we all spend less, fewer goods are bought and fewer get made. The nation's income is therefore lower. From this starting point, Keynes created a new explanation of recessions and unemployment.

Keynes first had to pinpoint why conventional economics thought that a nation's factories and workers would always be kept busy. He said that the belief came from a principle known as 'Say's Law' named after a nineteenth-century French economist. Keynes rejected it. Before we see why, we need to understand the law itself. Say's Law holds that everything that's made will get sold. The reason is that what people care about is the useful goods they have. Bootmakers sell boots to get money to buy coats and hats. Hat manufacturers sell hats so that they can buy boots and coats. The money from anything that's produced is used to buy something else. There can never be a situation in which a firm finds that it can't sell its goods and so has to sack workers and close its factories. Therefore, recessions and unemployment are impossible.

According to Say's Law, then, the economy has some level of spending at which the factories are running flat out and everybody has a job. Picture the level of spending as the level of water in a bath. Say's Law applies because people use all their earnings to buy things. But what happens if people don't spend all their money, saving some of it instead? Think of it as water flowing down the plughole of the bath (you've lost the plug). Savings are a 'leakage' of spending from the economy. You're probably imagining the water level now falling, so there's less spending in the economy. That would mean firms producing less and sacking some of their workers. Something stops that from happening. There's a hose running from the plughole to a tap that leads back into the bath. Savings don't simply flow down the drain. The leakage of water through the plughole ends up flowing back into the bath. The savings are lent to people who want to use them to invest in new factories and businesses. The investment – purchases of buildings, machines and so on – is an 'injection' of spending into the economy. The savings get spent on something and so leakages equal injections: the same amount flows out as flows in. Hence, the water level stays where it is; the economy continues to run with all its factories and workers fully employed.

What happens, though, if investors get cold feet about building new factories? Then the savings don't flow back into the bath. Instead they gather in the hose. Once more, it looks as if the water level will fall. There's something else that saves the day, though. How about opening the tap a bit more to encourage the water in the hose to flow into the bath faster? Open it up enough and leakages equal injections again and the water level – the amount of spending in the economy – won't fall. Here, the tap is the rate of interest: the price of taking out a loan. When the interest rate falls – the tap opens up – loans are cheaper and so more people want them. How does this happen? When investors stop investing they stop borrowing people's savings as loans. That means there's a large supply of savings available for loan but little demand for them. When the supply of anything is bigger than what people demand, then its price falls. In this case, the price of the loan, the interest rate, falls. The lower interest rate encourages investors to borrow the savings to spend on new machines and factories. The result is that excess savings – the water backed up in the hose – always gets turned into a new flow of investment. Again the water level stays where it is.

Keynes took an axe to Say's Law, asking: why assume that extra savings automatically turn into investment in new factory buildings and machines? The world is uncertain and you don't necessarily want your savings tied up in buildings and factories. You might want to stick some cash under your mattress just in case. According to Keynes the interest rate doesn't help to turn extra savings into investment. In fact, there's nothing that links them. The hose isn't attached to the tap leading back into the bath. It leads into a drain and the savings disappear down it – under people's mattresses – rather than flowing back into the bath.

Keynes said that recessions happen when more flows out of the bath than flows in. What happens is that businesspeople start to feel gloomy about the future and stop investing. That means that the amount of spending flowing into the economy as investment is less than that flowing out as savings. The water level of the bath begins to sink. Businesses produce less and sack some of their workers. The economy falls into a recession. This is what happened to America in the 1930s, thought Keynes. All this happens when no one's being stupid or reckless. In fact, recessions are caused by people saving rather than spending – what we often say is the sensible thing to do. The problem, then, is people being a bit too sensible! 'Whenever you save five shillings, you put a man out of work for a day,' said Keynes.

Keynes's point was that once the economy is in recession it has no means of escape. Economists who held to Say's Law thought that if businesspeople stop investing, the economy would soon sort itself out. It was like one of those round-bottomed roly-poly toys: push it off centre and it would always come back to a standing position on its own. Keynes thought it would clunk onto the floor and stay there. Because the depression went on for years, Keynes seemed to be correct. If the economy was like a self-righting toy then there couldn't be lots of people desperate for a job. Anyone who was out of work was so out of choice. They were simply unwilling to take a job at the going wage. But surely all the men and women leaving Oklahoma for the chance of a job in California weren't out of work by choice? By attacking the conventional theory, Keynes showed why they weren't.

So, thanks to Keynes, economists soon agreed on one thing: the millions of unemployed people during the Great Depression, and in the many recessions since then, were the victims of spending going down the drain. Keynes's ideas had another significant effect: after him, economics became divided into 'macroeconomics' (the study of the economy as a whole, such as employment levels, which he helped develop) and 'microeconomics' (the study of how individual consumers and firms make choices).

Keynes didn't want to invent a new theory just for the sake of it. He wanted to use it to improve the world. In the 1930s that meant doing away with the misery of unemployment. The leaky bathtub shows his diagnosis of the problem; in Chapter 27 we'll come to the cure. The gist of it was that because the economy couldn't right itself, the government had to. It had to take on a larger role in the economy than ever before, in the hope that a disaster like the Great Depression would never happen again. Capitalism survived the storm, but it was changed forever.

CHAPTER 19

Creative Destruction

The Austrian economist Joseph Schumpeter (1883–1950) loved to show off his brilliant intellect and keen wit. He once said that he had three ambitions: to be the greatest economist in the world, the finest horseman in Austria and the best lover in Vienna. He regretted, he said, that he'd only succeeded in two of them, adding that, unfortunately, things hadn't been going so well with the horses lately.

The joke points to a contradiction in Schumpeter the man. On the one hand he'd attended the finest schools and mixed in high society. This gave him old-fashioned manners, harking back to times when daring men rode around on horses and wooed maidens. On the other hand, he aimed to become a great scientist in the most modern field of economics, a very new intellectual discipline compared with the old ones of philosophy and mathematics.

Schumpeter's students marvelled at his old-world flamboyance and his love of cutting-edge economic theory. At one university in a small town on the edge of the Austro-Hungarian Empire he fought a duel with the librarian to get better access for his students to the latest economics books. (He won, nicking the librarian in the shoulder with his sword.) Later, at Harvard University, he was known for his theatrical entrances into class, sweeping into the room, removing his coat, hat and finally his gloves – finger by finger – then whirling round and dazzling his students with the finer points of economic thought in his aristocratic Viennese accent.

The contrast between old and new also runs through his theory of capitalism, which he set out in his book *Capitalism, Socialism and Democracy*. According to Schumpeter, the fruits of modern capitalism – the vast array of goods on offer and the new technologies used to produce them – are created by heroic figures who are modern-day versions of the swashbuckling knights of old. They're entrepreneurs, men like the railway owner Cornelius Vanderbilt, or Andrew Carnegie, who amassed a huge fortune through expanding the American steel industry. Thorstein Veblen had seen Vanderbilt and his type as throwbacks to ancient societies of violent barbarians, 'robber barons' whose aggression made them rich but didn't benefit society as a whole. But Schumpeter said that it was because they'd channelled their excess energy into industry instead of battle that they'd become society's wealth creators.

It's entrepreneurs who, through daring and determination, make the innovations necessary for economic advancement and so help raise living standards over the long run, thought Schumpeter. They create new products using inventions (light bulbs that make use of the new discovery of electricity), or use new technologies to produce goods more easily (cheaper coal as a result of mechanical digging machines). Their motivations are about more than just money, said Schumpeter. They want to conquer, fight and show themselves to be superior people. Schumpeter had one in his family, his great-grandfather, who brought a steam engine to the town where Schumpeter was born and used it to power the first textile mill there.

In order to make their visions a reality – to build factories to make new kinds of refrigerators and radios – entrepreneurs need to lay their hands on bricks, iron and workers. How do they get hold of them when they're being used by other businesspeople to make the goods that consumers want now, in order to use them to produce new things, goods that people don't yet know that they want? They can do it because banks lend them money, which allows them to buy what they need. Therefore, money is more than just an aid to buying and selling – it's the heart and the blood pumping around the economic organism, directed by its brain, the entrepreneur. Schumpeter had practical experience of this when he became the director of an Austrian bank in the 1920s. He used his position to put money into all sorts of business schemes. (His experience shows the risks of entrepreneurship, too: in 1924 the economy turned bad and he was left with huge debts which it took him years to pay off.)

When they succeed, entrepreneurs get rich. Their new goods ripple through the economy as people realise that they'd like a gramophone player or a television and then go out to buy one. Henry Ford made a fortune out of discovering how to make cheap cars for the masses, Andrew Carnegie from introducing new ways of making steel.

Soon, imitators copy the original entrepreneurs, making the same cars, furnaces or dyes that they introduced. The new goods revolutionise whole industries and the economy expands. Eventually, some businesses fail and the economy starts to contract until a new round of innovation begins. Boom and bust, the up-and-down cycles of the capitalist economy, come from successive waves of innovation, the ebb and flow of entrepreneurship and imitation. New technologies kill off old ones – the horse-drawn cart gives way to the car, the candle to the light bulb. Companies like the camera film manufacturer Kodak rise, then decline, and new leaders appear, like Samsung, who put digital cameras into mobile phones. Schumpeter called it 'creative destruction'. In Schumpeter's view, capitalism is nothing but the constant change caused by restless entrepreneurs.

Unlike most economists, Schumpeter thought that monopolies helped the economy to advance. Economists usually view monopolies as inefficient because they charge too much and produce too little. They recognise a few exceptions, though. In some industries huge investments need to be made to begin producing a good. A water supplier has to lay a network of pipes before it can supply any water, for example. A single firm supplying the whole market can spread the costs of the pipes over a large output and so supply water at a low cost. It would be much more expensive for ten firms to each lay their own network of pipes to supply a tenth of the market. Schumpeter believed that monopolies were especially important for bringing about innovation because they give entrepreneurs big rewards for the risky activity of trying to create new things. When an entrepreneur invents a new engine valve, they're the only supplier of the valve: they're a monopolist for it and so can earn high profits. The possibility of earning high profits encourages entrepreneurs to create all sorts of new products. Without monopolies it would be much harder for new technologies to even get invented. Monopolies propel the technological progress that transforms the economy and eventually leads to more and cheaper products.

Schumpeter's view of capitalism differed, too, from the conventional view held by Marshall and Jevons, whom we met earlier. Their view was of an economy at rest: a snapshot. Schumpeter saw the economy as ever-changing, more like a film. In the standard snapshot, everyone knows what goods are available to buy and sell, and most of the time demand balances supply. Firms don't earn high profits because there's competition between lots of them to supply goods to consumers. The economy is said to be in 'equilibrium'. Conventional economics takes the resources in the economy as given and then looks at how it all comes into balance. There are no entrepreneurs who invent new things, just people who buy and sell what they know in order to maximise their utilities. Schumpeter shows us that equilibrium is really just an economy caught in a freeze-frame. 'What a pathetic figure is the economic actor who is always searching anxiously for an equilibrium,' says Schumpeter. 'He has no ambition and no entrepreneurial spirit. He is, in short, without force and life.' To Schumpeter the most important thing about capitalism was that entrepreneurs are constantly throwing rocks into the pond. The waves of creative destruction never die down. In Marshall's economy, firms compete on the price of oil lamps. In Schumpeter's, successful entrepreneurs blow away their competitors by inventing light bulbs.

In fact, capitalism is a bit like Schumpeter himself: bold and vital, fizzing with new ideas, never at rest. Underneath Schumpeter's surface of sparkle and wit, however, was a troubled mind, and in the capitalism that he tried to understand he perceived a dark side. 'Can capitalism survive?' Schumpeter asks. 'No. I do not think it can.'

Capitalism's liveliness contains seeds of gloom that will destroy it. To explain why, Schumpeter did something unusual for an economist. He made an argument about the politics and culture of capitalist society, not its economics. Karl Marx explained why capitalism was doomed in terms of economics: as the capitalists take more and more of what's produced as profit, the workers get less and less until the whole system shatters. For Schumpeter, however, there was no problem with the economy of capitalism. The problem was in the effect that capitalism has on people's broader attitudes, especially when firms get bigger. When entrepreneurs are successful, firms grow. Eventually giant corporations appear. They use advanced technologies to spray out new goods. Innovation can then be carried out using rational methods, often in specialised company research departments. Think of one of today's big companies, such as Apple. It has various research teams: some produce new software, some develop faster and lighter iPhones, others create more powerful laptops. What used to be visualised in a flash of genius by an entrepreneur now gets done using tried and tested procedures. Economic progress becomes automated in company policies and committee meetings.

From an economic point of view all this is a good thing: the creation of new products is planned in advance and becomes predictable. The problem is that it's so boring! Firms turn into vast organisations full of people in grey suits (or in the case of Apple, matching T-shirts). Schumpeter's entrepreneurs start off as daring heroes, but end up rather like bored teenagers who hate school and refuse to do their homework. They loathe having to go to work in a tie and having to sit in tedious meetings. They detest the way that life has become so dull and dreary under capitalism. So they start to distrust business and moneymaking in general. Some end up as anti-capitalist 'intellectuals' who teach in universities and write books criticising capitalism. They argue for the government to take over the economy from businesspeople and to create a socialist society. Schumpeter thought that this was starting to happen in the 1930s and 1940s when many intellectuals were hostile to capitalism and the state started to play a greater role in the running of the economy (see Chapter 21).

Schumpeter's predictions about the end of capitalism didn't come to pass. Capitalism has functioned to this day with significant state involvement – what's termed the 'mixed economy' – without an end to the system. Still, Schumpeter taught us something important: that the economy is constantly moving. Here he echoes Marx. And, like Marx, he said that socialism was inevitable. (He lived in a castle and praised rather than condemned the millionaires, so he's been called the rich man's Marx.) According to Schumpeter, the end of capitalism comes about because of the frustration of people at the top of society, the dissatisfied intellectuals. For Marx, it's the unhappy workers who topple the system. Marx's socialism comes out of capitalism's economic failure; Schumpeter's out of its success as firms get bigger. And unlike Marx, Schumpeter was a strong defender of capitalism, and didn't welcome a drift towards socialism.

Schumpeter was also opposed to the new theories of Keynes, which said that the government could stop the economy from slipping into recessions like the deep one of the 1930s. If capitalism is change, it has no end point; you can only begin to reckon its achievements in the long run, along the sweep of history that takes us from the messenger on horseback to the smartphone. The problem with calls for the government to sort out the economy is that they view capitalism in the short run and so favour quick fixes. Schumpeter thought the fixes would only suffocate entrepreneurship, put capitalism on a life-support machine for a while, and then kill it off.

CHAPTER 20

The Prisoners' Dilemma

Imagine two countries threatening to blow each other up. One arms itself with missiles to aim at its enemy, and because one does, so does the other. Each country tries to gain an advantage by buying weapons. The result is an 'arms race'. Both end up with huge stocks of missiles aimed at their enemy. The arms race is an example of 'game theory', a field of mathematics and economics that emerged in the 1940s and 1950s. Game theory looks at how countries, firms and people behave in situations in which what one side does affects outcomes for the other. When your enemy buys missiles it puts you at a disadvantage and makes your country less safe; when you buy missiles you do the same to your enemy. Each side needs to decide what to do, taking into account what their enemy might do. Game theorists call it 'strategic interaction': we affect each other (we 'interact') and so we decide what to do in the light of what our enemy does (we're 'strategic'). Game theory is the study of strategic interactions that are found everywhere, from simple games like rock-paper-scissors to the search for profit by businesses and the wars fought between nations.

After the Second World War, the United States and the Soviet Union became arch-enemies. The era became known as the Cold War: the two sides were involved in a huge arms race and threatened each other with deadly nuclear weapons. *Dr. Strangelove* was a 1964 film that poked fun at the rivalry, and as well as being a gripping story, it's an excellent introduction to the era of game theory and to some of the basic ideas. During the Cold War, the American military paid for research into areas helpful to national security and game theory was one of them. Many game theorists worked for the RAND ('research and development') Corporation, a military research organisation. In the film, Dr Strangelove is the American president's director of weapons research, an eccentric genius with dark glasses and a funny accent who advises on military tactics. He's said to have been inspired by a real genius, the Hungarian-born mathematician John von Neumann (1903–57), one of the founders of game theory who worked for RAND and became President Eisenhower's adviser on defence strategy. Von Neumann was so clever that at the age of eight he could divide eight-digit numbers in his head. As an adult he wrote scientific papers on shockwaves, aerodynamics and the distribution of stars. In his spare time he started the field of game theory.

Imagine you're a general and that you have to decide whether to buy more bombs. You know that an enemy general has to do the same. How do you actually decide what to do? A big part of deciding is understanding what your enemy is likely to do. Once we know what you're going to do and what your enemy is going to do, we can say what the outcome of the game is going to be – everyone buying bombs, no one buying bombs or some other outcome. Von Neumann took a big step by working out a method for finding the outcome of games. But it only worked for some kinds, such as those in which participants were able to negotiate and make firm agreements with each other. Two enemy generals wouldn't be able to do that. So there was a need for a method that worked for other kinds of games, including ones where the players wouldn't necessarily stick to any promises they made to each other.

In 1950 a mathematician named John Nash (1928–2015) came up with a solution. Nash thought of his idea when he was still a student at Princeton University. He decided to pay a visit to von Neumann, who was then a Princeton professor, to tell him about it. Even though von Neumann was by then very famous, it didn't deter Nash. (Before that, he'd popped in to see Einstein to discuss some new ideas he'd had about the expansion of the universe.) The great von Neumann sent Nash away, telling him that his idea was trivial.

In fact Nash's idea became the most important in game theory, still used all the time today. He said that the outcome of a game – its 'equilibrium' – is that in which each player does the best for himself given what the other player does. When everyone's doing that, no one has any reason to change what they're doing, so that's the equilibrium of the game. Nash proved that most games have an equilibrium – what became known as a 'Nash equilibrium'. Take me and my enemy. Given that my enemy buys missiles, then my best response is to do the same: the worst thing would be to be unarmed in the face of enemy threats. The same reasoning applies to my enemy: if I arm, then they should definitely arm. Both of us building up our stock of missiles is the equilibrium of the game.

The arms race is a version of a really famous game, the 'prisoners' dilemma', which was invented by mathematicians at RAND. In the game, two gangsters are arrested for robbing a bank. The police don't have much evidence but know that they can at least convict the gangsters of tax evasion. The gangsters are questioned separately. Each can confess to the robbery or deny it. The police tell the gangsters that if one of them confesses and the other denies then the police will take the denier to be the ringleader and use the confessor as a witness against him. They'll give the denier a long prison sentence of twenty years and reward the confessor by setting him free. If both deny the robbery they'll each get four years in prison for tax evasion, and if both confess they'll each get a moderate prison term of ten years for the robbery.

What should the gangsters do? Suppose that one gangster believes that his partner will confess. Denying the robbery would be disastrous because he'd be given a twenty-year prison sentence, so he should definitely confess. Suppose, on the other hand, that he believes that his partner will deny the crime. In that case he should confess too, because that gains him his freedom. When both reason like this then both confess to the robbery. The prisoners' dilemma has a clear equilibrium: both gangsters confessing.

There's something odd about the equilibrium, though. The players make their best responses but end up in a position which isn't the best available for both. Both denying the robbery is better for both but it isn't the equilibrium: either gangster always does better by cheating his partner and confessing in the hope of being released. By acting rationally the gangsters do worse than they could. It's the same in the case of the arms race: the outcome of the game is that both countries build up stocks of missiles. In the end, neither has an advantage over the other but both have spent huge amounts arming themselves. It would have been better for both if neither had bought any missiles in the first place.

Prisoners' dilemmas crop up in economics all the time. Take a big product like the turbogenerators used in power stations. In the 1960s two of the leading American manufacturers, General Electric and Westinghouse, wanted to get good prices for their generators. One way was to get together and agree to sell fewer generators and charge a higher price for them. The problem is that when the price is high there's a temptation for a firm to cheat by undercutting its rival a bit and selling a few extra generators. The danger is that the price plummets and both firms end up with lower profits. It's the firms' equivalent of both gangsters confessing. The same problem faced oil-producing countries. In the 1960s, they'd promise each other to sell less oil in order to make it more expensive. But again, once prices were high, countries were tempted to produce a bit more oil to sell.

In business, politics and life, people sometimes compete and sometime cooperate. Game theory provides a way of thinking about that complexity. When are people likely to try to work together and when will they fight tooth and nail? In prisoners' dilemmas, for example, cooperation is always at risk of breaking down.

Some games allow for particularly complex tactics, especially when decisions are made in sequence so that you can see what the other person has done when you're deciding what to do. You could say that you'll punish your rival if they do something you don't like. In the 1970s two American coffee companies, Maxwell House and Folger's, battled each other for control of the US market. Folger's expanded eastwards into areas where Maxwell House was the main supplier, intending to take over business there. Maxwell House began a price war, cutting its prices low to drive Folger's out of its market. The sequence is: if you enter my market then I'll slash my prices; my hope is that this will put you off from entering the market in the first place. The problem with threats is that they aren't always believable. You might think that I'll never follow through on them because low prices would lose me too much money. In the case of Maxwell House and Folger's, though, the threats worked: Maxwell House succeeded in discouraging Folger's from expanding into New York City.

But the story of *Dr. Strangelove* shows how hard it is to make effective threats. To discourage a nuclear attack, you tell your enemy that you'll definitely retaliate. But once your enemy has launched their missile they know you won't launch yours because two missiles would wipe out life on the planet. In the film, a rogue American general orders a nuclear bomb to be dropped on the Soviet Union. The American president tries to call off the attack, but the general has shut himself off from communications. The president summons the Soviet ambassador who reveals that the Soviets have installed a 'doomsday machine', a massive bomb that will destroy all life if detonated. It's set to go off automatically if an attack is launched on the Soviet Union, and there's no way of turning it off. Dr Strangelove explains to the president the logic of the machine: by making it automatic and irreversible the machine creates a believable threat and so should deter your enemy from attacking. The film's grim joke is that this works only if everyone knows about it: 'Vy didn't you tell za vorld?!' yells Strangelove at the ambassador.

The doomsday machine illustrates a basic lesson of game theory: influencing what your opponent thinks about you is critical. A firm threatening to retaliate against a rival needs to show that it's tough rather than weak. An economic equivalent of installing a doomsday machine is to build a much bigger factory than the market needs. Once built, it's worth retaliating against competitors by flooding the market, even at rock-bottom prices, to get back some of the money spent building. In the 1940s, the Aluminum Company of America, which controlled 90 per cent of American aluminium production, used this tactic to keep out competitors.

Nash presented his ideas in a handful of mathematical articles written when he was a young man. Then he disappeared. He was suffering from a serious mental illness and spent decades in and out of hospital, but his ideas revolutionised economics in his absence. (The 2001 film *A Beautiful Mind* tells his extraordinary life story.) Strategic interactions occur very often in the economy, but until game theory was invented they were overlooked by economists. The leading theory of markets was that of perfect competition in which there's no strategic interaction at all. There are so many buyers and sellers that no single one of them can have any effect on the price. When thousands of apple-sellers serve thousands of customers they sell whatever number of apples they want to at the market price, so sellers don't have to worry about what their competitors are doing or thinking; they don't have to outwit each other to survive. Game theory allowed economists to analyse all sorts of more complex, realistic situations in which people and firms do have to outwit each other. Nash's method for analysing these sorts of situations is now used in pretty much every area of economics. Gradually Nash recovered from his illness and in 1994 was awarded the Nobel Prize for economics in recognition of his truly groundbreaking idea.

CHAPTER 21

The Tyranny of Government

One night during the Second World War, two men sat on the roof of the ancient chapel of King's College, Cambridge. They'd climbed up there to protect the building from bombs dropped by German planes. The chapel had taken five English kings over a hundred years to build. Now the pair were going to defend it against enemy bombs – using shovels. (The idea was to use them to push off any bombs that landed on the roof.)

The intrepid duo were two of the most famous economists of the twentieth century. They must have made an odd couple, though. For one thing, they were totally opposed to each other in their economic thinking. The older of the two, John Maynard Keynes, whom we met in an earlier chapter, was already famous – a brilliant, persuasive and supremely self-assured Englishman. The younger was Austrian-born Friedrich Hayek (1899–1992), a quieter man with a formal, precise way of talking. After the outbreak of war, the London School of Economics, where Hayek was a professor, had been evacuated to Cambridge and he ended up living in Keynes's college. The two neighbours had very different responses to the catastrophes of the 1930s and 1940s, the mass unemployment around the world, and the rise of the Nazis in Germany which sparked the great conflict and was the reason for their night on the roof.

Nazism was, of course, a dreadful system of cruelty and murder. It's easy to believe that, while the Nazis were pure evil, the countries opposing them were completely different – good and just societies. Is it enough to leave it at that? Hayek thought not. In fact he said something rather uncomfortable – even shocking. Yes, Britain and America were sworn enemies of the Nazis and fought and defeated them, but they had more in common with the Nazis than they'd care to admit. The German economy was tightly controlled by the Nazi government. In Britain, too, many believed that the government should run things. Hayek said that this belief could eventually lead to complete control by the government, not just of the economy but of life in general. The end result would be 'totalitarianism', a society in which the government is all-powerful and requires everyone to be totally obedient to it. If you disobey, you face prison or even death. It happened in Germany, and if people weren't careful it would happen in Britain too.

How could Hayek compare Nazi Germany with free, democratic countries like Britain and America? Surely the comparison is ridiculous? To understand what he was getting at we need to look at what happened to the economies of Europe during the Second World War and after it. When the war broke out, governments took over. In Britain, the government ordered factories to produce more guns and aircraft for the military and fewer ordinary goods like clothes and shoes. That meant that there was less for people to buy. Shoppers were allocated a fixed amount of basic goods like butter, eggs and sugar rather than being able to purchase whatever they wanted with the money in their pockets.

It was a big change to the normal system of free markets, in which the government lets firms make what they want, and people buy what they want and work wherever they want. But these were extraordinary times, and economic life couldn't continue as normal. A wartime poster said: 'Increase British Production. Speed

Nazi Destruction.' Government control of the economy helped to do that. Many people felt that the government should continue to play a big part in the economy once the fighting was over, and by the 1940s economists had come to the conclusion that governments had an important role, war or no war. Keynes had argued that the economy could get stuck in a state of high unemployment with no way out on its own, and only the government could correct the problem.

Many ordinary people had started to think along similar lines. You'd imagine that to pass the time in the air-raid shelters people would have turned to an exciting escapist novel. Surely the last thing that anyone would have wanted to read about was economics and government finance? But at the height of the war, a bestselling book in Britain was a thick government report about just those things. It was called *Social Insurance and Allied Services*, and the night before it went on sale people queued in the street to get hold of a copy. Why were they so keen to read such a heavy-sounding book? Because they'd been gripped by the very idea that Hayek had warned about: that the government should be heavily involved in the economy. The report explained what the government was going to do after the war ended. It was written by William Beveridge, a well-known academic and writer who, when a young man, had worked helping the poor in London's East End. The report made him a national hero, and people flocked to hear him talk about it. Before the war, the government had helped the poor, but the help was patchy. Beveridge wanted the government to properly protect people from the uncertainties of markets – from losing their jobs, not having enough to feed their children, and so on. The government had to battle five 'giant evils': want, disease, squalor, ignorance and idleness. It would set up a system of 'social security' that would support the unemployed and the sick. It would provide hospitals, schools and housing, and it would follow economic policies that helped to create jobs.

Hayek disagreed with this vision of the economy. His mentor had been Ludwig von Mises, the Austrian economist we met in Chapter 16 who'd said that socialism could never work. But Beveridge and Keynes hadn't proposed a socialist economy. The postwar economy was a 'mixed' economy, a middle way between capitalism and socialism. The government owned big industries like coal and the railways, controlled the prices of some goods and paid for schools and hospitals, giving the economy a socialist flavour. But a strong capitalist tang remained: there was a large number of privately owned firms ruled by profit. Hayek rejected the compromise. He said that state control of the economy would deprive people of their freedom, even under the middle way of the mixed economy.

The problem as Hayek saw it was that the spectacular economic progress of the last few centuries had given people a sense of power. The progress had been generated by the thousands of markets that make up an economy, which weren't created by any one person. People become impatient and want quicker progress. Governments start to interfere with markets in the hope of developing the economy faster. Why would this destroy freedom, especially if it's designed to free people from economic hardship as Beveridge hoped it would? It does, thought Hayek, because people have different desires and disagree about which ones are most important. Some people want more art galleries, others more swimming pools. It's impossible to reflect every person's desires in a single plan. If the government takes control of the economy it ends up deciding for you. You're no longer able to choose and your personal freedom gets trampled on.

Hayek said that the loss of freedom could even cost you your life. 'The last resort of a competitive economy is the bailiff,' he said, but 'the ultimate sanction of a planned economy is the hangman.' What he meant was that in a free-market economy if you're lazy you lose your own money (by getting fired or by making a loss). If things go really badly the worst that can happen is that an official of a law court (a bailiff) could give your possessions to the people you owe money to. In an economy controlled by the state, if you do your work badly you don't lose your own money but that of the nation as a whole. The entire community pays for your mistakes. You can't repay your fellow citizens with your own possessions because the state owns everything. You must pay by going to prison or, in an extreme case, with your life. What begins as an attempt to get rid of the unfairness of capitalism ends in tyranny.

For Hayek, it wasn't enough for Britain to fight the Nazis with tanks and planes – or with a pair of shovels. It had to fight them with ideas too. The idea that had to win was that of economic freedom – for the government to let people decide what to do themselves. Without economic freedom, political freedom was impossible. Without political freedom, people can't think for themselves anymore. The government tells you what to do, what to think, how to live. Hayek made his warning towards the end of the war in his book *The Road to Serfdom*. He felt that he had to write it to warn people of the danger, even though he knew that it would annoy a lot of them. Hayek said that if we allowed the government to control us, we'd eventually end up rather like medieval serfs: peasants controlled by a lord, who weren't allowed to decide anything for themselves. Modern Western civilisation itself was based on the freedom of the individual, said Hayek. If we forget that, then civilisation might collapse.

Hayek's book was a sensation (and rather more fun to read than Beveridge's), and it made him famous. The British wartime prime minister and Conservative Party leader, Winston Churchill, mentioned it in a radio broadcast during the 1945 election campaign. He criticised the opposing Labour Party's policy of having the government run the economy, comparing them to Hitler's ruthless secret police, an echo of Hayek's warning about big government. But the book did annoy a lot of people. It came out just as economists were coming to a firm belief in the importance of the government being involved in the running of the economy. Herman Finer, one of Hayek's colleagues at the London School of Economics, called the book 'sinister' and 'bigoted'. As opinion moved away from him, Hayek abandoned economics. He became famous again a few decades later when free-market economics came back into fashion (see Chapter 29).

In the end, bigger governments in Western democracies didn't lead to a new Hitler (although Hayek didn't say that it would inevitably do so, only that it would take us closer to that point). Today, most economies are a mix of private business and government action. Much of the debate among economists is about where to draw the line. Hayek drew it further towards the free market than most. But even he said that some government spending in the economy was needed: to guarantee a basic living to the unemployed and to provide goods that markets can't. It wouldn't threaten freedom if done sparingly. This brought ridicule from those who thought he hadn't gone far enough. The free-market philosopher Ayn Rand scrawled rude comments about Hayek in the margin of her copy of *The Road to Serfdom*: he was an 'ass' and an 'absurd fool'.

Most economists today disagree with Hayek's basic position that more government means less freedom. When the government provides schooling for every child, surely it increases people's freedom? When people can read and write they can participate fully in society – they can get good jobs and understand the policies of the leaders who they vote for. After the war, spending by governments on health and education helped disadvantaged groups like women and black people like never before and enabled them to shape their own lives. In the end, much of the debate comes down to what we mean by freedom – a difficult question that economists often leave to others. For Hayek, it had to be faced head on. It was the central question, not just for philosophers, but for economists as well.

CHAPTER 22

The Big Push

Just before midnight on 6 March 1957, the president of Ghana, Kwame Nkrumah, stood on a podium gazing down on a cheering crowd of his fellow citizens. For the previous eighty years Ghana had been a colony (a nation ruled over by a foreign country), but as the clock struck twelve Nkrumah declared that Ghana was free forever. In that moment his country became the first colonised black African nation to gain independence. At the polo ground in the capital city of Accra, where the official celebrations were taking place, the British Union Jack – the flag of Ghana's old colonial ruler – was lowered and a new red, yellow and green one was raised. 'Children of Ghana arise and uphold your cause,' sang the crowds. Ghana was a trailblazer. A few years later the British prime minister, Harold Macmillan, talked of 'winds of change blowing through this continent' and during the 1960s dozens of colonies in Africa and further afield gained their independence.

Nkrumah made a single, independent nation out of a patchwork of provinces and peoples. An arch built in Accra, carved with the words 'AD 1957 Freedom and Justice', marked the new era. Nkrumah knew that the words meant much more than a colourful flag and a new national anthem. Freedom and justice would only exist when his people had enough to eat, were healthy and housed, and could read and write. Before independence, Ghana had earned a lot of money from selling its cocoa. Some of this wealth had gone into building roads and railways. Even so, like many of the newborn nations, Ghana was a poor country. Nearly a quarter of children died before their fifth birthdays and average incomes were a tiny fraction of European levels. Nkrumah promised that Ghana would become a paradise within a decade.

Taking part in the independence celebrations was Nkrumah's economic adviser, Arthur Lewis (1915–91), who'd been raised in a poor backwater of the British Empire, the island of Saint Lucia in the Caribbean. As a teenager he'd hoped to become an engineer, but soon realised that the white-run sugar plantations would never employ a black engineer. After he graduated from London University in the 1930s, *The Economist* magazine turned him down on the grounds that he'd have to interview people who wouldn't want to talk to a black journalist. Later came triumphs: in 1938 he became the first person of African descent to be appointed a lecturer at the London School of Economics, and in 1979 he won the Nobel Prize for economics, to this day the only black person to have done so.

Lewis observed that unlike those of rich countries, poor nations' economies are full of contrasts between the 'modern' and the 'traditional', for example between luxury shops and the street sellers hanging around outside them. The modern part consists of capitalist farms and industries that hire workers in order to make goods to sell at a profit. The traditional part consists of family farms and businesses that share their proceeds among relatives and friends instead of maximising profit. In a poor country, most of the economy is traditional. Lewis called it a 'dual' economy: 'heavily developed patches . . . surrounded by economic darkness'.

The traditional economy has lots of workers, many of whom add little to production. There are aunts doing odd jobs on the family plot, young men offering to carry travellers' bags and messenger boys lounging outside office doors. In fact, said Lewis, the traditional sector contains an 'unlimited' supply of workers, in the sense that you could probably halve their number without hurting production. Here, though, lies the root of economic progress. The modern sector can employ the plentiful labour for a low wage, and then earn high profits. The profits get invested in machines and factories. The modern sector of the economy expands and the traditional one shrinks. Economic darkness recedes.

Lewis helped start the field of 'development economics'. Development suggests advancement and improvement: a baby becomes a toddler, learns how to communicate and eventually turns into a socially sophisticated adult. In the nineteenth century, Britain grew up from an agricultural society into a vigorous industrial economy. Now the nations of Africa and Asia were trying to do the same. Another founder of development economics was the Polish-born British economist Paul Rosenstein-Rodan (1902–85), who, during the Second World War, far from the front lines in an elegant mansion on a quiet London square, gathered a group of colleagues to mull over the economic prospects of the new nations. They believed that the rapid development of Africa and Asia was essential to the creation of a better world after the war.

All the great economic thinkers, such as Adam Smith and David Ricardo, were fascinated by how economies advance. Why, then, the need to talk of 'development economics' specifically? Isn't all economics about development? In a sense, yes. But Ghana and other newly independent states such as India and Egypt were born into a different world from nineteenth-century Manchester where Britain's first railway lines were laid. By the 1950s, Europe and America had pulled far ahead of the rest of the world. They'd worked out how to generate cheap electricity and make everything from radios to sugar cubes on long production lines. The emerging nations wouldn't have to reinvent it all. 'What other countries have taken 300 years or more to achieve, a once dependent [colonised] territory must try to accomplish in a generation,' said Nkrumah.

Rosenstein-Rodan and Lewis believed that the new nations were far from achieving their economic potential. They called them 'underdeveloped' or 'developing' countries. Crucially, they believed that there were policies that could make the countries richer. The development economists and the leaders of the developing nations thought it was essential to create industries. Nkrumah said that his people would be happy only when factory smoke prevented them from seeing from one side of the River Volta to the other. The task, then, was to turn developing countries like Ghana, societies consisting mainly of small farms and scattered villages, into industrial ones churning out cars and chemicals.

Until the 1940s, most economists believed that markets would be enough: the promise of profit would encourage businesspeople to build factories and telephone networks. But the new development economists thought that markets didn't work at all well in poor countries. Lewis showed how developing economies needed to take the plentiful labour in the countryside and to place it in factories, but Rosenstein-Rodan said that this wouldn't happen automatically.

The problem is that to be profitable, a factory depends on there being other factories. To make money, a new sardine-canning factory needs to sell its sardines. Who'll buy them? People in the traditional part of the economy earn very little and don't have the money to buy tinned sardines. The factory's own workers will spend some, not all, of their wages on them; they'll want to buy shoes as well. If at the same time a shoe factory opened, then its workers would buy some sardines and the sardine factory's workers would buy shoes. Each creates a market for the other's products. For industrialisation to happen, then, workers need to be taken from the land and put into many different industries at the same time. Together the factories would be profitable, but on their own they wouldn't be, so if you were a businessperson thinking about setting up a sardine factory, you'd be put off by a lack of other industries in the country. Ports, metal plants and shipyards depend on each other and need to be built together. Developing countries had to go from having nothing to having everything, and Rosenstein-Rodan argued that only the government could time the leap accurately. It had to make massive investments in many areas of the economy. He called it the 'big push'.

Ghana tried it. The government built power stations, hospitals, schools and a modern harbour. Factories and industrial plants sprouted. The biggest project was the construction of a dam on the River Volta. Eighty thousand people had to be moved to make way for it, and it created the largest manmade lake in the world. Rich countries gave 'aid': money to help pay for the projects. The government had high hopes that wealth was just round the corner.

But a big push is a tall order, especially for new governments with little experience. In Ghana it did give people hospitals, telephones and clean water, but it also created lots of inefficient firms. Many were complete duds. Mango-processing plants were built even though there were few mangoes to be had. One huge factory could make more glass than the entire country would ever use. The firms didn't propel take-off; instead the engines sputtered and the economy crashed. The big push ran into trouble in many other countries in Africa and in Latin America and Asia, too. One reason was that politics and economics became linked in a way that hurt development. As the government put money into the new industries, businesspeople would do everything to make sure that it kept coming. They'd support the government to stay on its good side. Some of them would put in more effort persuading state officials to give them money and favours than in making their factories efficient.

A few countries were successful, however. South Korea was one. At the end of the Second World War, Korea was divided into two countries, the communist North and the capitalist South, and they went to war at the beginning of the 1950s. South Korea emerged from the fighting in chaos. Millions of people had been killed and the survivors lived in deep poverty. Many of them had lost their homes and had to forage in the hills for food. In 1961 an army general called Park Chung-hee seized power and initiated South Korea's own big push, aiming to turn the country into an industrial powerhouse. Park organised South Korea's push through *chaebols*, large businesses with close links to the government. The government directed the *chaebols* into particular industries and gave them cheap loans. At first they were protected from foreign competition, but the government insisted that they become competitive and eventually export their goods.

South Korea's economy took off. The country developed its own textiles and clothing industries before moving into steel, cars and shipbuilding. In the 1950s, North Korea had the stronger economy, but before long the South had overtaken it and left many other developing nations behind as well. A couple of decades after Park took power, the economy was ten times bigger. Two of its *chaebols*, the electronics firm Samsung and the car manufacturer Hyundai, have become household names in Europe and America. Today South Koreans enjoy standards of living on a par with the rich nations. People called Park's feat the 'Miracle on the Han River'. What was exceptional about South Korea was that the government was able to stop the new industries from getting lazy. When rewarding businesspeople with cheap loans they made sure that the firms performed well, and Park even took away loans from firms that failed to become competitive enough to sell their goods abroad. A few other Asian countries – Singapore, Taiwan and Hong Kong – also took off after the war. For their amazing achievement these countries became known as the Asian Tigers.

Sadly, in some countries state involvement in the economy turned into something much worse than a stalled big push. The leader of Zaire (now the Democratic Republic of the Congo), Mobutu Sese Seko, stole millions of dollars of his country's money, built himself a dozen palaces and cruised down the Zaire River in a huge yacht furnished with oyster-shaped sofas in pink silk. Meanwhile, his people struggled to survive and the roads fell apart. So economists turned against the idea of the big push. In the 1980s they told governments of both rich and poor countries to stop interfering in their economies. New free-market policies for the development of poor nations were drawn up, like 'privatisation', the selling off of companies owned by the state to private business-people. They, too, proved a disappointment and economists began to see that there was no single ignition switch for economic take-off to be pressed whenever governments chose.

CHAPTER 23

The Economics of Everything

If you own a shop, then when you're at work your mind is constantly calculating. Are there enough eggs? Should we buy an extra drinks freezer? Would it be worth hiring a new shop assistant? All day you add up sales and costs to try to make as much profit as you can. After you close up for the day, you come home and prepare dinner and clean the house. You might think that at this point your calculating mind takes a rest. Surely family life – cooking, cleaning and playing with the kids – has nothing to do with business and economics? Other social scientists study the non-economic aspects of life – its 'social' aspects. Anthropologists look at people's customs and cultures, sociologists at the workings of society in the broadest terms. Anthropologists and sociologists think about things like marriage and the family, and about the darker subjects of crime and racism. Economists are different, you might assume: they deal with strictly economic topics to do with industries and firms, prices and profit.

In the 1950s, Gary Becker (1930–2014) broke down the divide between the 'economic' and the 'social'. He was a leading economist at the University of Chicago, whose department of economics became so famous that people talk of the Chicago school of economic thought. Chicago's philosophy was that markets and prices are the basis of how society works. Becker took this further than most. At work, shopkeepers calculate costs and benefits to earn the most profit. At home they're busy calculating costs and benefits too, thought Becker. They make the children turn off the television and do their homework because children who do their homework end up earning more when they're adults, and adults with money are better able to look after their elderly parents. In fact Becker saw economic calculation everywhere. One of his lectures was called 'The Economic Way of Looking at Life'. Becker thought that economics could be used to understand pretty much any area of life.

One afternoon, Becker was running late for an important meeting. If he parked his car in the designated car park he'd definitely miss the start of the meeting. It was quicker to park illegally on the street. He noticed himself weighing up the costs and benefits of different courses of action. If he parked on the street he'd just make it to the meeting on time, but he'd risk a parking fine. The cost to him of parking illegally was the size of the fine adjusted by the probability of getting caught. He reckoned that the cost was low compared to the benefit of getting to the meeting on time and so he decided to park on the street. His lawbreaking was a matter of economic calculation.

The experience inspired Becker's economic theory of crime. Becker rejected the argument that criminals are different from law-abiding people, that they commit crimes because they're mentally ill or have been treated badly by others, that they're in some sense victims of circumstances. According to Becker, criminals aren't that different from the rest of us. They're not necessarily evil, ill or wild, but people with logical, calculating minds. Becker doesn't deny that the causes of crime are complex. His point is that costs and benefits matter, just as they do for a shopkeeper, and crime prevention needs to take account of them. For example, the parking authority could save money by simply raising fines rather than spending a lot trying to catch people by sending out traffic wardens to find illegally parked cars. When motorists calculate logically, a high fine with a low chance of being caught can come to the same thing as a small fine with a high chance of being caught. The best way to get rid of crime is to make it unprofitable. For illegal parking that might mean a higher fine, for burglary a longer prison sentence.

Becker used standard economic principles to analyse all sorts of human behaviour. One principle was that people have a clear set of preferences that don't change much: today you prefer rock music to jazz, and most likely next week you will, too. Another is that people are rational: they calculate the course of action that best satisfies their preferences. They do the best for themselves given how much money they have and how much things cost. This implies that there are trade-offs everywhere. The shopkeeper compares the benefit of opening a new shop with the cost, the car thief the value of a stolen Mercedes with the risk of being imprisoned for stealing it.

While a student, Becker used the same economic principles to look at racism. His colleagues were shocked. Surely racism was to do with people's attitudes and the injustices of society? It was a topic for sociologists. What on earth did economics have to do with it? Becker was convinced that economics could explain a lot.

In the 1950s, black people in America suffered from severe discrimination in employment and wages. Becker viewed a racist employer's dislike of black people as a sort of preference. If you prefer rock to jazz, then compared to rock you dislike jazz, and you wouldn't be prepared to pay as much for a jazz album as for a rock album. In the same way, racist shopkeepers aren't willing to pay a black person as much as a white person to do the same job. Suppose that a black person has to accept a wage $50 lower than that of a white person to stand a chance of getting a job with a racist shopkeeper. Becker called that $50 the 'discrimination coefficient'. Racist shopkeepers are willing to pay $50 extra to white workers. They therefore end up paying more for their staff compared to non-racist employers who get employees who are just as good for a fraction of the cost. It's often assumed that discrimination by whites against blacks keeps black people poor and white people rich. Here Becker showed that the racists lose out too.

Jews also suffer from discrimination in employment. But they make up a small share of the population and so suffer less because they can make sure they only accept employment from non-racist employers. In America, black people make up such a large share of the population that not all of them will be able to find work with non-racist employers. Many will have no option but to work for racist bosses. Becker's theory therefore showed that on average the wages of black people will be lower than those of Jewish people even if racist employers hate Jews just as much as they hate black people. The larger the discriminated-against group, the more its members end up working for low wages for racist bosses who pay more to employ people from the favoured racial group. That's why, said Becker, the apartheid system in South Africa, in which the oppressed blacks made up the majority of the population, was economically wasteful as well as being immoral.

Becker also applied economics to the positive aspects of life, to marriage, families and raising children. At home, things aren't bought and sold for money, but Becker believed that economic principles worked here just as well.

A house is a small factory in which inputs such as flour, vegetables and cooking skills are used to produce an output: a family meal around the kitchen table. To economists, flour and vegetables are scarce: even though you can easily find them in the shops, there's a limited amount of them and so there's a limit to how much each of us can have. A crucial input to household production is time, which is also scarce. Some household outputs need a lot of it. Becker called them 'time-intensive'. Staying at home and watching the *Star Wars* films is time-intensive because it takes you many hours. The main cost of doing it isn't how much you paid for the electricity and the popcorn you ate. It's the other things that you could have done with the time (visiting a friend, perhaps) – the opportunity cost. For someone on a high wage the opportunity cost of watching the *Star Wars* films is high because in spending the day watching them instead of working they give up a lot of money.

Becker applied the idea of time intensity to the decision to have a child. He said that a child is a bit like a good that you buy. When you buy a car you pay a cost and receive a stream of benefits over time. Having a child is the same. (When he first made this comparison at a conference, the audience laughed at him.) Children are time-intensive goods because of the many hours needed to look after them. The cost, then, of having a child, just like watching films all afternoon, is the wage income you give up when you stay at home to look after your child. The cost of a child is therefore higher when you earn a higher wage. Often the earnings that are given up are those of women when they stop working to look after their children, so during the twentieth century, as more women went out to work, the cost of children rose. The result was that women began to have fewer of them.

In the nineteenth century, the economist Alfred Marshall described economics as 'not a body of concrete truth, but an engine for the discovery of concrete truth'. This view sees economics as a method of analysis, the application of principles of rationality and choice to any situation you like. To Becker, too, economics was a 'tool' rather than a 'thing'. It didn't have to be about 'the economy' – the people and firms that consume and produce goods. It could be about pretty much any area of life, including those like crime and child-rearing that had always been thought of as off limits to economists. Following in Becker's footsteps, economists have analysed the legal system, terrorism, even tooth-brushing and Japanese sumo wrestling! Many economists think that this is a very good development. The strength of the economic method is that it's versatile and can be applied anywhere. It's a powerful way of explaining all sorts of human behaviour.

Others think that economics is overstretching itself. By putting all their energy into learning how to use their method, economists neglect the study of the economy itself, how it functions day to day and how it has developed over time. (If you study economics at university you'll spend a lot of time learning how to apply the principles of rationality and choice, rather than learning about how, for example, the American or Japanese economies actually work.) Then there's the question of how powerful the economic method really is. When we met the economist Thorstein Veblen in Chapter 17 we saw that he rejected economists' standard theories of rationality and choice. Unconventional economists like him say that economics needs to incorporate richer models of human behaviour that go beyond calculations of costs and benefits. And many economists now believe that shopkeepers managing their stock are in fact far from rational, let alone people cooking dinner at home (see Chapter 36).

Nevertheless, many of Becker's ideas have become so influential that it's easy to forget how controversial they once were. Today economists constantly talk about 'human capital', the idea that people contribute to production like a machine does, and that people can enhance their human capital and job prospects by getting educational qualifications. People were outraged when Becker proposed the idea. Today, the notion that students go to university to gain skills that will help them get high-paying jobs when they graduate is barely questioned.

CHAPTER 24

Growing Up

When you were a young child, your parents might have made a mark on the wall every year on your birthday to show how much you'd grown. You took pride as the marks got higher: as you grew up and got taller you'd be able to do more things than when you were small. If you had a younger brother or sister, then their mark would have started off way below yours, but gradually caught up. Economists think about economies in the same way.

Economies are like growing humans: some, often the 'young' ones, grow fast and catch up with the old. And like children, when an economy grows it can do more: there are more goods for people to consume and more resources available to build schools and to fight disease. In a way, how and why economies grow is the central question of economics. When an economy grows it gets better at overcoming scarcity. So even if they didn't use the modern term 'economic growth', many of the thinkers we've met so far were concerned with it. They wanted to know how societies get richer and more sophisticated over time, and a big part of this is how economies get bigger – how they grow.

After the Second World War, economists started to think about economic growth in a new way. In the 1930s, during the Great Depression, economies had done the opposite of growing. They got smaller: countries produced less, firms went out of business and millions lost their jobs. If the Great Depression was a crisis, then economic normality was something else: the situation in which a country uses all of its resources to make goods, so that there's little unemployment and few idle factories. Over time, the economy grows; its capacity to make things increases, and society gets wealthier. Between crises, this is often what happens. Up until the First World War, many of the world's leading countries grew steadily without huge economic turmoil; after the Second World War a new period of growth dawned.

The American economist Robert Solow (b. 1924) is today one of the few economists to have lived through the economic growth that came after the war as well as the Great Depression that came before it. At the end of the war he was discharged from the army and returned to his interrupted education at Harvard University, where he'd been studying sociology and anthropology. On a bit of a whim – his wife suggested that he might find the subject interesting – he turned to economics. It was good advice. Solow used mathematics and statistics to put a modern twist on old economic questions. What are the forces that cause economies to grow so that over time the living standards of the population improve? Why do some countries grow faster than others?

Solow – and in parallel with him, a now overlooked Australian economist, Trevor Swan (1918–89) – devised a theory to explain how economies grow during normal times when they're using all available resources to produce goods. They ask us to imagine a simplified world in which goods are made using capital (machines and factories) and labour. A society can produce goods using different combinations of capital and labour: it could dig a train tunnel using a few mechanical diggers and hundreds of people with shovels, or using lots of mechanical diggers and only a few people to drive them. Rich countries are those with a lot of capital compared to the population. That means they're able to produce a lot of output for each person. It's output per person that's the proper measure of how rich a society is. A society of ten people that produces goods worth £100 is twice as rich as a society of twenty producing the same amount. The society of ten can provide on average double the amount of goods to each of its people, and they have a higher standard of living than the society of twenty. Solow's theory is about explaining growth in the crucial measure of income per person.

If you invest in a bit more capital – in another bread oven, for example – you add to the output of the economy because more bread gets made. In Solow's theory, as you add more capital to the same number of workers, the extra output you squeeze out gets smaller and smaller. The effect is called 'diminishing returns to capital'. Imagine a country that has only a few bread ovens. Investing in an extra one adds a lot to bakers' production. As more ovens are installed, though, it becomes harder to find people to run them, so the hundredth oven adds a much smaller amount to production than the tenth one did.

Diminishing returns to capital means that as an economy adds more to its stock of capital and produces more, its rate of growth tapers off. Eventually, all the gains from extra capital are exhausted. If capital was the only thing that created economic growth, then the economy would end up in a position in which there was no growth in income per person. In fact, there is something that creates growth in income per person in the long run: technological improvements. In economic terms, technology is a recipe that makes inputs, such as cloth, thread and metal, into outputs, such as a pair of jeans. The recipe is knowledge: how to cut cloth, how to sew the pieces together, and so on. Knowledge advances when someone invents a more efficient sewing technique. Jeans can then be made more easily. The economy becomes more 'productive'. Technological progress allows more to be made with the capital and labour that a country has. It also creates completely new goods. Societies progress as they move from stone tablets to parchment, from parchment to paper and from paper to digital tablets. It's higher productivity stemming from technological advancement, says Solow, which is the true engine of growth.

Solow's theory is an optimistic one. It says that living standards in poor countries tend to catch up with those of rich countries, just as a small child eventually gets closer in height to its older sibling. A poor country that has little capital grows faster than a rich country that has lots of it and so has already exhausted most of the gains. Because the poor country grows faster, its living standards catch up with those of the rich country. Both countries close in on a position in which the only source of growth is from improved technology; the further away from that position a country is, the faster it moves towards that endpoint.

After the Second World War, America was the most economically advanced nation in the world. Europe caught up with it, just as Solow said. European countries used new technology like transistors and computers and built big automated factories like the ones in America. At the end of the war Europe's income per person was less than half of America's, but by the mid-1970s it was nearly three-quarters. Outside of Europe, Japan made massive gains.

The steady progress went on for decades, and there was no repeat of the Great Depression. Economists looked on those years as a 'Golden Age' for growth and living standards. In the early 1950s only 20 per cent of French families owned cars, but by the early 1970s, 60 per cent did. Fridges and televisions, which were rare in France just after the war, soon became common. And while people consumed more, they worked less. Even Britain – no longer the economic leader as its European neighbours overtook it – saw the gains. Days off and trips to the cinema became normal. A hit British film in 1963 was *Summer Holiday,* in which a group of mechanics borrow a bus during their lunch hour and drive it south, ending up on a beach in Greece. These were years in which mechanics and bus drivers, no longer just rich people, hoped for a summer holiday in the sun. In 1957, the British prime minister, Harold Macmillan, caught the mood: 'Most of our people have never had it so good. Go around the country . . . and you will see a state of prosperity such as we have never had in my lifetime – nor indeed in the history of this country.'

But it was only a Golden Age for some. While Europe did well, most of the world stayed poor. A few countries, such as South Korea, did start to catch up, as Solow's theory predicted, but much of Asia and Africa lagged behind. Before Solow, economists thought that poor countries got richer when they built lots of factories, roads and ports. In an earlier chapter we saw how developing nations tried to do that. Solow showed that investing in more capital – factories and machines – would at best only boost growth temporarily. To grow in the long run, an economy needed better technology. But Solow's theory didn't explain where the new technology came from. It left technology as 'exogenous': something that comes from outside of the economy and that's not controllable, rather like the sunlight that makes a garden grow. It's assumed that technology is available to all economies equally, whether that of Malawi or Switzerland. Once Malawi makes use of new technology it becomes more like Switzerland. In reality, there are all sorts of barriers to a poor country adopting the latest technological methods. The country might lack the skills needed to use them properly or they might not be cost-effective in its businesses.

What's more, technology isn't exogenous: it's created by a society's inventors and engineers. In the 1990s, the American economist Paul Romer (b. 1955) started off a new wave of growth theory which treated technology as 'endogenous' – produced within the economy. Romer's point is that technological progress isn't like sunlight. People invent better car engines because they can make money from selling them. Technology is special because once discovered it can be used over and over again. When an aeronautical firm spends money on research into the melting point of a metal it uses the knowledge to make a lighter aircraft wing, which it can then sell and make money from. The same knowledge can then be used by a kitchen appliance manufacturer to make a better oven. The appliance manufacturer doesn't need to spend money on doing the research again. This makes knowledge quite different from most things that people buy and sell. Economists call it a 'non-rival' good. Contrast it to a drill: if you're using the drill, I can't use it, and drills wear out and must eventually be replaced. Once discovered, however, the melting point of metal is known forever, and new discoveries add to it, increasing our stock of knowledge without limit.

Because technology is non-rival and can keep on increasing, it leads to ever greater wealth. There's a hitch, though. Since some of the benefits of a new idea go to people other than the original inventor, there tends to be too little research and development compared to what would be best for the economy as a whole. (This is an example of a market failure, an idea we saw when we met Professor Pigou back in Chapter 14.) Romer's theory of technology and growth implies that governments can play a role by paying for research and development to bring about the creation of more new ideas than private markets alone create.

Where in Solow's theory growth tends to slow down, in Romer's it can keep on going as new ideas spread through the economy. That means that big economies – ones that are good at creating new ideas – can keep on getting bigger without slowing down. The smaller ones won't automatically catch up. Unfortunately, this has been the fate of many of the poorest countries around the world. In the end it means that they don't have as many resources available to feed, educate and house their people. That's why growth is so vital, and why the American economist Robert Lucas said that once you start thinking about it, 'it's hard to think about anything else'.

CHAPTER 25

Sweet Harmony

When classes start for the day, maths students turn up at Room 15 to spend an hour doing fractions and students learning geography go to Room 12. When the class ends, students stream into Room 12 for history and others head over to Room 3 for English. It goes on like this, day in, day out. How do the students know where to go? Because someone sat down and worked out a timetable, obviously. It's chaos if it doesn't work: teachers try to teach French to students learning physics and students from different classes end up jostling for seats in the same room. When it works, though, a day of lessons is a day of harmony.

Timetables coordinate people with different objectives: students studying different subjects. The person drawing up the timetable has to get the objectives to match up given the number of rooms and teachers available. The economy is a giant problem of coordination. Right now, you want a new pair of headphones, your friend wants a computer game and I want a cup of coffee. There are people out there who want all sorts of strange things that we'd probably never want, like meatball-flavoured bubble gum (yes, it does exist). If you and your friend go down to the high street, there'll be shops there selling headphones and computer games, and if I stop writing and head outside I'll definitely find someone willing to sell me coffee. Even people with strange bubble gum obsessions can find what they fancy in the right place.

The economic equivalent of students turning up to the right room is firms supplying exactly the right amount of the many different goods that people want: headphone manufacturers making a total of a million pairs of headphones when people want to buy a million pairs, and the same for suppliers of coffee and computer games. So who sets the timetable for the economy? Who tells the headphone manufacturers to make a million pairs? In capitalist economies, nobody does. We're so used to it, in fact, that we hardly give it a moment's thought. Often we're only really made aware of the issue of economic coordination when things go wrong: when a firm making computer components goes out of business and you discover that the laptop you want is out of stock. But under our noses something really rather extraordinary is going on, week in, week out. Most of the time the economy works well without anyone setting a timetable for it. Why isn't it in constant chaos, then?

In the 1950s a group of economists led by the American Kenneth Arrow (b. 1921) and the French-born Gérard Debreu (1921–2004) tried to answer the question. The basic theory of markets perfected by Alfred Marshall in the nineteenth century looked at supply and demand in a single market. The demand and supply for headphones depend on the price of headphones, those for oil on the price of oil. When the demand for oil is bigger than the supply, the price of oil is pushed up, encouraging people to demand less of it and oil firms to supply more of it. Eventually supply and demand are brought back into balance, into equilibrium. At equilibrium the price is that at which oil producers supply exactly the amount that buyers want. If supply and demand are two ends of a see-saw, then equilibrium is the see-saw when it's perfectly balanced and at rest.

The problem is that the price of oil doesn't just affect the oil market. Arrow points out the various effects of the low oil price that resulted from the discovery of new oil in Texas and the Persian Gulf in the 1930s. People started to heat their homes using oil rather than coal, and employment in the coal mines fell. Oil refineries got bigger, which pushed up the demand for steel. Cheap oil encouraged people to buy more cars, which led to the decline of the railways. Movements in one market created ripples in many others. Marshall's theory of demand and supply is a theory of 'partial equilibrium': it ignored the ripples.

Capturing the ripples is difficult. Under the partial equilibrium theory, we think of movements of the oil market see-saw as depending on the price of oil only. How can we take account of the interactions between different markets? Imagine the oil market see-saw being connected to the car market see-saw. When one see-saw moves, so do the others. Each see-saw is connected to dozens, perhaps hundreds, of other see-saws.

'General equilibrium' is the analysis of the connected movements in the see-saws. It was begun in the nineteenth century by the French economist Léon Walras (1834–1910). The equilibrium of a single market can be written as a simple equation: supply = demand. In Walras's theory, the supply and demand for oil depends on every price in the economy, as do the supply and demand for headphones, coffee and everything else. If there are a million goods, you end up with a million equations, each depending on a million prices. When supply equals demand in every single market, then all the see-saws are at rest. In Walras's mathematical terms it happens when all the equations are solved at the same time. Walras didn't manage to work out the solution to his mathematical problem; Arrow and Debreu did.

In the 1940s, when Arrow and Debreu were learning economics, the subject wasn't very mathematical. Open an economics book from the time and you'll find most of it written in words. Arrow and Debreu were mathematicians who'd moved into economics. In the 1950s they worked at a research institute at the University of Chicago, the Cowles Commission, which became an important centre for mathematical economics. In their writings many mathematical symbols were woven amongst the words (much like the writings of today's economists, in fact). When Arrow received a prize for his work in the 1950s, one of his colleagues suggested that he begin his speech of thanks after collecting the award with the words 'Symbols fail me.'

Arrow and Debreu start off with assumptions about people's behaviour and then, using strict mathematical reasoning, see what they imply for the economy. Some of the assumptions are to do with people being rational or consistent in their choices. For example, if you prefer bananas to pears and you prefer pears to peaches, then you must prefer bananas to peaches. They found that when people's preferences are rational then it's possible for all the markets in an economy to be at rest. In the technical language of economists, a general equilibrium exists. The discovery was important because if an equilibrium was impossible there wouldn't be a set of prices under which everyone's demands were being satisfied by the economy's firms. In mathematical terms, the economy would be 'inconsistent'. The collection of interconnected see-saws would never be at rest. They'd crash onto the ground, bang into each other and get all tangled up. Chaos would result.

But the question of whether markets work is about more than whether they're 'consistent'. Imagine that we know that the economy is at an equilibrium. As well as describing the situation, economists wonder how well it serves the needs of society as a whole. Let's suppose that after a morning's shopping at the local market we each return home with a bag of fruit. Is it a good thing that I have this many pears, you that many bananas? At the beginning of the twentieth century an Italian economist, Vilfredo Pareto (1848–1923), came up with a method for judging. An economic outcome is undesirable or 'inefficient' if it's possible to make at least one person better off without hurting anyone else, he said. Suppose that I have four pears and you have four bananas. You like pears and bananas equally, but I like bananas twice as much as pears. If we swapped your bananas for my pears, then I'd be twice as well off and you'd be as well off as before. It's called a 'pareto improvement'. If we didn't make the swap, the economy's resources wouldn't be being put to their best use: the bananas could be used to increase my happiness, but aren't, and so in a sense are wasted. An economic outcome is 'pareto efficient' when all the swaps have been done. From that position it's then impossible to make one person better off without making someone else worse off. The idea is that an economy shouldn't contain 'wasted' resources like your bunch of bananas.

Arrow and Debreu proved that if there's a general equilibrium in the economy then it must be pareto efficient. It's a cherished result in economics. Economists give it a special name: the First Welfare Theorem. It means that when an economy is in equilibrium there are no wasted resources like your bananas. At the prices that brought about the equilibrium, I'd be able to sell my pears and use the money to buy bananas and you'd be able to sell your bananas and buy other things. In fact, millions do the same for all sorts of goods. Once the trades are done no one can gain any further: there are no more wasted resources. So Arrow and Debreu showed that even though no one organises it, an economy of markets is like a well-organised school. It leads to harmony: people's desires are brought into balance and nothing gets wasted.

Be careful not to get carried away with all of this, however. First, pareto efficiency is a minimal notion of what's good for society. All it does is to rule out cases in which resources are wasted. But there are many pareto-efficient outcomes. One of them would be that in which one rich person owned everything and everyone else had nothing. A transfer of goods from the rich person to the rest would make the rest better off but would reduce the rich person's welfare. It wouldn't cause a pareto improvement even though we might think it very much desirable. The outcomes of markets, even if efficient, can be very unfair.

Second, the assumptions on which Arrow and Debreu's theory is based are far from the reality of how markets really work. They depend on markets being competitive so that no buyer or seller can influence the price on their own. In practice, there are powerful firms that do influence the market price, often because of 'economies of scale'. An aircraft manufacturer, for example, has to invest in expensive equipment before it can produce a single aircraft. As it produces more, the large initial costs are spread over the greater number of aircraft that it sells. Such a firm will often expand until it takes up a large portion of the market; at that point, the market is no longer perfectly competitive and the First Welfare Theorem doesn't hold. Neither does it when one person's consumption or production affects someone else's but isn't counted in prices, for example if the pollution produced by a power station reduces the harvests of nearby farms.

Arrow and Debreu put a modern twist on an old question in economics: why millions of people doing their own thing leads to harmony in the economy. Adam Smith described it as the 'invisible hand', and some economists have taken the First Welfare Theorem as proof of Smith's idea. But because the assumptions needed to prove the theorem are far from what's true in reality, you can also take the message of the theorem to be that in practice markets are unlikely to be efficient. Perhaps, therefore, the government will have to step in to help push the economy towards efficiency. Governments sometimes try to break up monopolies to make markets more competitive, for example, or tax pollution to make the economy better reflect society's desire for clean air. Beyond the advanced mathematics, though, general equilibrium theory has a basic and important message: that it can be dangerous to examine a market in isolation. Changes in one market cause changes in others. Economically speaking, everything is connected.

CHAPTER 26

A World in Two

In November 1956, eighty-two men set sail from Mexico in an old boat meant for only twenty and laden with food, rifles and anti-tank guns. The passengers got terribly seasick, the boat leaked and one man fell overboard, but seven days later the group made it to Cuba. On board were two young men who would go on to count among the most famous revolutionaries of the twentieth century. Fidel Castro, the leader of the group, had earlier made an attempt to overthrow the government of Cuba. The ship's doctor was an Argentinian, Ernesto 'Che' Guevara, who'd spent his student years travelling through Latin America on his motorbike. He was angry about the poverty and suffering that he saw on his journey.

Guevara and Castro hated the Cuban government. They said that it cared nothing for the poor of the villages whose children went barefoot and unschooled. It cared more about the American companies that made money in Cuba and the rich people who enjoyed themselves in Havana's casinos. Guevara and Castro wanted to be rid of it for good – that's why they'd undertaken their dangerous journey. Their boat landed at a thick swamp where many of their men were killed by the Cuban army. Guevara, Castro and a few others managed to escape into the mountains. From there they began a war against the government.

Guevara and Castro believed that the poverty in Cuba, and in the other countries of Latin America, was caused by the greed of rich countries, especially the United States. They said that rich countries 'exploited' the poor ones. Karl Marx said that capitalists exploit the workers by making them do long, hard shifts and then taking most of what they produce as profit. The very word 'exploitation' suggests something that's unfair and wrong. But how could the idea apply to whole countries? How could an entire nation like America – made up of millions of workers and firms – exploit a poor one such as Cuba?

The economist Andre Gunder Frank (1929–2005) devised a theory that showed how. Frank was born in Germany and in the 1960s made his home in Latin America. Before heading south he earned a PhD at the famous centre of free-market economics, the University of Chicago. To Frank's teachers, Marx's ideas were dangerous and wrong; it was probably better not to even open his books. The whole idea of exploitation, whether between bosses and workers or between different countries, made no sense at all. (When workers take a job, they freely accept the wage offered. No one is exploiting anyone else.) Frank rejected the lessons of his teachers, however. Like Guevara, he said that he got his real education on the road, hitchhiking thousands of miles around America. Later, he moved from one Latin American country to the next, using his theories to advise the radical new leaders who were then coming to power.

Standard economics held that trade with rich countries helped poor countries get richer. Frank thought the opposite: trade actually harmed them. The problem, said Frank, is that profits from the export of goods from poor countries – things like bananas and coffee – don't go into real economic development such as new schools or industries. Poor countries' economies are dominated by big foreign companies. In Cuba, for example, these companies owned three-quarters of the farmland. Foreign companies ran the plantations and the mines and it was they who got the profits from trade. Some locals did get rich, like the powerful landowners and the lucky few who worked for the companies; they blew their money on imported cars and fancy foreign clothes.

Frank viewed the foreign companies as modern versions of the European explorers of the fifteenth and sixteenth centuries who discovered South America and then looted it, taking hoards of gold back to Europe. One of the modern-day conquerors was the United Fruit Company from the United States, which by the early twentieth century ran a commercial empire across Latin America. The company built entire towns next to its banana plantations, complete with railways to transport the fruit. It even had its own police force. Latin American newspapers referred to United Fruit as 'the Octopus' because of its reputation for exploiting its workers and for controlling government officials, sometimes entire countries. When its Colombian workers went on strike in 1928, troops shot them. The company's tentacles reached everywhere, sucking out the continent's riches and suffocating the people.

Frank thought that over time the differences between rich and poor countries become bigger, not smaller. World capitalism divides into two. At the centre of the system is a 'core' of rich countries in Europe and North America. At the edge of the system – on its 'periphery' – are the poor countries of Latin America, Asia and Africa. The core wins at the expense of the periphery. The fate of the poor countries – to get poorer – therefore 'depends' on the efforts of rich countries to make themselves richer. That's why Frank's idea became known as 'dependency theory'. Instead of the development and progress preached by conventional economics, Frank believed that world capitalism led to the opposite. He summed up his theory in the title of one of his works: *The Development of Underdevelopment.*

An Argentinian economist, Raúl Prebisch (1901–86), had another theory about the pitfalls of trade for poor countries, of how the rich end up dominating the poor. Prebisch became the director of Argentina's central bank and later an important official in the United Nations. Prebisch wasn't as radical as Frank but his idea still contradicted conventional economics. It was to do with the prices that poor countries are able to sell their goods for. The conventional view of trade was based on the theory of the nineteenth-century British economist David Ricardo. If nations specialise in the production of goods that they're relatively better at making (in other words, in their comparative advantage) and trade with other nations, then all nations are made better off, said Ricardo. If Cuba found it easier to grow sugar than to make cars, then Cuba should sell sugar to America and buy American cars. Free trade would help poor countries like Cuba to achieve standards of living closer to those of the rich countries, so the theory went.

Prebisch said that this was wrong. Poor countries like Cuba tended to export 'primary' products such as sugar, coffee and bananas. Rich countries tended to export manufactured products like television sets and cars. When people get richer they spend more on television sets and cars but they don't spend nearly as much extra on sugar and coffee. (Imagine your income going up tenfold. You might spend ten times as much on cars and jewellery. On the other hand, although you might buy an extra cup of coffee each day, you probably wouldn't buy ten times as many cups as before.)

Prebisch saw that this had a disturbing implication for poor countries. When the economy of a poor country grows, its demand for the cars that it imports from rich countries rises. But when a rich country grows, the country's demand for the sugar that it imports from poor countries rises much more slowly. In consequence, the price of cars rises faster than the price of sugar: the poor country's 'terms of trade' worsens. So when the population of the poor country demands more cars the country has to export ever more sugar to pay for them. It turns into a vicious cycle: the poor country specialises more in sugar production to pay for cars, but over time each tonne of sugar buys fewer cars. In the end the poor country can't grow as fast as the rich country. A high rate of growth would create a high demand for cars that the country wouldn't be able to satisfy with the revenues from its sugar exports.

What a contrast with the cheerful outlook of the nineteenth-century economists! Now it seems that trade between rich and poor traps poor countries into exporting cheap sugar and coffee, and into always lagging behind the rich world.

What was the way out for poor countries? Prebisch said that they shouldn't specialise, they should diversify – that is, make lots of different goods. They needed to produce sugar and coffee, and cars and television sets, too. Instead of using the money from exporting sugar to buy foreign cars they should close their borders to foreign cars and use it to build their own car factories. In the 1950s and 1960s this is what many countries did, in Latin America and in Africa and Asia too (see Chapter 22).

Prebisch wasn't a revolutionary. He believed that with the right economic strategy, capitalism could help poor nations. In contrast, Frank, like Guevara and Castro, believed that capitalism couldn't be fixed. Revolution was the only answer. The people had to seize power and set up a socialist system that ends exploitation. That's what Castro and Guevara tried to do after winning the war against the Cuban government. In the hills, they'd built up a band of 800 men who defeated Cuba's army of 30,000, and entered Havana victorious in the first days of 1959. Castro formed a government and took control of the hated foreign companies.

By the 1970s the free-market economists of Chicago were on the rise, and dependency theory fell out of fashion (although Frank's idea of exploitation is still important for many critics of capitalism). Violent military coups unseated socialist governments across Latin America. Frank was living in Chile when the army took over there. He fled, arriving back in Germany forty years after he escaped from the Nazis. In Chile the turn back towards capitalism was led by Chilean economists trained at Chicago, who, unlike Frank, had taken on their teachers' message of free markets; they became known as the 'Chicago Boys'. Only Castro in Cuba soldiered on with the socialist revolution. By then Guevara was dead, executed in 1967 by the Bolivian army – with the help of the Americans – while trying to start another revolution. Today you often see his picture on T-shirts and posters, and he's usually remembered by his nickname, Che. His flowing hair and beret have become symbols of the fighter who'll stop at nothing for revolution.

It wasn't just free-market economists who rejected Frank's theory; even some Marxists did. Marx said that only by reaching a high level of capitalist development could societies make the leap into socialism. True socialism had to build on capitalism. The poor countries of Latin America weren't anywhere near that level. Frank had taken on Marx's idea of capitalist exploitation but had forgotten that capitalism was a necessary stage on the road to socialism, the critics said.

The dependency theorists were certainly right to point out the many injustices in the global economic and political system. Rich countries have often enforced a system whereby their exports are sold freely to poor countries, while being slow to allow the same for poor countries' exports. Another injustice is the meddling by the United States in the commerce and politics of independent countries in Latin America and elsewhere. The American government supported coups against socialist governments like that of Chile because America was competing for influence with its enemy, the communist Soviet Union, which was an ally of the socialist governments. The United States invaded other countries – Grenada and the Dominican Republic – and waged a long war in Vietnam to reduce the influence of communists.

But saying that there is unfairness is one thing. It's quite another to claim that this is an inescapable part of capitalism, as Frank does. The rising fortunes of Asia show that poor countries can get richer in a capitalist world. The 'Asian Tigers' – South Korea, Singapore, Hong Kong and Taiwan – transformed themselves from poor countries in the middle of the twentieth century to advanced industrial nations by the end of it. They managed to quickly diversify their economies, eventually producing ships, cars and computers, as Prebisch had recommended. Trade with richer countries didn't impoverish the Tigers: it was the lever for their development. Today, China is repeating the feat.

CHAPTER 27

Fill Up the Bath

One of the most influential books about economics ever written was Keynes's *The General Theory of Employment, Interest and Money*, published in 1936. It's also one of the most difficult, and economists still argue over exactly what Keynes meant. After the Second World War the followers of Keynes helped make his ideas into the accepted economic thinking. One of them, the American Paul Samuelson (1915–2009), took stock of the book a decade after it came out. He called it badly written, arrogant and full of confusions. Its analysis was obvious, but also completely new. 'In short,' Samuelson concluded, 'it is a work of genius.' Samuelson, along with another American, Alvin Hansen (1887–1975), and in Britain, John Hicks (1904–89), boiled down Keynes's big untidy book into a few neat graphs and equations. Their version became the Keynesian economics that was taught to generations of economics students and used for economic policy-making by governments after the war. Keynes had argued that to avoid a repeat of the Great Depression of the 1930s, governments needed to intervene in their economies. The young Keynesians went into the government ministries and showed the officials what to do.

In 1946, the year in which Samuelson praised Keynes's genius, there came a milestone in the Keynesians' influence on real-world policy-making. America passed a law that gave the government responsibility for making sure that the economy kept growing and created enough jobs to employ its people. Another milestone came in the early 1960s when President Kennedy adopted a radical Keynesian policy.

Kennedy said that the economy was then capable of greater production. If people spent more, then it would produce more, and the unemployed would be put back to work. He planned huge tax cuts to achieve that, and they were implemented in 1964 by President Lyndon Johnson, who appeared on television to announce them. The cuts would give consumers $25 million more to spend each day, he said: 'the money will circulate through the economy, raising the demand for goods several times the amount of the tax cut'. This, in a nutshell, is how Keynesian economic policies work.

According to Keynes, recessions happen when savings don't get invested in factories and machines. When people save rather than spend and businesspeople stop investing, there's less spending overall and the economy stops growing. In Chapter 18 we pictured the spending as the water level in a bath. When more flows out as savings than flows in as investment, the water level falls and the economy goes into recession. If people don't spend, then the government must, said the Keynesians. It can stop the downward spiral by spending money on roads, on hospitals, on new pot plants for its offices, on pretty much anything in fact. (Keynes said that the government burying banknotes in the ground would be better than doing nothing. That would generate spending and jobs when businesspeople employed workers to dig up the money.)

If the government pours enough of its own spending into the bath it can offset the spending flowing out as savings. In fact, what the government does is to borrow the unspent savings that are sloshing around the economy and spend them itself; it redirects them back into the bath. In doing this, it spends more than it

collects in taxes (a bit like when someone borrows money from a
bank to buy a car and so spends more than they earn). The government runs a 'budget deficit'. Later, when the economy picks up and
more people are in work and earning money, the government
collects a greater amount of taxes and the deficit disappears.

Another way is to cut taxes – Kennedy's policy. It does much the
same thing by putting more dollars in the hands of consumers.
Even though consumers save some of the dollars, they also buy
things, which pushes up spending in the economy. In his television
address, Johnson imagined what happens to the dollars. Instead of
going to the government's Treasury they end up in a shop when
someone uses them to buy groceries. The shop uses them to pay its
milk supplier. The milk supplier pays them to one of its clerks. The
clerk spends them on a cinema ticket, and so on. An initial dollar
of spending, whether created by a tax cut that puts extra money in
the hands of a consumer or by the government spending the dollar
itself, flows through the economy, creating more than a dollar's
worth of new spending. The spending effect is called the 'multi-
plier': the eventual impact on the economy is a multiple of the
original spending boost or tax cut. Soon firms start to produce
more and hire new workers. The economy starts moving again.

Economists call any policy to do with government spending
and taxing 'fiscal' policy. In ancient Rome, the *fiscus* was the
treasure chest of the emperor, so fiscal policy is about the state
filling up its coffers with taxes and emptying them by spending. It
fills them by putting taxes on the incomes that people earn and
empties them by buying things – medicines, textbooks, tanks.
Kennedy and Johnson's policy was a Keynesian fiscal policy that
seemed to do its job. Afterwards, economic growth increased and
unemployment fell.

Another type of policy is 'monetary' policy: anything that alters
the amount of money in the economy or the interest rate charged
for borrowing it. The simplest type is the government printing
more dollars. The Keynesians' view of monetary policy was based
on their theory of the interest rate. The starting point is to see that
people have choices about what to do with their wealth. They can

choose to keep it as plain old money, simple notes and coins that don't earn them any interest. Alternatively they can buy financial products like bonds. Bonds are certificates that pay interest to whoever owns them. Firms or governments sell them to the public when they want to borrow money. When there's a high rate of interest on bonds then people don't want to keep their wealth as money that doesn't pay them interest – they'd rather buy bonds. In this case, we say that the demand for money is low. In contrast, when interest rates are low, people's demand for money is high. Suppose now that the government prints more dollars (increases the supply of money). For people to hold on to the extra, rather than use it to buy bonds, the interest rate must fall. The fall makes the supply of money equal the demand for it. What's important here is that the lower interest rate affects businesspeople's decisions. It isn't worth building a new factory that promises them a certain profit when they have to pay a lot of interest on the money they borrow to build it. But when the interest rate is low enough, it is worth it. So a lower interest rate stimulates business investment. That means more spending in the economy and so higher national income and more jobs.

The Keynesian theory about the effect of money on the economy – higher money supply → lower interest rates → higher investment → higher national income and employment – was different from what had come before. The conventional economics of the day, which Keynes criticised, was based on the 'classical' economics: the thinking of the economists of the eighteenth and nineteenth centuries. Classical economics said that money had no 'real' impact on the economy, on how many cars or bricks are made and on how many people are in work. Money was simply what people used to buy and sell things. If the government doubles the supply of it then people have twice as much to spend; the only result is that all prices double. This is the 'classical dichotomy', a contrast between two completely different things: the 'real' side of the economy, which is totally divided from the 'money' side. Keynesian economics tore down that divide. Now the real and the money sides were connected. The amount of money in the economy affected real things: how much was produced and how many workers had jobs.

In practice, however, Keynesian economists were much keener on fiscal than on monetary policy. They were influenced by the experience of the Great Depression in the 1930s when interest rates were very low. If they were so low, why did the depression go on for so long, they wondered? They concluded that money and interest rates don't affect overall demand in the economy that much. Keynesians came to believe that what really spurred investment was businesspeople's feelings of optimism (what Keynes had called their 'animal spirits'), not a low interest rate.

The conventional economic thinking, which Keynesian economics replaced, said that attempts by the government to keep the economy moving, whether through fiscal or monetary policy, would be useless. The economy would find its own way back from a recession to 'full employment', the situation in which all the workers and factories were employed. How would it? Wages would fall, encouraging firms to hire more workers, and so would prices, encouraging people to buy up unsold goods. The Keynesians didn't claim that the classical theory was totally wrong, just that it only applied in a situation of full employment. Keynes had looked at what happens when the economy is in a recession, at less than full employment. He said that prices and wages wouldn't fall easily – they've already been agreed upon by firms and workers – so they don't help goods to get sold and unemployed workers to get hired. Instead, in a recession when people stop spending, firms cut production and employment.

After the war, the Keynesian economists blended the two approaches. Suppose the economy is in a recession; factories and workers lie idle. The government spends more or cuts taxes, which boosts demand in the economy. Firms produce more and hire more workers. Because there are so many unemployed workers, the extra demand can be satisfied without prices going up. This is the Keynesian economy. Later, all the factories are running and everyone is employed. This is the classical economy of full employment that you eventually get to in the long run. What happens if the government tries to boost demand? Because the economy is running at full capacity, it can't make any more goods and the extra demand simply pushes up prices. The point of Keynesian economics was that before we get to the long run, governments must step in to help. 'In the long run we're all dead,' Keynes said.

In reality, the shift from the Keynesian to the classical economy is gradual. The economy doesn't suddenly go from prices being completely level to them rocketing. The New Zealand economist Bill Phillips (1914–75) studied actual patterns in the economy and found a smoother relationship. When unemployment was high, indicating a lot of unused resources in the economy, then inflation – how fast prices increase – tended to be low. When unemployment was low, inflation tended to be high. There was a curve linking the two extremes: a bit less unemployment came with a bit more inflation. The 'Phillips curve' became another part of the Keynesian system, and it provided important guidance for government policy. If the economy was depressed, governments could spend more, cutting unemployment at the cost of higher inflation. On the other hand, if the economy was running too fast so that inflation was high, then the government could reduce spending or raise taxes to slow it down.

Keynesian economics seemed secure when in 1971 President Richard Nixon, whose Republican Party was often wary of Keynesian fiddling with taxes and spending, said 'I am now a Keynesian'. Despite some ups and downs, the decades following the Second World War hadn't seen a repeat of the terrible depression of the 1930s. Economies grew steadily and brought rising living standards. But in the 1970s Keynesian economics lost its shine. Economists questioned whether Keynesian policies really were responsible for the good economic performance. Perhaps too much government spending was causing economies to become more unstable by pushing up inflation. New schools of economics emerged that attacked Keynesianism – we'll come to them in Chapters 29 and 30. Many of their ideas were in tune with the older tradition of economics that Keynes had attacked. The classical theorists were about to strike back.

CHAPTER 28

Ruled by Clowns

In November 1863, during the American Civil War, President Abraham Lincoln made his most famous speech at the site of the Battle of Gettysburg in Pennsylvania. He hoped that the slaughter going on around him wouldn't be in vain, that out of the ashes of war would come a new freedom: 'government of the people, by the people, for the people'. His words present the task of government as intensely moral, even heroic. Lincoln called on those who take hold of the levers of power to use them in the service of society as a whole.

Nearly a hundred years after Lincoln spoke, Charlie Chaplin said: 'I remain just one thing, and one thing only, and that is a clown. It places me on a far higher plane than any politician.' Had America's rulers gone from heroes to clowns in just a few generations? Perhaps Chaplin was thinking about the antics of the mayor of Chicago, William Hale 'Big Bill' Thompson, who in the 1920s and 1930s made Chicago politics a laughing stock. Gangsters bankrolled his election campaign and his administration was beset by scandal after scandal. To divert attention, Big Bill once organised a bogus expedition to the South Seas to find a fabled tree-climbing fish; the expedition achieved its real objective of keeping him on the front page of the newspapers.

A few years after Big Bill's reign, a farmer's son graduated from the Middle Tennessee State Teachers College, paying his fees by milking cows. It hardly seemed a likely start for a Nobel Prize-winning economist, but that's what James Buchanan (1919–2013) became years later, through writings that shattered the image of the virtuous politician. Buchanan believed that politicians' claims to be working for the good of society, like Big Bill's, were just a large puff of hot air.

This was a big challenge to the economics of the time. After the Second World War when Buchanan was starting out, most economists had come under the influence of the ideas of Keynes, who'd argued that governments needed to play a major role in the economy. In particular, they needed to spend money to stop the economy from falling into recession. Economists also saw another role for government: that of redistributing wealth by taxing the rich and giving money to the poor, and by supplying health care and schooling. After the war, many governments started taking on these tasks, spending more money in the economy and getting bigger than ever before. Economists didn't really question whether governments were actually capable of carrying out these policies. Once the correct policies were worked out, they assumed that the government would be willing and able to implement them.

As a young man, Buchanan had believed in the power of the state to fix things and had even flirted with socialism. His family was poor: he grew up on a run-down farm without electricity, and was driving a tractor at the age of six. Even so, his grandfather became the governor of Tennessee under a short-lived political party that wanted to challenge America's elites, its most powerful and influential groups of people like the rich bankers. Buchanan's interest in the workings of society was stoked by reading the piles of dusty political pamphlets that his grandfather had left in the back room of the family home. But when he arrived at the University of Chicago to study for his PhD he had a conversion. Six weeks after the start of classes he came to recognise the power of markets and abandoned socialism. What he did retain from his grandfather's old pamphlets was a dislike of elites. To Buchanan, though, the real elites weren't the rich industrialists and bankers, they were people from influential families who studied at famous universities like Harvard. Many of them became politicians and government officials. From their positions of power they'd meddle with society and decide on what was good for everybody else.

His dislike became a theory one summer after he'd finished his exams. He was browsing for books in the university library and there, once again, his life was changed by a piece of writing that had been left to gather dust. The book he pulled from the shelf was in German and written by the Swedish economist Knut Wicksell (1851–1926). It electrified Buchanan and he immediately decided to translate it into English. In short, Wicksell had torn up the notion that governments were completely unselfish, only concerned with carrying out the policies that are best for society as a whole.

Buchanan developed Wicksell's idea into a new field of economics. Economists assumed that the state could fix things. But what actually is the state? Buchanan said that it's just a group of people: officials, advisers and ministers. The problem with standard economics was that it viewed those people as having split personalities. When looking for the best-value pair of shoes or working out how much to sell their car for, government officials behave as 'rational economic man' does: they act firmly in their own interests by maximising benefits and minimising costs. But as soon as the officials enter their ministry building it's assumed that they think only about the good of the nation, and no longer about their personal interests. They carry out the correct policy without question. They never snooze at their desks or take three-hour lunch breaks. It's as if selfish 'economic man' has disappeared and been replaced by someone else, 'political man', a totally unselfish person who always acts according to what's in the best interests of society.

Buchanan said that this was inconsistent. The actions of governments had to be examined in the same way as those of businesses trying to make money. Politicians and government officials were people who pursued their own interests like everybody else. Buchanan's new field of economics was called 'public choice'. He described it as 'politics without romance'. Politicians weren't unselfish heroes – to Buchanan that was a silly, romantic notion. In reality they were more interested in protecting their positions, and were quite a bit grubbier, more selfish and unreliable, than economists had believed them to be.

The American government went on a spending spree during the 1960s, and Buchanan's theory put a new perspective on it. The growth of government was more to do with politicians and bureaucrats looking out for themselves than with helping markets to work better, he said. The problem with government wasn't just seen in the ridiculous capers of Big Bill. Grey-suited officials and respected political leaders in Washington were just as bad. (When John F. Kennedy was elected president in 1961, Buchanan observed that Kennedy's father, a rich and ambitious man, had as good as bought the presidency for his son.)

What all politicians want, above all else, according to Buchanan, is to stay in office. To hold on to power they create 'rents' and then give them to their supporters. Rents are revenues over and above what it's possible to earn in a competitive market. For example, if the government puts a tax on foreign cars then domestic car producers, protected from overseas competition, make big profits. By giving privileges to special groups of people, politicians hope to gain political support, perhaps even money.

The prospect of earning extra profits for doing very little encourages 'rent-seeking'. Businesses spend money trying to persuade the government to give them privileges. They might take government officials out for expensive lunches to try to get them to do what they want. They might set up an organisation to help their case, the American Association of Umbrella Manufacturers, perhaps. Organisations like this are often defended on the grounds that in a healthy democracy they help to air the views of varied groups of people. In public choice theory, they're rent-seekers whose activities use up resources that could have been employed more usefully in a different way.

Rent-seeking hurts consumers because if the markets for cars and umbrellas are protected from foreign competition then people have fewer cars and umbrellas to choose from. The problem is that consumers, being so many scattered people, would never find it individually worth their while to spend time organising their own group to prevent protection. (Why not let others do it, and reap the benefits later?) Producers, though, are often big and few. Each is powerful enough to exert pressure on the government to give them concessions. But businesspeople aren't the ones to blame, said Buchanan. The problem lies with having a too-powerful government which is able to meddle in the economy to help get itself re-elected.

Buchanan savaged the Keynesian economists, too. They said that governments should boost the economy during recessions by spending more money. The boost tips the government's budget into deficit because spending exceeds the taxes that the government collects. This isn't a problem, according to Keynesians, because the policy gets the economy moving again, and then the government can reduce spending, so eliminating the deficit. The problem was that government spending is popular with voters. Politicians want to stay in power and so will do anything to avoid cutting spending and annoying them. In the end, spending keeps going up and up, and so does the government's deficit. This is what Buchanan believed was happening in the 1960s.

Meanwhile, he argued, the bureaucracy of the state – its officials, its committees, its ministries – grows like pondweed. Officials can't maximise profits like firms do because they're not selling a good or service for money. Instead they want the power and status of running a large organisation. They try to make their budgets as big as possible, which they can do because they have more information about their own spending programmes than outsiders. They can always say that they need more limousines, chauffeurs and conference rooms to get the job done properly.

For the public-choice economists, not much can be done to make politicians and officials into unselfish people. This is the fate of day-to-day politics. There's a sphere of politics that lies above the day to day, however: the broad 'rules of the game' that everyone agrees to and that particular governments or politicians can't easily change. One of them, for example, is that people should be allowed to express their opinions without being thrown into jail. Some of these sorts of rules are contained in documents like the American constitution. To improve the government's behaviour, Buchanan argues for constitutional rules such as one that makes it a legal requirement for the government not to spend more money than it collects in taxes – to have a 'balanced budget'.

Buchanan and the other public-choice theorists remind us that it's naive to assume that governments are always reliable and unselfish. To them, the problem isn't that markets go wrong, but that governments do. Critics of public choice, though, say that much of what governments do is essential. A lot of the growth in government over the last couple of centuries was the result of an increase in social spending, particularly that on public health and education, which was needed to build an advanced economy. It's an exaggeration to say that it was all about government officials trying to increase the size of their departments.

Opponents of Buchanan also question the idea that a person can only ever act as 'rational economic man'. In reality, people's lives involve many roles. People are consumers, rulers, parents and voters all at the same time. They can act according to different principles in each role. For example, political life often involves acting out of sympathy to causes. You might vote for a political party because it wants to help the poor or improve the environment, for example. The value of the causes to you are about much more than your personal interests. If not, you might wonder why anyone would ever go to the bother of voting, given that a single vote rarely changes an election result. And if you act in this way, isn't it possible that politicians can too?

CHAPTER 29

Money Illusion

During the winter of 1978–79, Britain was covered in unusually thick snow and ice – and was experiencing a blizzard of strikes by workers. In Liverpool, the dead were turned away from cemeteries when the gravediggers threw down their shovels. In other places, supermarket shelves were bare because lorry drivers refused to drive. Newspaper headlines warned of economic ruin. The miserable months became known as the 'winter of discontent' and have often been looked back on as the point at which Keynesian economics, dominant since the Second World War, lay down and died.

Economic problems were brewing in Britain and America long before the end of the 1970s, though. Keynesian policies had been based on the Phillips curve, which showed that lower unemployment went with higher inflation, and higher unemployment went with lower inflation. Economists thought that by spending, governments could boost the economy and reduce unemployment while pushing inflation up a bit. During the 1960s inflation had been creeping up, and by the 1970s economists were scratching their heads because the high inflation came alongside persistent high unemployment, not the low levels that the Phillips curve predicted. 'Stagflation' became the name for an unhappy combination: high unemployment – economic 'stagnation' – and high inflation. The Phillips curve was breaking down, and with it the foundation of Keynesian economics.

Economists searched for explanations. Some thought that the inflation was caused by unusually high oil prices that increased firms' costs and so the prices of their goods. Others blamed the labour unions (organisations that represent the workers) for demanding high wages. The high wages forced firms to charge higher prices. On the surface, the strikes did seem to have something to do with it. The government was trying to keep inflation down by encouraging the unions and employers to agree on modest wage rises. Often, though, they'd settle on bigger increases and sometimes the unions would end up calling a strike.

Keynes had been the giant of economic policy thinking in the twentieth century. Into the economic confusion of the 1970s stepped a new giant: a small, determined American called Milton Friedman (1912–2006), who put forward a new explanation, one that revolutionised economics. He was born in Brooklyn, New York, to poor Jewish immigrants from Hungary, and came of age during the Great Depression of the 1930s. Like Keynes, many of his ideas were a response to that economic disaster; it inspired Friedman to become an economist. But Friedman's theories were in opposition to those of Keynes and they defined new battle lines in economics. Friedman believed that the problems of the 1970s were the result of too much government, not too little. Like Keynes, he didn't want to think up economic theories just for the sake of it – he wanted to change the world. Eventually, Friedman's economics conquered the Keynesian way of thinking.

Friedman was one of the most famous champions of capitalism and the leading economist of the Chicago school of economics, which held that the principles of markets should govern society. In his book *Capitalism and Freedom* he criticised many kinds of government interference in the economy: for example, controls on rents and the setting of minimum wages should go. At first, economists dismissed him and his followers as oddballs. Friedman, though, was a lively debater – quick, tireless, razor-sharp. He'd pounce on errors of logic and demolish his opponents' arguments. He thrived on dispute and controversy. Many hated him for his free-market views. Worse, in the 1970s he visited Chile and with a group of colleagues had a short meeting with President Augusto Pinochet, a dictator who killed and tortured thousands of political opponents and who was then pursuing free-market policies. For years, Friedman had to dodge groups of protestors who accused him of being the brains behind Pinochet's nasty regime. While he was being presented with the Nobel Prize for economics in 1976, a protestor stood up and shouted 'Down with Capitalism! Freedom for Chile!' The man was ejected from the hall and Friedman received a standing ovation.

Friedman's ideas were to do with the effects of money on the economy. The Keynesians had said that an increase in the supply of money could stimulate the economy, but in practice was unlikely to be a powerful force. More powerful was fiscal policy (government spending and taxes). Friedman brought money back to the centre of economics and his school of thought became known as 'monetarism'.

He revived an old idea: the quantity theory of money. To understand it, let's do what economists often do – imagine a ridiculously simple economy to illustrate a theory. Picture an island with ten pineapple sellers. Each sells one pineapple a year for $1. With ten $1 transactions, the national income of the island is $10. Now suppose there are five $1 bills on the island. For the ten transactions to be made, each bill has to change hands twice each year. The stock of money ($5) multiplied by the number of times each dollar changes hands (twice) equals national income. Economists call the rate at which the dollars change hands the 'velocity of circulation'.

Suppose that the velocity of circulation doesn't change much. If the central bank of Pineapple Island prints five more $1 bills, then the money supply doubles to $10. With a velocity of circulation of two, each of the ten $1 bills changes hands twice, generating $20-worth of transactions. National income has doubled.

Without a stable velocity, the link between money and national income is weak. That's why Keynes thought that money wouldn't have a great effect. What if velocity fell, so that any extra money that the central bank injects into the economy ends up getting hoarded in people's wallets? If velocity fell enough – on Pineapple Island, from two to one – then national income stays the same as before. (Ten $1 bills each changing hands once adds up to the same national income as the original position in which five $1 bills each changed hands twice.) Friedman, however, believed that the velocity of money was fairly stable, and therefore that money does influence national income.

There's a further step in Friedman's argument. Does Pineapple Island's doubled national income come from higher production or higher prices? The higher income could have come from a doubling of production to twenty pineapples at the existing price of $1. On the other hand, it could have come from a doubling of the price of pineapples to $2 at the existing production of ten pineapples. Alternatively, the doubled national income could have come in a combination of higher production and higher prices.

Friedman said that in the short run, an increase in the supply of money encourages spending and leads to higher production; money has 'real' effects. Pineapple sellers employ more people to help them harvest pineapples and so the rate of unemployment falls. This is how the Keynesian Phillips curve was supposed to work, in fact. When the government boosts the economy by increasing the supply of money then unemployment falls as the economy picks up. (The same would happen through the policy that Keynes preferred, of the government spending more.) When more people chase after pineapples, prices start to creep up, hence the link between low unemployment and high inflation. Friedman believed that this was only possible for a little while, however. People work more because pineapple sellers offer them higher wages. But soon the price of pineapples rises. People's 'real' wages – measured by how many pineapples they can buy – aren't any higher. The problem is that workers have confused 'money' wages with 'real' wages. Economists call it 'money illusion'. Once workers realise their mistake, they stop working as much and the economy returns to its original, lower level of employment. The only effect is that inflation is higher.

So although the boost might work for a bit, then comes the hangover: a return to the original level of employment along with higher inflation. There's only one way for the government to sustain the boost to employment, but Friedman likened it to the actions of an alcoholic. Just as an alcoholic treats hangovers with another shot of whisky, so the government can try to pump up the economy again. Wages and prices rise still higher and, as before, employment rises as long as workers incorrectly believe that their higher money wages are higher in real terms. When they see their mistake they reduce their supply of labour. Again the economy reverts to its original level of unemployment with even higher inflation. The original level of employment is the economy's 'natural' level – the number of workers that firms employ in total given how much they're able to produce. Trying to boost the economy beyond that is pointless. All it does is to cause ever higher inflation.

To Friedman it was no surprise that the Phillips curve was breaking down. In his view, after the war governments had got addicted to boosting the economy and pushed up inflation. During the 1930s, it was the opposite problem. America's central bank created the century's worst recession – the Great Depression – by pumping too little money into the economy. The money supply declined by a third between 1929 and 1933. Keynes argued that the depression was caused by too little spending. Friedman said that had nothing to do with it; the problem was too little money.

If money can affect the economy in the short run (if not in the long run) is there scope for the government to use it to regulate the economy? The government might increase the supply of money when the economy slowed down, and reduce the supply when it ran too fast. No, said Friedman. The short-run effects of money don't kick in immediately. By the time they do, the direction of the economy might well have changed. It's impossible for the authorities to accurately predict future conditions and to match today's policies with them. They'll end up doing more harm than good.

The best thing is for the government to commit to a fixed rate of growth in the money supply, say 3 per cent a year, in line with the growth of the economy. When the pineapple sellers plant new trees, the economy grows. With the velocity of circulation of money constant, the money supply needs to expand in line with the expansion in pineapple production, but by no more. Friedman even suggested abolishing central banks that decide on the amount of money in the economy and replacing them with robots that would spew out money at the required steady rate. The hoped-for result? A steadily growing economy with low inflation.

In 1979 Britain voted in Margaret Thatcher as its new prime minister. Soon afterwards Ronald Reagan became president of the United States. Thatcher and Reagan tried to follow Friedman's recipe for bringing down high inflation by tightly controlling the supply of money. But controlling the money supply was tricky and the governments of Britain and America turned out to be bad at doing it. Many economists blamed the policy for making the recession of the early 1980s worse than it needed to be, even if inflation was eventually reduced. In 1981, 364 of them wrote a letter to *The Times* newspaper condemning the British government's economic policy.

Still, Friedman's broader philosophy that government interference in the economy leads to trouble lived on in Thatcher and Reagan, and in their successors. Keynes believed that the economy was unstable and that doses of government intervention would steady it. His recommendation was to make sure that there was enough spending in the economy – enough demand. Friedman was convinced that the economy, when left alone, was really rather stable. Instabilities – runaway inflation in the 1970s, depression in the 1930s – were the result of government meddling. Let markets breathe and a healthy, stable economy would result. The route to that was to enhance the economy's supply (what its businesses were able to produce), not its demand. Economists thought that if governments removed company taxes and loosened restrictions on markets, businesses would be encouraged to produce more and employ more workers. These ideas became known as 'supply-side economics'. And in the decades following the winter of discontent, these were the sorts of things that governments tried to do.

CHAPTER 30

Future Gazing

In life you have to make guesses all the time about what's going to happen. You know that it takes twenty minutes to get to town, so if you need to be there at 9.00 a.m., tomorrow you'll be at the bus stop at 8.40 a.m. How do you know that the bus will take twenty minutes? Because that's how long it took today, yesterday and for as far back as you remember. One day, the gas company announces that from Monday it's closing a road to lay new pipes; traffic will be diverted onto your route. On Monday your journey takes thirty minutes because of the extra traffic. You thought it would take twenty minutes because that's how long it took in the past, so you arrive in town ten minutes late. The same happens for a few more days until you realise what's going on and then start arriving at the bus stop at 8.30 a.m.

In the 1970s economists got interested in how people predict. That's because economic activities take place over days, months and years. A tyre factory built today might only start to make a profit in five years. A worker accepts a wage, calculating that it will cover the cost of rent in six months. Firms and workers have to predict the future. How big will the market for tyres be in five years? How much will rents go up in the next six months?

When planning your journey, you used 'adaptive expectations': you predicted by looking at what happened up until now. Sometimes it works fine, but it didn't when the gas company dug up the road. Economists began to worry about the theory of adaptive expectations, which was what most of them used. You weren't being fully rational when you planned your journey. You would have done better if you'd checked the travel reports and immediately taken into account the effect of the gas works on your journey. Firms and workers lose out too if they don't predict using all the information available. If a car tyre firm doesn't take into account new restrictions on the production of cars, it's too optimistic about the future size of its market and builds a factory that turns out to be unprofitable.

Economists adopted a new theory: 'rational expectations'. The idea was introduced by an American economist and maths whizz named John Muth (1930–2005), a man who was unusually cagey about his work. He was rumoured to have had piles of research papers hidden away which he thought weren't good enough to show to people. His groundbreaking article, 'Rational Expectations and the Theory of Price Movements', which appeared in 1961, was at first ignored. The ideas were far ahead of their time and he wasn't that bothered about promoting them. He turned down invitations to talk at conferences, preferring to stay at home and play the cello. In the 1970s a new generation of economists realised that Muth's idea was revolutionary. A few won Nobel Prizes for developing it.

Muth's idea is simple to state. With rational expectations you're no longer caught out. Instead of predicting your journey time on the basis of how long it took in the past, you use all the information available today, including the gas company's announcement. So on Monday you'd have predicted that the bus would take thirty minutes. Your predictions won't be perfect every time. One day the bus takes twenty-eight minutes when there's slightly less traffic because the staff of a local company have been given the day off.

On another it takes thirty-two minutes because an accident slowed the traffic down. When you're a little off, it's because of random factors that affect the speed of the traffic. On average your prediction of a thirty-minute journey time is a good one.

One of the first to apply Muth's idea was the economist Eugene Fama (b. 1939). He wondered what rational expectations implied for how financial markets worked. The financial system's banks and stock exchanges channel money from savers to borrowers. A saver wants to put £300 into a bank account and withdraw it after six months. A corporation wants to borrow those savings, but needs a loan of £10 million to dig a mine which it will repay in five years. The financial system sorts all this out by bundling up the savings of millions of people into the larger pots of cash that companies need, and managing the timing of inflows and outflows of money. A bank does it by acting as a middleman between savers and borrowers. In a stock market, companies do it by selling shares. Buyers of shares then own a fraction of the company. Shares are potentially profitable, but also risky. When the firm does well its value increases and the holders of its shares make a profit if they sell, but if it does badly, or goes bust, the shareholders lose.

To make money in the stock market an investor needs to have an expectation about whether the price of a share will go up or down. Stock market traders wanting to get rich sometimes study graphs of a share's past price movements in search of patterns that might reveal where the price will go tomorrow. While an undergraduate, Fama was employed by one of his professors to devise ways of predicting movements in share prices. None of them worked.

Fama's theory showed why. It implied that the forecasting methods were as reliable as those of astrologers who predict when you'll get married by looking at the position of the stars. Suppose that stockbrokers see an upward trend in their charts. They conclude that the price of the share will rise next week. If brokers have rational expectations that's impossible, says Fama. If they knew that a share price was going up then they'd buy it today. If they didn't they'd lose some of the gains to be had from buying something cheap and selling it dear. By buying the share today, brokers push up its price, so its rise over the next week won't be as big. If there's still some price rise expected then the logic applies again. In fact, the whole of the original expected price rise must get swallowed up in today's price. If not, brokers would be missing out on a profit opportunity.

Fama's reasoning implies that share prices can't be predicted. If you think that something is going to happen to the price, then that must have already been taken into account in today's price. But surely, you might think, we could reasonably expect a rise in the share price of Nifty Wrap Limited, a company which you heard had just invented spray-on wrapping paper (wrap your presents in under a second). Wouldn't it be a good idea to buy its shares? Not necessarily. The biggest traders in shares are professional stock-brokers, whose job it is to be informed about economic trends and about the companies whose shares they deal in. Having rational expectations, these investors use every scrap of information available in making their buying and selling decisions. It would be impossible for you or me to consistently beat the market by trying to guess next week's movement in a share price. Unfortunately for us, the price of Nifty Wrap's shares will already have jumped up to take account of the new aerosol wrapping paper.

Fama's theory is called the 'efficient markets hypothesis'. It says that the prices in financial markets reflect all available information. When all information is factored into share prices then investors have exploited all profit opportunities. This doesn't mean that prices don't change – far from it. What it means is that you won't be able to predict them. Changes are the result of unpredictable, random factors. They're the equivalent of your bus being delayed by two minutes because of an accident. When people are rational, the market becomes not more but less predictable. So professional financial advisers who tell you which shares to buy are a waste of time. (An American newspaper once asked some of them to choose the best shares for the coming year. It also got an orangutan to 'pick' its preferred shares. At the end of the year, the orangutan had done as well as the humans!) You might think that randomness equals chaos, but according to Fama's theory the more random prices are, the more efficient the market, and the more efficient financial markets are, the better they do their job of channelling money around the economy.

Rational expectations put another nail in the coffin of Keynesian economics. Remember that Milton Friedman hammered in the first. He argued that the Phillips curve, the basis for Keynesian policy, would break down. The curve implied that the government could spend to boost the economy, bringing down unemployment while pushing up inflation. Friedman said that it could only work temporarily. A boost to the economy would lead to higher wages and cause more people to take on employment. The problem was that workers hadn't factored in the impact of higher inflation. Once they realised that their real wages (the amount of goods they could buy) hadn't risen, they'd go back to the old lower level of employment.

The American economist Robert Lucas (b. 1937) said that the workers were being caught out, just like you were on Monday morning. They're forming expectations by looking to the past. The government's ability to boost the economy, even temporarily, depended on them getting fooled. When people have rational expectations that's impossible. They immediately anticipate the effects of the government's actions. When thinking about whether to work more, they expect higher inflation in future. They under-stand that it means that their real wage won't go up and so they don't work more. It's pretty much impossible for the government to boost the economy, even in the short run. People are too clever to be fooled over and over.

Lucas also believed that markets quickly got to an equilibrium: there'd rarely be too little demand or supply of a good. Prices adjust to make sure of it. Economists call it 'market clearing'. Lucas said that it applied in the labour market too: the price of labour (wages) would adjust so that the supply of labour (the number of people looking for a job) equalled the demand (the number of people firms wanted to hire). There'd rarely be a shortage of labour. There'd rarely be a shortage of jobs, either. Unemployment couldn't happen, at least not for any significant length of time – wages would quickly fall and firms hire more workers. Market clearing, combined with rational expectations, was a strong attack on Keynes. He'd argued that economies could get stuck in situations where many people were looking for jobs but couldn't find one. Market clearing meant that anyone who wanted a job at the going wage could get one; workers without jobs were unemployed out of choice. And rational expectations meant that the government could do nothing to increase employment. Lucas's school of thinking was called 'new classical economics'. It revived ideas that Keynes had fought against, those of the classical school which had said that the economy would always quickly adjust to eliminate unemployment and that there was no point in the government trying to boost it further.

The new classical economics is controversial. Were the millions of unemployed workers during the Great Depression in the 1930s or the recessions since out of work voluntarily? Do markets really adjust so quickly? Many doubt it. The efficient markets hypothesis, too, has been questioned. Are people really able to quickly gather and understand vast amounts of economic information, so that there are no unexploited profit opportunities in financial markets? Here, some refer to the story of the student and the economics professor, a believer in rational expectations theory, who are walking together to class. The student spots a £10 note on the ground and goes to pick it up. The professor tuts and says, 'Don't bother. If there really was £10 there it would already have been picked up!'

Towards the end of our story, we'll look at the economic crisis at the start of our century when the financial system stopped working. It turned out that people weren't fully informed and financial markets were far from being efficient. This, too, deepened doubts about theories of rational expectations and efficient markets.

CHAPTER 31

Speculators on the Attack

The traditional bank manager in the 1950s was usually a respected pillar of the community, a cautious, careful sort of person who probably went to bed early and didn't drink too much. You might have found him rather dull and stuffy. But from the 1970s a new kind of banker appeared – loud, flashy and arrogant. These bankers loved taking big risks. They wanted to get rich quick and blow their money on fast cars and expensive champagne. They made their money through what's called 'speculation'. Normally, people buy things because they want to use them, such as wheat to make bread and petrol to run the car. But when people speculate they buy things even when they have no interest in using them. They might buy a load of wheat simply because they think that its price is going to rise when a drought is predicted in wheat-growing areas. If their guess is right they later sell the wheat for a profit.

Speculation has gone on for centuries. But from the 1970s onwards it really took off. Banks had whole teams of people whose job was to trade in pretty much anything in order to make money. Some speculators ran their own companies known as 'hedge funds', which were completely dedicated to the business of speculation. One of these companies, the Quantum Fund, was set up by a philosophy-loving Hungarian-born banker named George Soros. He was rather different from many of the speculators, who were more interested in Rolex watches than books, and he became one of the most famous financiers of the century.

One way in which speculators like Soros make money is by trading in currencies – dollars, euros, yen and many others. Today, the currency market is the biggest financial market in the world. A currency's price is its 'exchange rate': how many dollars or euros a Mexican peso is worth, for example. To pay for American jeans, a Mexican shopkeeper uses pesos to buy dollars. If the jeans cost $10 and a peso is worth ten cents, then the jeans cost the shopkeeper 100 pesos. If a peso is worth only five cents then the jeans cost 200 pesos. Like anything that gets bought and sold, currencies are subject to supply and demand. If American jeans become particularly fashionable in Mexico, then Mexicans demand more dollars to pay for them, pushing up the price of dollars. When the supply and demand for currencies bounce around, so do exchange rates.

When the value of pesos in dollars moves around a lot it's hard for a Mexican shopkeeper to know what price to agree for an order of American jeans over the next six months because an affordable dollar price today could be unaffordable in six months if the peso loses value. Some countries live with this: they let their exchange rates move up and down, what's called a 'floating' exchange rate. Others try to stop it moving and 'peg' their exchange rates – in other words, fix them at a certain value of a leading currency like the dollar. The hope is that this will bring more certainty to consumers and businesspeople. They know how much they'll be able to get for their goods abroad and how much foreign goods will cost.

A pegged currency creates an opportunity for speculators to make money – by 'attacking' the peg. In the 1970s the American economist Paul Krugman (b. 1953) devised a theory about this. To see what it means to attack a peg we first have to understand how a government fixes its currency. It does this by buying and selling the currency to maintain its value. The same would be true if the authorities wanted to fix the price of petrol at fifteen pesos a litre. If at fifteen pesos the supply of petrol exceeds the demand, then the authorities have to spend money buying petrol to stop the price from falling. If, on the other hand, demand exceeds supply, then the authorities have to supply extra petrol, otherwise the price will rise. The government needs to keep a stock of petrol in reserve to do so.

In the same way, suppose that in May the Mexican government sets a price for pesos in dollars. If in June the demand for pesos is higher than usual, then the government can print more pesos to keep their value from rising above the price it set. But if in July people buy a lot of dollars, and so sell more pesos than usual, then the price of pesos is in danger of falling. To keep it up, the government must buy pesos using its stock of dollars. Economists call this stock a country's 'foreign currency reserves'; they're crucial for regulating the level of exchange rate.

In Krugman's theory, speculators attack pegs when governments go on spending sprees. In the 1970s, Mexico pegged its currency to the dollar. The government was also spending huge amounts on social security, housing and transport projects. The government didn't want to put heavy taxes on the people to pay for its spending. Instead, it printed money. Because more pesos circulated for each dollar than before, the value of the peso in dollars looked set to fall. But a fall would break the peg. The government had to stop it by buying pesos using dollar reserves to keep constant the number of pesos in circulation. It worked for a while – until the government ran out of dollars. It continued to print more money to pay for its spending programmes, and because it could no longer buy pesos, the supply of pesos rose. The value of the peso in dollars then had to fall.

In fact, in Krugman's theory the fall happens before the dollars run out because of the actions of the currency speculators. They know that the government is printing money and using up its stock of dollars. They know that in sixty days there'll be no dollars left.

On day 60, when the currency starts to lose value, speculators have to sell all their pesos, otherwise they'd make a loss. This is the attack. In fact it happens earlier: on day 59 speculators know what's going to happen on day 60 and so will get rid of their pesos then, and reason in the same way on day 58. So some time before the government has completely exhausted its dollar reserves, the speculators sell their pesos and buy up the remaining reserves. The peso's peg breaks. Economists call it a currency crisis. The speculators gain because they've shifted their wealth into more valuable currencies like the dollar. Mexico reached crisis point in 1976 and the currency crashed. With the currency worth so little, imports cost people a lot. That reduced the real value of their incomes and they stopped spending: the economy fell into a recession.

Later, the American economist Maurice Obstfeld (b. 1952) showed how countries can have currency crises even when they're not printing money. It happens to the richest of them. In the early 1990s the currencies of a number of European countries were pegged to the Deutschmark, then the currency of Europe's leading economy, Germany. But the countries were in a dilemma. Take Britain, for example. On the one hand the government wanted to keep the peg. Prime Minister John Major had staked his reputation on it, and if the country abandoned it, banks might not trust Britain as much and be wary of lending it money. On the other hand, the government wanted to abandon the peg and let the pound fall. To maintain the pound's value the government had to keep interest rates high: high rates mean that people earn a lot from keeping their money in pounds and so they buy pounds, helping to keep its value up. But the high interest rates were hurting British homeowners who'd taken out huge loans to buy houses and were now struggling to pay back the large amounts of interest.

Britain's crisis hit when the speculators stopped believing that the government would maintain its peg. They expected that the pound would drop. The attack came in September 1992 on a day that's been called Black Wednesday. It was a battle between the speculators – people like Soros who'd predicted that the pound would fall – and the government. The speculators began selling pounds in huge volumes. The Bank of England tried to hold back the tide by buying up pounds. John Major met his ministers and they decided to increase interest rates from 10 to 12 per cent, a very big increase. After the meeting, Home Secretary Kenneth Clarke was being driven back to his office. His driver turned to him and said, 'It hasn't worked, sir.' The driver had heard about the interest rate increase on the radio, and now the news was bad: the pound was still plunging. Within minutes Clarke was back with the prime minister. They raised interest rates to 15 per cent. The rises were paper boats in a storm. The speculators could see that the government was eventually going to give up, and they kept on selling pounds. That evening, the government abandoned the peg, and John Major thought about resigning. Chancellor of the Exchequer Norman Lamont said that he slept soundly for the first time in weeks because he didn't have to fret about the value of the pound. The government had spent billions defending the pound. George Soros came away with a profit of £1 billion and acquired the nickname 'the man who broke the Bank of England'.

Some economists think that speculation is a good thing. Currency speculators are only responding to the reality of what's going on in countries' economies. They attack pegs when governments pursue bad policies, such as going on spending sprees or setting impossibly high interest rates. If so, Soros made money out of a crash that was going to happen anyway. Some say that speculative attacks might even encourage governments to adopt more sensible policies. But in the late 1990s, people squarely blamed speculators for a series of economic disasters in Asia. The Malaysian prime minister, Mahathir Mohamed, said that the speculators were criminals. He called Soros a moron and said that currency trading should be banned; Soros called Mahathir a menace and someone who shouldn't be taken seriously.

The problems in Asia began at the end of the 1990s when Thailand's economy crashed. Firms and banks were going bust, and half-finished buildings around Bangkok were frozen in time when their owners ran out of money. Malaysia and other countries in the region, such as South Korea and Indonesia, soon caught Thailand's economic illness.

But what did the problems of Thailand have to do with those other countries? Economists believe that economic crises can spread between countries as flu does between people. They call it economic 'contagion' and it's the speculators who spread the illness. Seeing what had happened in Thailand, speculators started worrying that something similar might happen in Malaysia and other nearby countries. If it was going to happen they'd want to get rid of their Malaysian currency. But they weren't just worrying about the health of Malaysia's economy; they were worrying about what other speculators were thinking. If speculators think that other speculators are worried and will therefore sell Malaysia's currency, then they'll sell theirs too. If enough of them think like that, the currency really does end up crashing. It's a bit like shouting 'Fire!' when there's no fire and creating a stampede. Economists call it a 'self-fulfilling crisis'. Some, like the American economist Jeffrey Sachs (b. 1954), think that it's possible for speculators to trigger crises when there's nothing seriously wrong with the economy. The Asian economies were doing well and were being managed sensibly by their governments; they weren't like Mexico in the 1970s. The attack was all an unnecessary panic among the speculators, their critics say. That's why Mahathir was so furious.

We'll come across the speculators again later. Many of them deal in financial products far more complicated than dollars and yen. As we'll see in Chapter 38, by the beginning of the twenty-first century speculators were trading in products so hard to understand that people began to suspect that finance was dangerous hocus-pocus. They said that the speculators were wild and reckless, and needed to be stopped.

CHAPTER 32

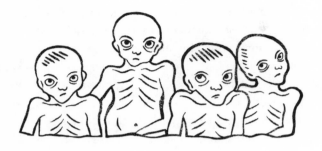

Saving the Underdog

When he was only 11 years old, the Indian economist Amartya Sen (b. 1933) witnessed the aftermath of a murderous attack in his hometown of Dhaka, today the capital of Bangladesh. Riots were going on in the city and Muslims and Hindus were killing each other. A Muslim labourer called Kader Mia, who'd been working nearby, rushed into the garden of the Sen family home, which was located in a Hindu area of the city. He was covered in blood after having been stabbed in the back by a local gang. Sen gave him water and raised the alarm. On the way to hospital Mia spoke of how his wife had told him not to venture into a Hindu area where he might come to harm, but his family was hungry and he had to take the risk in order to earn money. The man died later that day.

The murder shattered the young Sen. It made him see that poverty was about more than a lack of money or food. The poor lacked many freedoms that richer people take for granted. Because he was poor, Mia struggled to provide enough food for his family. But his poverty also meant that he couldn't rely on the freedom that comes from knowing you're in a place of safety. People who are well off don't have to go somewhere dangerous to earn money; they can always take a job somewhere else or buy food using their savings. Mia, on the other hand, had no choice – and he paid with his life.

The experience shaped Sen's thinking as an economist. He wanted to understand the situations of economic underdogs, of people like Kader Mia. Sen is both a philosopher and an economist – unusual for a contemporary economist, but it puts him in the company of the very first economists, philosophers who got interested in humans' material well-being. Sen's philosophical curiosity has led him to question the most basic assumptions of economics.

When thinking about the poverty faced by people like Kader Mia, Sen asks the question: poverty of what? The conventional economic answer is poverty of money or poverty of food and shelter. People are poor when they lack material goods. To Sen the problem is broader than this. Think about the benefit of owning a bicycle. The bicycle allows you to get to the places you need to go. What adds to your well-being isn't the bicycle itself, but having a means of transportation. Sen calls transportation a 'capability'. A good life needs a variety of capabilities: being nourished, being healthy, being part of a community, being safe and so on. The connection between material goods and capabilities is complex. A bicycle creates the capability of transport for an able-bodied person, but not for someone who has a disability that prevents them from cycling.

If we say that someone is poor when they live on less than 2,000 calories a week, we're using an 'absolute' measure of poverty. There's a definite amount of food below which you can call someone poor. If poverty is 'relative', on the other hand, then someone is poor when they lag far behind the average. In a rich country the average is high and so under the relative definition a poor person might well own a television and have a mobile phone. Sen's idea of capabilities brings together the relative and the absolute: capabilities are absolute but the material requirements for achieving them are relative. For example, one capability that you need in order to properly take part in your society is being able to appear in public free from shame. This capability is absolute because the quality of being free from shame is the same for a New Yorker as for an Indian villager. The material requirements are different, though. For New Yorkers they include having a pair of shoes. It would be shameful for them to go to work barefoot because they couldn't afford shoes, while it might be perfectly fine for Indian villagers to do that. For Indian villagers, being free from shame depends on other things, such as who their children marry.

In Sen's view the development of society is the expansion of capabilities. When more people are able to take part in their communities and are safe and healthy, then society advances. Education in particular offers the freedom to turn into the person you can be when you're able to read, write and think about things. Democracy, too, gives people the opportunity to influence how their society is run, and so for Sen it's another freedom that's part of development itself. Real development is more than economic development measured in the production of goods. It's human development: more people experiencing the freedom that comes from having the capabilities needed to live a good life.

Does this mean that more factories, better technology and cheaper goods and services are irrelevant to human development? Not at all. For a society to have schools or hospitals it must have the resources needed to set them up. But economic development isn't the same thing as Sen's broader notion of human development. Pakistan, for example, even after decades of economic growth, still has low rates of literacy, particularly among women. So greater national income doesn't guarantee greater human development. Sen has therefore pressed for new measures of economic progress. He was able to put his ideas into practice in the 1990s when he helped the United Nations improve on the traditional measure of development – gross domestic product. Gross domestic product measures a country's national income and is calculated by adding up what it produces each year. Sen came up with an alternative that included life expectancy and literacy along with income. It was called the Human Development Index and it highlighted the difference between human and economic development: Sri Lanka was ranked higher than Saudi Arabia in human development even though Saudi Arabia was much richer. Now most economists agree with Sen that development isn't just about a country's income, but about the health and education of its people too.

The most basic of all the capabilities is that of nourishment. It means having enough to eat, and the most extreme deprivation is a lack of food, leading to malnutrition and death. Here, Sen's experience once again went back to his boyhood. In 1943, just a year or so before the murder of Kader Mia, he helped give out rice to victims of the Great Bengal Famine in which nearly 3 million people died. Memories of the widespread starvation came back to Sen when he was developing his theory of famine decades later. At the time, in the 1970s and 1980s, there were terrible famines in Africa and Asia. The most obvious cause seemed to be a lack of food: people starve when the rains fail and the crops die. Or perhaps there were simply too many mouths to feed as a result of rapid population growth, the conclusion of Thomas Malthus in the eighteenth century.

Sen saw defects in the common explanations. Droughts happen in America from time to time, but no one ever starves there. And while Malthus warned of the consequences of too many people, famines have happened in Ethiopia and Sudan, places where the populations live thinly scattered over vast areas of land. Sen said that people not having enough to eat isn't the same as there not being enough food available overall. Food isn't just food: it's a commodity that people obtain through the market, and so there are all sorts of reasons why people might not be able to get enough of it and so go hungry.

Sen argued that famines happen when people's 'entitlements' to food collapse to a level too low to feed them adequately. People's entitlements are how much food they can afford to buy given their incomes and the price of food. Entitlements also include the food they grow at home and any that they're given by the government. Food entitlements can collapse even when there's no overall shortage of food, drought or explosion in population numbers.

None of these are necessary for a famine to take place. Sometimes the poor are simply priced out of the market. This helped to make sense of the questions raised in Sen's mind by what he saw during the famine in Bengal. If famines were caused by too little food, then why did people starve in front of well-stocked food shops and why didn't the famine affect his well-off friends and relatives?

Sen used the idea of entitlements to explain the famines of the 1970s and 1980s. During a famine in Bangladesh in 1974, food production was high but a flood had disrupted agriculture, which led to a lot of labourers in the countryside being laid off. Others, worried by the flood, started buying up food, causing food prices to shoot up. Many of the poorest people then couldn't afford to buy food because of the high prices and their lack of income, and some starved to death. When prices returned to normal, the famine ended.

Sen argues that by better understanding how fluctuations in markets can cause famines, more can be done to prevent them. For example, in the early 1970s a drought led to agricultural workers losing their jobs in the Indian state of Maharashtra. The government employed them to build roads and dig wells, which gave them a wage and protected their food entitlements. Famine was therefore averted.

Sen says that democracy and a free press are essential to preventing famines. When journalists can write about the hardship faced by the poor, the government has an incentive to do something about it, otherwise it risks getting voted out of power at the next election. Sen believes that this is why there's been no famine in India since its independence. On the other hand, the biggest famine of the twentieth century – that in China in the late 1950s, in which 30 million people died – went on for so long and killed so many because journalists weren't free to write what they wanted. The Chinese government had launched its Great Leap Forward programme that aimed to modernise the economy, part of which was a disastrous reorganisation of agriculture. Without anyone reporting what it was doing, the government was able to go on with its policies at the cost of so many lives.

A more recent famine was the one in Ethiopia in 1984. Television reports about it shocked the world, and began the trend of rock stars making records and holding big concerts to raise money for Africa. But although it was horrendous, the Ethiopian famine was small compared to China's mid-century famine or the one in the Soviet Union in the 1930s, which killed 8 million people. Thankfully, famines on the largest scale now seem to be in the past. Nowadays, famines tend to be confined to regions in Africa where there is fighting. Often in these famines, people die less of starvation than of the deadly diseases that are spread amidst the chaos of war.

People often think of economics as the study of stock markets, major industries and the decisions made by businesspeople. They're certainly important, but Sen showed that economics was about more than these. In the nineteenth century, Alfred Marshall said that economists needed to have warm hearts as well as cool heads. Sen is an example of Marshall's kind of economist: he uses logic to think about the plight of the people at the very bottom of society, the millions like Kader Mia who have to scrape by and who so often lose the struggle for survival. To Sen, economics is about the varied things that the poorest people desperately need to live happy and fulfilled lives. Money for food is important, but so is knowing how to read, being healthy and having the opportunity to participate in the running of society. Real human development is about the growth of freedom itself.

CHAPTER 33

Knowing Me, Knowing You

At a glittering banquet in Stockholm to celebrate his receipt of the Nobel Prize, the American economist George Akerlof (b. 1940) explained his economic thinking to the guests, who included the king and queen of Sweden: 'Bring a sad old nag to market. Put a live eel down her throat. She will be frisky.' Sellers of nags (worn-out old horses) use all sorts of tricks to make their horses look lively. These can have bad consequences, though: 'On one side of the market are the tricksters. The other side avoids the tricksters. In the extreme, markets totally collapse.'

Akerlof became famous for a 1970 article, 'The Market for Lemons', which looked at the modern-day version of the horse-buyer's dilemma: how to buy a second-hand car. The car that you're thinking of buying from your local dealer might be a good one. It could, however, be a dud (a 'lemon'), one that looks fine on the garage forecourt but is sure to break down if it's driven more than a few miles down the road. You will never know until after you've bought it. The seller knows whether the car is a lemon, but will always tell you that it's in excellent condition. Buyers and sellers would be willing to trade good cars for a high price, bad ones for a low price. The problem is that buyers don't know which cars are good and which are bad. Assume that half are good and half are bad; there's then a 50 per cent chance that the car you're thinking of buying is a lemon. You'd be unwilling to pay the high price for it; you'd only be willing to pay a price halfway between the high and low prices. The problem is that the owners of good cars wouldn't be willing to sell their cars at the intermediate price, well below the high price that their cars are worth, so they stop offering their cars for sale. The owners of lemons, on the other hand, are willing to sell; the fact that someone puts their car up for sale shows that it's suspect. Hence, the bad cars drive out the good ones. It's a failure of the market because there are plenty of people willing to pay a high price for a good car.

Akerlof's idea is that in the economy some people know more than others. Perhaps that sounds ridiculously obvious, but when he wrote his article it wasn't well understood. The standard model of the economy showed that markets worked well. They'd bring about an outcome in which people's desires were satisfied as well as they could be with the resources available. (We looked at how they do that in Chapter 25.) This depended on big assumptions, though. Markets had to be competitive and they couldn't suffer from externalities such as a factory's pollutant imposing costs on a nearby fishery. Economists knew that in practice markets often fell short. Akerlof saw that there was another assumption of the standard model that had been overlooked. For markets to work well, people had to know everything: what cars cost, what quality they were, whether an employee was hard-working, how reliable a borrower was. If we're going into business together you want to know whether I'm competent and I want to know the same about you. The assumption of 'perfect information' – that people do know everything – was rarely questioned. When Akerlof tried to get his article published, journal after journal rejected it. One editor said that the idea was trivial. Another said that if it was true, economics would have to change. Eventually Akerlof's article was published and economics did change. It helped start off the new field of 'information economics'.

Economists had a technical name for the lemons problem – 'adverse selection' – and found it cropping up all over the place. Take health insurance. When you buy health insurance you pay a company a monthly amount (a premium) and the company promises to pay your medical bills if you get ill. In insurance markets it's the buyers – the people who want to get insured – who know more than the sellers, the insurance company. A health insurance company would like to charge a high premium to unhealthy people because they're likely to need medical services often, and a low premium to healthy people. However, it's hard for the company to tell who's healthy and who's unhealthy. So, like the buyers of second-hand cars, they move to the middle and charge a medium level of premium to everyone. Just like the owners of good cars, healthy people then don't want to take part in the market. The premium is too high for them, given their low risk of ill health. The only people who want to buy the insurance are the unhealthy people. Hence, the unhealthy drive out the healthy. The insurance company then has to raise its premiums sky high to cover the increased costs from having to pay the medical bills of the many unhealthy people who buy health insurance from it. Eventually only the sickest people are willing to buy the expensive insurance on offer.

Adverse selection happens when important characteristics are unknown by buyers or sellers, such as when a buyer doesn't know how good a car is, or a seller of insurance knows little about the health of a potential customer. Markets also get disrupted when people's actions are unknown. Economists call it 'moral hazard'. After you've bought insurance against the loss of your mobile phone you might get careless with it because you know that you'll get a new one if you leave it on the bus. Insurance companies know this, but can't check up on you. As a consequence, they won't want to insure you completely. They might ask you to cover some portion of any loss. Again, it's a failure of the market because you'd like to have full insurance coverage, and the firm would like to sell it to you, but a lack of information stops the trade.

Buyers and sellers find ways of dealing with some of the glitches. People do manage to buy and sell decent second-hand cars, for example. Buyers try to find out about the history of the cars that they're thinking of buying, and sellers of good cars offer guarantees. Another pioneer of information economics, Michael Spence (b. 1943), investigated how people get round lack of information by 'signalling' to each other. For example, firms want to hire the most productive people, but people's ability is hard to observe. One way that people signal their ability is by obtaining educational qualifications. Pushing the idea further, education might not make people that much better at their jobs; qualifications merely help employers to distinguish between productive and unproductive people. Sometimes, though, there isn't an easy solution to a lack of information. If a bank has no way of telling whether it's giving out loans to responsible business-owners or crooks, it might stop giving out loans altogether. As Akerlof warns, when information is very poor markets might seize up completely. They stop supplying the useful things that people and businesses need.

While at the Massachusetts Institute of Technology in the 1960s, Akerlof made friends with a fellow student, a future pioneer of information economics, who'd go on to share the stage with him in Stockholm. Joseph Stiglitz (b. 1943) hailed from Gary in Indiana, an industrial town founded in the early twentieth century by the United States Steel Corporation, the giant company created in 1901 by a group of American businessmen including Andrew Carnegie. The poverty, discrimination and unemployment that Stiglitz witnessed in Gary influenced his thinking as an economist. 'Having seen the downside of a market economy, it would be hard to be euphoric about its marvels,' he said. Conventional economics, to the extent that it championed free markets above all, was simply wrong.

To Stiglitz, information economics is relevant to the biggest questions in economics, for example how poor countries get richer. In the 1990s he was able to apply his theories in the real world. He became an adviser to President Bill Clinton, and later joined the World Bank in Washington, which provides loans and advice about economic policy to developing countries. Stiglitz wasn't your average government official; he often walked around with a wonky tie and didn't care about offending powerful people.

In Washington, Stiglitz took on the established officials and econo-mists who clung to the notion that free markets were the answer for poor countries.

The World Bank and a similar Washington organisation, the International Monetary Fund, had been pressing developing coun-tries to adopt free-market policies, including the opening up of their economies to foreign flows of money. They argued that the money would be invested in new factories and roads and so help economic development. Huge amounts of money flowed into the economies of East Asia but, as we saw earlier, in 1997 those coun-tries struck economic rocks. Foreign lenders hadn't worried enough about whether the people they were lending to would be able to repay the loans. They'd made the loans on the basis of poor infor-mation, and in the end many of the borrowers weren't able to repay. Moral hazard made things worse because lenders expected to be rescued by governments if things went wrong, so had no incentive to be careful about who they were lending to.

Well-functioning financial markets depend on lenders being able to accurately assess how reliable borrowers are, and on inves-tors understanding the riskiness of the projects they put their money into. Financial markets are all about information, much more so than markets for things like oil or wheat. When financial markets aren't well developed, as in East Asia, they aren't good at sorting out complex information. Stiglitz was scathing about the recommendations of Washington's officials. They completely ignored the risks of free-market policies that let money flow in and out of countries without any restrictions when the lenders didn't have good information about who they were lending to. He likened the policy to putting a Ferrari engine into an old banger, and then setting off without bothering about the state of the tyres or the skill of the driver.

Information economics is also relevant to the big economic challenges facing advanced economies. Since the Great Depression of the 1930s, economists have been puzzling over what causes unemployment. George Akerlof had been wondering about it since the age of 11 when his father lost his job. (He reasoned that when one father lost his job and so stopped spending, another one would be put out of a job, and so on – the resulting chain reaction turning into a downwards economic spiral. Without knowing it, the schoolboy had discovered one of Keynes's main principles of economics.) The postwar economics that was based on the work of Keynes said that wages tended not to fall easily during recessions and by staying high discouraged firms from taking on more workers. Why didn't they fall? Information economics provided a new answer. An employer can't watch its workers all the time and so doesn't know how hard they're working. To encourage them to work hard, the employer increases the wages it pays. When all employers do the same the overall wage level increases. At a high wage level, firms hire fewer workers and unemployment rises. The threat of unemployment then encourages the already-employed workers to work hard. This way of thinking about unemployment became part of a new interpretation of Keynes followed by many of today's Keynesian economists.

When Akerlof and Stiglitz began their new field of information economics, many economists thought that markets worked pretty well most of the time. They believed in the 'invisible hand', Adam Smith's idea that buying and selling in markets leads to the best use of society's resources. Breakdowns in the market because of information problems don't necessarily mean that people are being stupid or irrational. It's perfectly rational for people to stop buying horses because they suspect that they're being offered old nags. But the breakdowns mean that the invisible hand no longer works. On receiving his Nobel Prize, Stiglitz suggested that the reason that the hand is invisible is that it's not there – and if it is, it's paralysed.

CHAPTER 34

Broken Promises

People change their minds when it's better for them not to. This unremarkable statement is the basis of an economic theory that says that even with the best of intentions, governments can't help thwarting their own aims. They're like well-meaning school-teachers who change their mind about giving lazy students detentions even when that would encourage students to work hard and pass their exams. Teachers threaten detentions if the students don't do their homework, but then let them off when the students fail to hand it in. Why? Well, if they give detentions, teachers have to stay late, and they'd much rather go home on time. The students know that teachers don't follow through on their threats and so don't do their homework; they never shake off their laziness and fail their exams. If the students had believed the teachers' threats, they'd have done their homework and the teachers would have been able to go home on time. Because lazy students don't believe teachers' threats, everyone loses.

The effect that the teachers are trying to create – the threat of detention leading to students doing their homework – unfolds over time. On Monday the best thing for teachers to do is to threaten detention if homework isn't delivered by Wednesday. Once Wednesday comes, though, the best thing to do is to let the students off. The teachers say to themselves: the homework hasn't been done, so what's the point in giving out a detention and having to stay late?

The problem of trying to achieve an aim over time was studied by two economists in the late 1970s. Finn Kydland (b. 1943) grew up on a farm in Norway, the only pupil in his area to go beyond elementary school. When studying for his PhD at Carnegie Mellon University in Pittsburgh, he met the American Edward Prescott (b. 1940) and on his return to Norway persuaded Prescott to spend a year with him at the Norwegian School of Economics in Bergen. In the quiet of the building, long after everyone else had gone home, Kydland and Prescott worked out their new theory and coined a new term. Lenient teachers faced a problem of 'time inconsistency': what's best today is no longer what's best tomorrow.

Scientists trying to control the flight of rockets don't come up against the problem of time inconsistency. When they launch a rocket on Monday they give instructions to the rocket's computer to get the rocket to the moon by Wednesday while burning as little fuel as possible. They could preload a batch of instructions onto the computer on Monday to cover the entire flight, or they could give some instructions on Monday, some more on Tuesday and a final few on Wednesday. It doesn't matter how they do it. What's best on Monday is best on Wednesday. The rocket's computer always keeps its promises.

When you're dealing with people it does matter. On Monday teachers set a batch of instructions for themselves for the coming week: detention if no homework. On Wednesday they do something different. People are different from rockets because they anticipate the future. They know what's likely tomorrow and so they alter their behaviour today. Students know that teachers won't carry out their threats and so they don't bother to do their homework.

Kydland and Prescott were among a group of economists in the 1970s who argued that the principle of Keynesian economics which said that the government could easily control the economy was wrong because it assumed that the economy was like a rocket. This was true only if people weren't fully rational, they said. The new approach to economics examined how the economy worked if people had rational expectations, an idea we came across in Chapter 30. When people have rational expectations they make predictions about what's going to happen using all the information available, including about the government's economic policies. They don't make mistakes by forgetting to take account of important information. Kydland and Prescott discovered that rational expectations led to time inconsistency. The teachers' problem arises because their students factor into Monday's actions what they anticipate the teachers will do on Wednesday. Rocket scientists play a game against nature, but teachers and governments play a trickier game, one against crafty people.

The Keynesian economic policy followed in the 1950s and 1960s was based on the idea that the government could affect the path of the economy by adjusting how much it spent. (An alternative policy, less favoured by the Keynesians, was for the government to adjust how much money it put into circulation.) According to the Phillips curve, which showed that low unemployment went with high inflation, governments could use these policies to reduce unemployment at the cost of a bit more inflation. The rational expectation theorists said that this was impossible. If the government boosts the economy, rational people normally foresee that higher wages will get eaten up by higher prices, they said. People's real wages (the actual goods they can buy) won't change and, knowing it, they won't take on more employment. The only effect of the government's policy is to push up inflation. Under this view of the economy, the best thing that the government can do is to keep inflation low by not printing too much money or spending a lot.

Even when it knows this, however, the government can't stop itself from trying to pump up the economy. In January the government makes a promise: it says it will keep inflation low because it knows that in the long run trying to boost the economy is futile and will only lead to higher inflation. By May, though, the government is unpopular and an election is coming up at the end of the year. Although the government can't normally influence employment, it sometimes can in the immediate future if it suddenly boosts the economy without people expecting it. In May it tries to do so, hoping to gain politically from a lower level of unemployment. For a short while people take on more employment in response to higher wages, but quickly return to the lower level of employment when they realise that higher wages have been eaten up by higher prices. The government tries the same thing in June, July and August. Because its actions only have an effect when they surprise people, they only work sometimes (and then only for a short while); over time there's no less unemployment than if the government had kept its promise. The difference is that inflation ends up at 8 per cent rather than 2 per cent. People understand the government's dilemma and so don't believe in its promises to keep inflation low. Just like the teacher, the government wants to keep its promises, but when the time comes it can't follow through. The result of the broken promises is that the economy is more volatile: with prices shooting up it's less stable and more turbulent and unpredictable.

You might think that it would be a good thing for a well-meaning government (or teacher) to have as much choice as possible about what to do at every point in time. Economists call it 'policy discretion': complete freedom to decide. In May the government decided to do something in response to current circumstances, and decided to do something in June, July and August as well. Surely discretion lets the government assess current conditions and then act, bringing about the best outcome over time? Kydland and Prescott's theory shows why discretion actually reduces the power of government to carry out the best policy. The government doesn't fail because it's crooked or stupid; rather, its freedom to decide at every point in time leads it into self-defeating actions.

Kydland and Prescott said that instead of using discretion – making separate decisions in May, June and July – governments should follow a rule decided in advance, such as 'keep inflation low at all times'. But how can the government enforce it? It holds the levers of power and so will always break its own rule. The problem is that the more power it has, the less it seems to have. It doesn't matter how strongly it makes its promise, no one will believe it (just like the shouty teacher whose threats are ignored).

After Kydland and Prescott devised their theory, economists looked for solutions that would allow the government to enforce its rule and solve the problem of time inconsistency. Many of them were to do with changing the way that central banks operated. The central bank is the government's banker and the organisation that issues new notes and coins. Today, central banks carry out the government's monetary policies: actions that alter the supply of money and the rate of interest. Central banks started off as private companies. One of the oldest, the Bank of England, was founded in 1694 by a group of merchants who wanted to make sure that Britain had enough money to fight the French. Gradually, central banks got tied into government. In 1946 the Bank of England was taken into public ownership; Stafford Cripps, Britain's chancellor of the exchequer in the late 1940s, used to call it 'his' bank. Central banks were used by governments to pursue Keynesian policies. They'd come under the thumb of the government to be used as politicians saw fit.

A solution to the problem of time inconsistency is for the government to give up its power over the central bank. Make the central bank independent, so the argument goes, and monetary policy will no longer be in danger of manipulation by politicians. The heads of central banks aren't elected by the voters and have nothing to gain by actions which might make them popular in the short run, so they'll be able to carry out the rule of keeping inflation low. The government could even appoint as its central banker someone who's known for having a strong liking for low inflation and will do everything in their power to achieve it. It would be like the lenient teacher sending the lazy student to the office of a strict head teacher who everyone knows enjoys giving out detentions.

In the 1990s many governments made their central banks independent. They'd set targets for inflation – to keep it between 2 and 3 per cent, say. The central banks' job was to use the tools of monetary policy, now under their control, to hit the targets. The Banque de France was cut loose from the politicians in 1994, nearly 200 years after it was set up by Napoleon to restore financial order after the turmoil of the French Revolution. At a ceremony to mark its independence, its governor looked forward to a new era of a steady economy. When the Bank of England became independent in 1998, a committee of experts began meeting every Wednesday. They'd take a vote on whether to raise or lower interest rates to hit the inflation target. Some economists even recommended linking the salaries of central bank governors to the rate of inflation. When New Zealand made its central bank independent it did something similar by saying that it could sack the governor if the bank missed the target for inflation.

Many economists believe that central bank independence led to low inflation and steady growth. It was a big turnaround from the 1970s era of stagflation (high inflation and high unemployment). The talk was of a 'Great Moderation', a stable economy free from wild ups and downs. Did independence work, then? It's true that in countries with independent central banks, inflation has been low, but making a strong connection between the two is tricky. The low inflation of the 1980s and 1990s might have been a bit of luck rather than the result of a clever economic theory that solved the problem of time inconsistency. In the 1970s, economies were hit by shocks which made inflation rise, such as political crises in the Middle East that led to surging oil prices. It's possible that the economic stability of the 1980s and 1990s was the result of an absence of similar shocks. Moreover, the Great Moderation didn't last; it ended abruptly in 2008 when the global economy crashed. Economic volatility had returned.

CHAPTER 35

Missing Women

In the early 1990s, the economist Amartya Sen calculated that 100 million women were missing. Because women live longer than men, there should be more women in the population than men. In Britain, France and America there were around 105 women for every 100 men, but Sen found that in some countries the men outnumbered the women. In China and Bangladesh there were only 94 women for every 100 men, in Pakistan a mere 90. Adding up the shortfalls, Sen found that there were 100 million too few women in the world. Where had they gone? Sen said that they were victims of extreme economic deprivation: poor nutrition and a lack of medicine that shortens lifespans. His findings showed that economies didn't treat men and women equally: they were biased against women.

In the 1990s a group of economists tried to explain the bias. They combined economics with feminism – social and political ideas based on a belief in women's equal rights with men. The feminist economists said that the bias meant that women didn't get their fair share of society's resources. A bias also existed in the way economists think about the world. This is important because how we think about the economy can influence how it actually treats different people.

In a sense, the economic theories that we've looked at in this book – perfect competition, the law of demand and so on – are stories that economists tell over and over again. A famous one is Adam Smith's invisible hand. Of course there isn't really an invisible hand, just lots of people buying and selling things in an ordered way. It's a story, although a useful one. Diana Strassmann (b. 1955), a pioneer of feminist economics, points out that most of the economic stories were first told by men, often in the nineteenth century. Many of the male economists who told them shared their society's misgivings about women having an active role in the economy. (Nowadays attitudes have changed, but economics is still a profession dominated by men.) Strassmann argues that even if we don't know it, the stories we tell reflect biases that we've inherited from the past. Economics has come to see the world through a male point of view. Women don't play a big part in our economic stories and suffer from disadvantage in the distribution of real resources. To be truthful, economics must be aware of its own biases. Feminist economists try to shine a light on them.

A favourite story in conventional economics is what Strassmann calls the 'benevolent patriarch' – the kind male leader. Society consists not of isolated individuals but of households, usually a group of adults and children living together. Economics treats the household as a single unit, however. The 'head of the household', assumed to be a man, earns a wage and is responsible for a wife and children who don't earn money and are dependent on him. The household is a place of harmony. There are no arguments about food or money. The man gives his wife and children what they need. Economists can then concentrate on the behaviour of male wage earners without worrying too much about the people who depend on them. After all, with such a fair and wise man ruling over them, the women and children will always be looked after. In this way, wives and children become invisible to economists.

Strassmann says that the story is a distortion. Sen's missing women show that resources aren't distributed fairly. Not all men are fair, and sometimes they end up quarrelling with their wives, often about money. Often the arguments leave girls at the bottom of the family pecking order. In some societies, boys are favoured over girls in food and medicine, and sick girls are even left to die rather than being taken to hospital as a boy would be. Also, the heads of households are often women rather than men, and frequently it's the female-headed households that suffer the greatest hardship. By overlooking women, economics misses important ways in which resources are distributed inside the family.

Another old economic story is that of women as 'leisured'. If women stay in the house rather than getting a job, they're seen as not working. If they're not working for money they must be doing the only other activity that economics recognises, taking leisure: going out for lunch and having their nails done, perhaps. The economist Nancy Folbre (b. 1952) challenged that story in her book *Who Pays for the Kids?*

Folbre says that it's women who bear most of the costs of raising the future labour force. Standard economics ignores the costs because mothers looking after their children aren't paid in money. When a man pays a wage to his housekeeper for cleaning, cooking and looking after his children, her labour is counted as part of the national income of the country. If he marries her, she becomes part of his household. She continues to clean and cook but as his wife she isn't paid a wage. Her labour is no longer counted in national income. Under the conventional view she becomes an 'unproductive housewife'.

Think of all the labour that's invisible because it's not paid for: shopping, cooking, cleaning, caring for children. In poor countries women collect wood, heave water, plough land, grind corn, repair huts. Calculations by the United Nations show that unpaid work could be equivalent to 70 per cent of the world's economic production. Most of the unpaid work is done by women. If unpaid work is so significant, isn't it important for economists to try to capture it when measuring the economy? The New Zealand feminist economist Marilyn Waring (b. 1952) argued the case in her book *If Women Counted*. The book did influence the way that economists calculate the income of countries, but the calculations still leave out a lot of important unpaid work.

Other feminist economists emphasise the need to make it easier for women to get jobs. One of the biggest economic changes over the last century, particularly in Europe and the United States, was the entry of women into paid work. In America, only 20 per cent of women earned wages in 1890. Until the 1950s some jobs were closed to married women, and women would be fired when they got married. Gradually, society came to accept women as part of the labour force, and 60 per cent of them had jobs by 1980. Much of the unpaid work that women used to do was transferred to nannies and cleaners. Despite the trend, unpaid work done in the home remains of huge importance, and it's still women – even those with paid jobs – who do most of it.

Strassmann says that economists' favourite story – the story of free choice – also needs rewriting. Standard economics is based on the notion of 'rational economic man' who chooses what to buy according to what prices and earnings allow. People have clear preferences. They know that they prefer tea to coffee and opera to football. Their lives consist in best fulfilling their desires using the money they have. This theory of behaviour also comes from a male point of view, argue feminist economists. To conventional economists – for most of history, well-educated and wealthy men – the idea of making a choice from a set of options would have seemed perfectly natural. They had the money and power to do what they wanted. The prejudice and discrimination faced by women and other disadvantaged groups, however, often removes free choice. Free choice over what to study means little in societies where girls are killed for going to school.

When economists judge how good economic outcomes are, what they care most about is that people have choices. No comparisons need to be made between the welfare of different men and women: in fact economists assume that any comparison would be meaningless. Instead, they assess how good an economic position is using the notion of pareto efficiency, which we looked at in Chapter 25. The only improvements that register under the measure are ones in which at least one person is made better off, but no one is made worse off. But pretty much any change in the economy creates winners and losers. Pareto efficiency has nothing to say, for example, about a change which involves a few rich people becoming slightly less rich while hundreds of women are lifted out of poverty. So this way of judging the economy will tend to be conservative in the sense of not easily approving changes to how things are now. That, of course, tends to benefit the most powerful people in society.

Feminist economists argue that the whole approach is too narrow. In practice, people are emotionally connected and feel sympathy for one another. Obviously, mothers look after their children out of love, not from a balancing of their own costs and benefits. Even buyers, sellers and employees act out of a broad set of sympathies, not only in response to money. For example, when someone in San Francisco buys expensive 'fair trade' coffee, which is supposed to benefit coffee growers in developing countries, they pay the extra because they want to do something to help strangers thousands of miles away. If people behave like that, can we really claim that it's meaningless to make comparisons between the welfare of different groups of people?

The economist Julie Nelson (b. 1956) argues for a different way of judging how well the economy is doing. Instead of thinking about it in terms of pareto efficiency and choice she uses the idea of 'provisioning': how to provide people with the various things that they need to live well. She even turns to Adam Smith, the thinker so often associated with the idea of free choice and the exchange of goods, and points out that he talked about a healthy economy as one that produced what's needed to live a decent life. You might then define economic success as the provisioning of life for all, in food, medicine and the care of children and the elderly, rather than simply as people making free choices between as many options as possible.

Today, some of the worst deprivation faced by women is the result of the HIV/AIDS epidemic. In poor countries, young women are more likely to be infected than men and face the greatest barriers to getting treatment. Women also bear the burden of extra work when other members of their families become infected. Feminist economics tells us that without policies aimed at them, the problem of missing women will only get worse, but social change and good policy can help. Kerala stands out among Indian states in its efforts to educate its girls, and many women there now have paid work. Sen found that Kerala, unlike much of India, had found its missing women. There the women outnumbered the men by nearly as much as in Europe and America.

Conventional economics hasn't totally ignored women, but feminists often disagree with the answers that it gives. Why have women so often tended to earn less than men, for example? A conventional economist might say that men and women simply have different preferences. Men like to study the kinds of things that lead to better-paid jobs – law and science, for example. Women prefer literature and languages and become schoolteachers rather than judges and engineers. It's all just a matter of what men and women choose, so if women want to earn more then all they need to do is change the choices that they make. Feminist economists reject this view: all it does is justify women's economic disadvantages by seeing women's role in the economy as something that they themselves have chosen, not as something that society says is suitable for them. It's not women that need to change, they say, but economics itself. At bottom, both women and men act in more complex ways than the story of 'rational economic man' says they do. 'Rational economic man' needs a heart, say the feminist economists. Perhaps that could be the start of a new economic story, one that does better at helping to improve the lives of everyone, both men and women.

CHAPTER 36

Minds in Fog

How do you know how far away a tree is? Partly you'll judge it by how sharp and in-focus it looks. This often works fine, but sometimes you suffer from visual illusions: when it's foggy, for instance, you might think that the tree is farther away than it really is.

Daniel Kahneman (b. 1934) is an Israeli psychologist who studied the psychology of visual perception and later turned to economics. With a fellow psychologist, Amos Tversky (1937–96), he discovered that when people accept a job or buy a cup of coffee, a mental fog stops them from perceiving things logically. Economists have long believed that people are rational, that they accurately weigh the costs and benefits of the options facing them before acting. Kahneman and Tversky found that this wasn't so. They spent decades observing people's real-life decision-making and helped create the field of 'behavioural economics'. All economics is about behaviour, of course, but behavioural economics was new because it built its theories around the quirks in people's actual decision-making, rather than simply assuming that they were completely rational.

One quirk is that people weigh up gains and losses differently. Rationally, a gain of $50 should exactly offset a loss of $50. However, people seem to hate losses more than they love gains. When he was still a student, the behavioural economist Richard Thaler (b. 1945) noticed 'loss aversion' in one of his own economics professors! The professor, a wine lover, was willing to pay a high price for a bottle of a certain wine to add to his collection. But he really hated giving one up: even if you offered him three times what he'd paid, he wouldn't sell a bottle to you. Thaler and Kahneman did an experiment on a group of people to see what was going on. Some of them were given a mug and then asked how much they'd sell it for. The others, who hadn't received a mug, were asked how much they'd pay for the same mug. The two groups were being asked essentially the same thing: how much they valued the mug. Economic rationality requires them to have a single valuation. If their valuation is £5 they should be willing to buy or sell the mug for £5; what they think something is worth shouldn't be affected by whether they have it or not. But people's valuations *were* influenced by whether or not they had a mug. When they already had one they valued mugs more highly than when they didn't.

Just as a room seems lighter or darker depending on how bright it is outside, outcomes look better or worse depending on the 'reference point' you begin from. If you start off without a mug, your reference point is not having a mug; receiving one is a gain. But if you start off with a mug, your reference point is having the mug; giving it up is viewed as a loss and that's psychologically painful. Once you have something it becomes more valuable to you. You're a bit like a toddler who clutches a twig she found on the ground and wails when her parent takes it away. You'd need to be paid quite a lot to give up your mug, and so would Thaler's professor to part with his wine.

People's decisions can be influenced purely by how something is described or 'framed' in comparison to a reference point. Imagine that there's a disease that will kill 600 people. Two health programmes are available to fight it. One programme saves

200 people. Under the other programme 400 die. Which is better? Kahneman and Tversky found that people preferred the first, even though the outcomes of the programmes are identical. The first is expressed as a gain from a reference point of everyone being dead, the second as a loss from the reference point of everyone being alive. Reference points stop people making decisions rationally on the basis of absolute money outcomes. If a laptop on sale for $1,000 looks like a so-so deal, the same one discounted to $1,000 from $1,500 might look like a bargain. Supermarkets make use of this by inflating the prices of certain goods so that they can slash them later.

Another quirk in decision-making is to do with how people judge uncertainty. A worker thinking about taking a job at a local bakery needs to assess how likely it is that the firm will go out of business next year. A taxi firm wanting to open an office in a new part of town needs to judge how likely it is that people there will want to use its services. If people are rational then they should be good at assessing the probability of future events on the basis of the information they have. Kahneman and Tversky showed that they aren't.

Imagine a woman named Carole who is really into music and the arts and spent most of her student years going to gigs. Which of these two statements is more likely? Statement one: Carole is a bank clerk. Statement two: Carole is a bank clerk and plays saxophone in a local band. Think about it for a moment. Kahneman and Tversky found that when asked this kind of question people tended to think that statement two was more likely. In fact statement one is, because the probability of a broad event (Carole being a bank clerk) is always higher than a narrow one (Carole being a bank clerk and also playing in a band). (Compare with this: the probability of rain tomorrow against the probability of rain tomorrow between 2 p.m. and 4 p.m.) People thought that statement two better represented the description of Carole that they'd been given, but the description was a red herring and led them to incorrectly judge probabilities. If people get led astray in judging these probabilities, then they're even more liable to go wrong when judging more complex situations such as how many people in a certain part of town are likely to want to use taxis.

Some economists acknowledge the quirks in people's decision-making but say that they aren't important, and that describing the economy as rational is a useful approximation. Behavioural economists, on the other hand, argue that their special theories are needed to explain major economic events. For example, behavioural economics has been used to explain why in the 1990s the American stock market took off and then in 2000 crashed, bankrupting companies and wiping out fortunes.

The American stock market had been on the rise since the early 1980s. In the 1990s people rushed to buy shares in new technology companies that offered exciting products like web browsers, search engines and online shopping. When Yahoo! was launched on the stock market its share price rose by 150 per cent on the first day, so great was the demand for its shares; the two Stanford University students who set up the company from their trailer found themselves $150 million richer. But many of the companies earned tiny profits. Amazon warned investors that it was actually going to lose money but that didn't stop them from buying its shares. Investors believed that the new technologies would earn the firms huge profits in future. Eventually shopkeepers, cabdrivers and teachers were buying shares in their lunch hours. In the late 1990s, the stock market leapt by 20, even 30 per cent a year. The problem was that the income of the economy hadn't risen anything like as fast.

A few economists warned that the trend couldn't go on. One was Robert Shiller (b. 1946), who'd applied behavioural economics to financial markets. The market was being lifted up by overexcited investors and soon it would thud to the ground, he said. In March 2000 he was embarking on a tour to promote his new book *Irrational Exuberance* – just when, with perfect timing, the stock market was about to crash. One day Shiller took part in a radio talk-show. A caller rang in to tell him that she knew he was wrong: the market simply had to keep on rising. Shiller remembers the tremble of emotion in the woman's voice. To Shiller, what was happening in the stock market was more about emotion and psychology than economic logic.

Economics says that when a firm makes healthy profits, its shares should be worth a lot. Rational investors use all the information they have about firms' profitability to make their decisions about which shares to buy. When enough people in the market do this, share prices reflect all the available economic information. Rationality ensures that financial markets work efficiently. This is what economists call the efficient markets hypothesis, which we came across in Chapter 30, and Shiller rejected the idea. He noticed that share prices were more unstable than the hypothesis implied because they went up and down more than firms' profits did.

The findings of Kahneman and Tversky showed what was going on. In financial markets investors do something similar to the people who wrongly believed that Carole was more likely to be a saxophone-playing bank clerk. Instead of looking carefully at a firm's profitability so as to correctly assess the probability of its share price rising in future, people read across from a situation that looked similar. An obvious one would be what was happening to the share price in previous months. It rose for the last five months, so surely it'll rise over the next five. Let's buy shares, people say. What happened five months ago, however, might have nothing to do with current conditions, just as the description of Carole had nothing to do with the true probabilities.

Quirks in people's decision-making lie behind runaway stock markets. To Shiller, the stock market in the 1990s was more like the world of fashion than rational economics. One year big sunglasses are in fashion, and as more people wear them more want to join the craze. A runaway stock market is economic fashion expressed through share prices. Economists sometimes picture the market as a herd – thousands of us charging after the people in front – or as a soap bubble on a gust of air, with share prices being carried up and up. In the 1990s people saw their neighbours getting rich on technology shares and bought shares too, believing that prices were going to keep on rising. This pushed up prices still higher, confirming their beliefs. People weren't buying shares because they'd made a favourable assessment of a firm's products, and so prices had little to do with the true value of the firms. Investors were at risk of pouring money into unsound companies – not the best use of the economy's resources.

It's true that computers and the internet have transformed the economy, but in their excitement about the new technology investors cast off all reason. And not for the first time. In the nineteenth century the Scottish journalist Charles MacKay told of similar bubbles in his book *Extraordinary Popular Delusions and the Madness of Crowds*. What happened to technology shares in America in the late twentieth century had happened to Dutch tulips in the seventeenth. In Britain during the eighteenth century there was a mania for buying shares in companies promising crazy moneymaking schemes such as the importing of walnut trees from Virginia, a perpetual motion machine and even a profitable undertaking which was to remain a secret!

Like the previous ones, the American stock bubble popped. When it did, the herd started to run in the other direction. People saw others selling shares, so they did too, and soon the market was in a panic. When share prices crashed, investors' fortunes were wiped out and many of the new technology companies went out of business. Within a week, wealth worth $2 trillion vanished into thin air. Soon the next bubble floated into view. Shiller predicted it – this time it was houses. People scrambled to take out loans to buy houses as prices went up and up. And as we'll see later, when the bubble burst, the whole financial system was nearly destroyed.

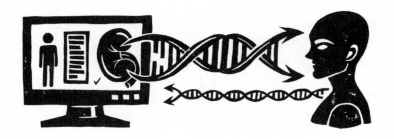

CHAPTER 37

Economics in the Real World

Should we allow the buying and selling of human organs – the hearts, kidneys and livers needed for transplants that can save the lives of seriously ill patients? Many of us would say no. We'd be horrified at the thought of poor people dying because they couldn't afford the kidneys that rich people could easily buy. That's why the sale of organs is illegal. Doctors decide which patients will benefit from transplants and then try to find them suitable donors, but patients often have to wait a long time. In the United States in 2006, 70,000 patients were waiting for kidneys but fewer than 11,000 transplants were carried out and 5,000 people died or became too sick to have one. The American economist Alvin Roth (b. 1951) used economic principles to come up with a way of increasing the number of organs available for transplant without people buying and selling them.

Roth's solution is based on the fact that humans have two kidneys but can survive on a single one, so if your brother needed a kidney you might decide to give him one of yours. The problem is that when the doctors do tests on you and your brother, they might find that your kidney isn't compatible – that it isn't a 'match' for him. Your brother has to go on waiting for a compatible kidney to turn up. Suppose there was another patient and another donor, completely unknown to you, who were in a similar position. What if your kidney was a match for the other patient and the other donor's was a match for your brother? Surely it would be a good idea to do a swap? This is the essence of Roth's solution. It's a version of a basic economic situation: if I have some fish and want some cheese and you have some cheese and want some fish then we can exchange our goods and both gain. The thing is, it's hard to find each other, which is why we use money: I sell my fish for £3 and then go and buy some cheese.

Roth designed a system that allowed advantageous exchanges of kidneys without any money changing hands. The first thing is to keep a database of kidney donors and kidney patients. The database is used to find matching kidneys and to exchange them. With advanced mathematics and computer programming Roth was able to calculate complex sequences of exchanges between patients and donors which found matching kidneys for many more patients than before. His method was used to create the New England Program for Kidney Exchange, which worked across fourteen kidney transplant centres in New England in the United States. Thousands of patients received kidneys who wouldn't otherwise have done.

Roth's system shows what a huge difference economics can make to people's lives. It's also an example of a different type of economics. So far we've thought about economics as describing how the economy works and judging how well it works. Economists like Roth go further: they use economic theories to create new parts of the economy out there in the real world. Even though it doesn't involve buying and selling, kidney exchange is like a market in the sense that it allows people to swap things with each other. When Roth set up his database and computer programmes he created something similar to a market where none existed before. It's an example of a new field of economics known as 'market design'.

Most of us will never need to get hold of a kidney, of course. A really famous example of market design – one to do with the mobile phones in our pockets – affects many more of us, and in contrast to kidney exchange it involved buyers paying huge sums of money to sellers. In the 1990s and 2000s, governments hired economists to help sell licences to companies who wanted to use the radio spectrum to set up mobile phone networks. When you're selling apples it's easy: you look at how much apples sell for and sell yours for that amount. But governments couldn't do that for spectrum licences: these kinds of licences had never been sold before and no one knew how much they were worth. Governments decided to auction them. In an auction one seller tries to get the best price from a group of competing buyers. Auctions have been used for centuries to sell artworks and crops. In ancient times there were slave auctions, and once the entire Roman Empire was put up for auction. What's different in today's auctions is that many of them were designed by economists using an important new field of economics called 'auction theory'.

In auctions, some people know more than others. In an art auction, bidders know how much they value a painting, but the seller doesn't. Bidders want the painting for as low a price as possible. They'd like to pretend that they value the painting less than they really do. Sellers, on the other hand, want to make sure that winning bidders pay their true valuations. Here, sellers and bidders are playing a game with each other in which some people have more information than others, so auction theory draws on the tools of game theory and information economics that we came across in earlier chapters. Designing auctions is about solving problems of strategy and information to make sure that the bidder with the highest valuation wins, and that the seller maximises profit.

Auction theory begins by looking at what happens in different kinds of auctions. You're probably familiar with the ascending auction, often used to sell antiques. An auctioneer stands behind a Ming vase and shouts out a price, inviting bidders to offer increasing prices until there's only one bidder left. The auctioneer bangs down her hammer, and the winning bidder pays the amount bid and takes home the vase. In the Netherlands, millions of flowers are sold each day using descending auctions. The auctioneer starts at a high price and then lowers it until someone offers to buy. Descending auctions are fast, and so are useful for selling flowers that need to be sold before they wilt. Houses are sometimes sold in 'sealed-bid' auctions in which each bidder submits a bid in a sealed envelope. The person with the highest bid pays the amount that they bid and gets the house.

Imagine you're taking part in a sealed-bid auction for a house which to you is worth £300,000. How much would you bid? Probably not £300,000. You'd be strategic about it and bid a bit lower, say £250,000, so that if you won you'd make a 'profit' of £50,000. Auction theorists call it 'shading' your bid. But the seller wants to get as high a price for the house as possible and so wants you to bid your true valuation of £300,000.

In the 1960s the Canadian economist William Vickrey (1914–96) worked out an ingenious solution to the problem of shading. He devised a type of auction in which bidders have every incentive to be truthful. In standard sealed-bid auctions the winning bidders pay an amount equal to their own bid, the highest bid. Instead of the 'first-price' sealed-bid auction, Vickrey proposed a 'second-price' auction in which the winning bidder is the highest bidder but pays an amount equal to the second-highest bid. Suppose that in a second-price house auction you bid £250,000, rather than your true valuation of £300,000. Shading your bid wouldn't affect how much you'd pay for the house should you turn out to be the highest bidder because you'd only pay the second-highest bid. But in bidding £250,000 you'd lose the house if someone else bid over £250,000, so the best you can do is to bid your true valuation. Vickrey wasn't the first to have the idea. In the eighteenth century, the German writer Goethe sold a publisher one of his poems using a second-price auction. Today, eBay auctions work roughly according to the second-price principle, although they're not true Vickrey auctions. One complication is that participants' bids are revealed as the clock ticks, which encourages tactics like waiting until the last moment to place bids.

The catch with Vickrey's auction is that the seller has to settle for an amount equal to the second highest rather than the highest bid. Which auction is the best? It depends. One factor is bidders' attitudes to risk. People are commonly scared of risky situations – those in which they have a chance of winning a lot or winning nothing. Shading your bid in a first-price sealed-bid auction is risky. If you bid £250,000 for a house that you value at £300,000 then you might win and make a £50,000 profit, but you might be outbid and end up with nothing. If you hate risk you'll tend to shade less, perhaps bidding £290,000. In the first-price auction your aversion to risk makes you bid close to your true valuation, and that's what you'll pay if you win. In the second-price auction, you'd only have to pay the second-highest bid. In this case it's possible that the seller would get more money in a first-price than a second-price auction.

There are many different kinds of auctions in theory, but in the real world economists have to tailor their designs to the context. The British economist Paul Klemperer (b. 1956) led a team that designed Britain's third-generation mobile phone licence auction held in 2000. The design was a bit like the ascending auctions used to sell things like antique vases. But the government had several licences to sell, so they were sold at the same time in repeated rounds of bidding. All bidders had to bid on something in every round, which helped keep the bidding lively.

One problem with this kind of auction is that bidders can be crafty and use early rounds of bidding to signal to each other about who should get which licences, then ease off on their bidding. This had happened in similar auctions held in America in the 1990s. Two companies, U.S. West and McLeod, were bidding against each other for a licence with the identifying code of 378 in Rochester, Minnesota. Bids were coming in round numbers: $200,000, $300,000 and so forth. Then U.S. West put in a bid of $313,378 for a licence in Iowa, which up until then it hadn't been bidding hard for, but for which McLeod had been. U.S. West was telling McLeod: drop Rochester or we'll mess up your plans in Iowa. It had the intended effect. McLeod dropped out of the

Rochester bidding and U.S. West dropped out of Iowa, each leaving the other an easy run.

Klemperer wanted to avoid this sort of thing, so in the UK auction bidders weren't allowed to bid for more than one licence. They had to go for the licence that they really wanted, so they couldn't play tricks with other bidders. Anticipating these sorts of problems is crucial to good auction design. Sometimes really bad designs can cause an auction to totally flop, like the one for a television station licence in New Zealand, which attracted a single bidder, a university student who got the license for NZ$1. Klemperer's design avoided the pitfalls and the auction was the biggest ever, raising £22.5 billion for the government. It was a triumph of economics in the real world.

Traditionally, arguments about economics have been to do with broad questions. Is capitalism a better system than communism? Why do the economies of some countries grow so much faster than others? Economists like Roth and Klemperer have turned economics towards questions that are narrower but still very important. The first economists were philosophers and political thinkers as much as they were economists. Many of today's economists see themselves more like engineers designing bridges and dams. Like engineers with cranes and measuring gauges, economists use their own tools – clever theoretical models and advanced mathematics – to solve specific problems. Perhaps it's no coincidence, then, that Roth and Klemperer started off as engineers, later turned to economics and helped turn economic principles into powerful tools for designing the real-world economy.

CHAPTER 38

Bankers Go Wild

In the late 2000s in San Antonio, Texas, a woman painted big letters onto the side of her house: 'Help!! Foreclosure!!' A bank was about to take ownership of her home (in other words, to carry out a 'foreclosure') because she couldn't repay the loan that she took out to buy it. In London, bankers walked out of the shiny offices of the investment bank Lehman Brothers clutching cardboard boxes containing the belongings from their desks. Their bank had just gone bust, the biggest company failure in history. In Athens in 2010, thousands of people stormed Greece's parliament, furious with the government for cutting wages and pensions. Three people died when some of the protestors set fire to a bank. These events, thousands of miles apart, were connected by a breakdown in the world's financial system, which after 2007 made the entire global economy tumble over. The collapse was given gloomy-sounding names: the Global Financial Crisis, the Credit Crunch, the Great Recession. Today we're still recovering and still arguing about how to fix things.

The crisis was a complete shock – even to economists. During the 1990s they'd hailed the Great Moderation, an era of steady economic growth with low inflation. Now it looked as if they'd been much too cheerful. Occasionally, though, economists step away from conventional thinking and are ahead of their time. The American Hyman Minsky (1919–96) was one. Although he was no longer alive when the crisis came, he was rediscovered when it hit; many people believed that his ideas explained what happened better than conventional economics could. Second-hand copies of his books started selling for hundreds of pounds. The crisis got yet another name: 'the Minsky moment'.

In the 1980s, free-market economics had made a comeback. Economists believed that when left alone the economy was fairly stable, without wild accelerations and crashes. Minsky, on the other hand, thought that capitalism runs into crises. This made him a bit of a radical. His attitude might have had something to do with his upbringing: his parents were socialists, Russian-Jewish immigrants who had met at a party to celebrate the centenary of the birth of Karl Marx. However, Minsky was inspired not so much by Marx but by Keynes, who believed that capitalist economies fall into slumps.

Even to Keynesians, Minsky was unconventional. He emphasised aspects of Keynes's thought that he believed the conventional interpretation had overlooked. One was that investment takes place in deep uncertainty. If you build a factory today you don't know how much money you'll make in five years when it opens. One way to view the position is as a set of probabilities about outcomes. There's a 50 per cent chance that your market will grow and a 50 per cent chance that it will shrink. Deep uncertainty is different because you don't know the probabilities, or even what the various outcomes might be. Investment therefore depends on people feeling optimistic – Keynes called it their animal spirits – rather than on a favourable mathematical calculation of the probability of profits in the future. When people's animal spirits dampen down, investment falls and the economy sags.

Keynes thought that money is what allows economic decisions to take place over time, especially when the future is so uncertain. A surprising feature of a lot of standard economic theory is that it says little about money and banks, the very things that you might expect it to be about. This is because the basic theory of markets is to do with the buying and selling of real things. You sell me potatoes so that you can buy yourself a scarf; what matters is how many potatoes you need to sell to get a scarf. Here money smooths the swapping of potatoes for scarves, but on its own it doesn't do much. To Minsky this was the wrong way round. Money, and the banks that help create it by making loans, are what power the economy – and what eventually lead it into a crisis.

Minsky said that as capitalism develops it becomes unstable. At first, banks are cautious about who they lend to. When you decide to open a business in the hope of a return you're betting on the future. You pay for the bet by taking out a loan from a bank. The bank tries to find out whether you'll be able to repay. Are you likely to earn enough to repay? Have you tended to repay loans in the past? It does the same when you borrow money to buy a house or a car. If you obtain the loan, every month you pay interest to the bank as well as some portion of the original loan. The amount of the outstanding loan gets smaller and eventually you pay it off completely.

Minsky says that cautious capitalism gives way to daring capitalism: more people want to borrow, and banks want to lend to them because it makes them a profit. Banks start to compete for borrowers and so they invent new kinds of loans to give to borrowers with less ability to repay. They give loans for which borrowers only have to pay the interest each month. When the original loan comes up for repayment the bank extends it. In the years leading up to the financial crisis, banks began giving out housing loans on these terms. Minsky called it 'speculative lending': the loans are a bet that house prices won't fall and that interest rates won't rise, so borrowers won't get into trouble with their loans.

Daring capitalism then turns into reckless capitalism. The economy is racing ahead and even more people want to borrow. The banks start giving loans to people with very little ability to repay – borrowers on the lowest incomes or with histories of not repaying. These are loans for which they don't even have to pay the interest. Each month the bank adds the interest to the original loan, and the size of the loan grows. The banks and the borrowers count on the price of houses continuing to rise so fast that they'll stay larger than the size of the loans. After a few years, when borrowers sell their houses, they'll have made enough on the value of their houses to repay.

Now lenders and borrowers' animal spirits are fired up. Banks give out loans hoping that house prices will keep rising, but by lending so much money they help to push up prices. In the ten years leading up to the crisis, American house prices more than doubled. Lenders and borrowers were creating a self-fulfilling upwards spiral, what economists sometimes call a bubble. Minsky called the reckless system of lending 'Ponzi finance' after a famous Italian swindler named Charles Ponzi whose crooked schemes worked by creating bubbles that pulled in more and more gullible investors.

The problem with bubbles is that they burst. Then comes the Minsky moment, when lenders get cold feet and start asking for their loans to be repaid. They stop lending to risky borrowers and house prices stop rising quite so quickly. That undermines the system of Ponzi finance, which depends on fast rises. People start selling houses, and prices fall. Borrowers find that they can't make their repayments and the banks start to take possession of their homes. Construction companies stop building new houses, invest-ment in the economy stops and the country falls into a recession. This is what happened after 2007.

Minsky said that innovations in financial markets help cause speculative and Ponzi finance. An important one in the run-up to the financial crisis was 'securitisation'. A security is a financial asset, such as a share in a company that can be bought and sold. When a company sells you a share, the share entitles you to an annual payment (a dividend). When you sell the share, the person you sell it to receives the payments. In the years before the financial crisis, housing loans were used to make securities that could be bought and sold. The securities were a financial cocktail of different loans. Whoever bought a security received the loan repayments from the owners of the houses. However, many of the loans were 'subprime' loans: ones made to people who were at a high risk of not being able to repay them.

Given how fast house prices were rising, the securities looked like rather tasty cocktails. They were also incredibly elaborate ones. (To properly understand what some of the securities contained you'd have had to read a billion pages of documents!) So the investors buying them didn't really know what the ingredients were – and didn't foresee what an almighty headache they'd give them. In times of cautious capitalism, banks keep hold of the loans they make and find out as much as possible about their borrowers to make sure that they can repay. At one time bank managers knew their customers personally and would only lend to people who they thought were trustworthy. When loans are packaged into securities and then sold on, why bother being so careful? To buyers, the securities looked like safe investments. The result was that information stopped flowing through financial markets and, as we saw in Chapter 33, without information markets stop working properly.

Because of securitisation, the loan payments of the woman in San Antonio weren't necessarily received by the San Antonio branch of her Texan bank. They might have ended up with an investment bank in London that had bought some of the securities into which her loan had gone. The bank knew nothing about the woman, but when she stopped paying back her loan it lost money. Lehman Brothers had bought so many of the securities that the bank fell when millions of homeowners stopped repaying. Banks stopped lending to each other because they feared that other banks might go bust. They also stopped lending money to people who would have been perfectly capable of repaying their loans. The whole system of finance – the channelling of money from savers to people who use the money to buy houses or set up businesses – ground to a halt.

In response to the crisis, America, China and European countries embarked on policies that signalled the return of the thinking of Minsky's intellectual ancestor, John Maynard Keynes. As Keynes had recommended, they increased spending to revive the economy, and their efforts seemed to help. During recessions, governments' deficits – the gap between their spending and their revenue – typically rise because when people and businesses earn less, the amount of tax collected goes down. Governments borrow to fill the gap, so their debts rise too. After a few years of Keynesian policies, governments in Europe began to worry about their rising deficits and debts. They reversed the policy to one of 'austerity': cuts to spending on public services and welfare benefits. Keynesians argue that austerity came too soon. The time to reduce the deficit is when the economy is firing again, they say. Then high employment and profitable firms increase tax revenue. Until then, austerity will only slow growth.

In Greece an austerity policy was a condition for getting help from the European Union when the government found that it couldn't repay its debts. When Greece's government cut spending on public services like hospitals, the protestors flooded onto the streets. Economists even started to wonder whether Europe's currency, the euro, would survive the turmoil. In Greece over a quarter of the population ended up out of work. Many fell into poverty, unable to afford food and medicine, and became sick and depressed. Greece was one of the worst affected, but the suffering went on around the world as people lost their homes and jobs. By 2009, an extra 30 million people were out of work.

Minsky's theory tells us that the financial crisis and the recession that followed weren't exactly the result of greedy borrowers or bankers. The deeper reason was to do with the effects of finance-based capitalism. The decades of economic growth after the Second World War sowed the seeds of crisis. Capitalism became more reckless as the centres of banking – New York's Wall Street and the City of London – helped to fuel growth with fancy financial products, especially since the 1980s, when governments had removed restrictions on what the banks could do. Perhaps, then, it's more accurate to talk of a Minsky era than a moment. It took decades for capitalism to evolve from its cautious form into its reckless one.

CHAPTER 39

Giants in the Sky

Imagine you're watching an hour-long procession of the population lined up in order of income, from the lowest to the highest. Each person's height represents their income: someone earning the average is of average height and someone earning half the average is only half as tall. You're of average height and you're standing on the pavement watching the parade go by. What do you see? You might expect to see some short people first; then, about halfway through the parade, people as tall as you are (those on an average income falling halfway along the population); then to gradually see taller figures in the later stages as the high-earners go past.

In fact, if the parade was of America's population today, you'd see something different. First of all, you wouldn't know that the parade had begun because you wouldn't see the people right at the front. They're people with loss-making businesses or debts to repay. They have negative incomes, so they're burrowing along underneath the ground. Pretty soon, though, you find yourself looking down on minute figures passing in front of you at the level of your feet.

They're people doing low-paid part-time work, old people on small pensions and the unemployed on welfare benefits.

The first really major event of the parade is the approach of an army of dwarves stretching off into the distance. They're the lowest paid members of the full-time labour force, the backbone of the economy. You see thousands of burger flippers, dishwashers and cashiers walk by. They barely reach your waist. Gradually the people get bigger. Taxi drivers, meatpackers and receptionists pass you, then couriers, filing clerks and decorators. Thirty minutes in – midway through the population – the people going past still just come up to your chest. Only after the forty minute mark are the people in the parade able to look you in the eye; you smile at the flight attendants and sheet metal workers as they go past.

After that the parade looks down on you. Firefighters are a bit taller than you, and you find yourself having to crane your neck to wink at the scientists and web designers. After fifty minutes, immense figures sweep past: lawyers five metres, surgeons nine metres tall. In the last seconds, giants towering miles into the air thud past. Some are executives in big companies like Apple and Facebook. You even glimpse a few gargantuan pop stars and sportsmen – Katy Perry, Floyd Mayweather – the soles of their shoes as high as the buildings, their heads breaking the cloud cover.

The 'distribution of income' is the amount of money that goes to the rich, the middle and the poor, and it's sometimes pictured as this kind of parade. The parade illustrates something important. People at the top earn hugely more than the rest, pulling up the average level of income, which means that most people in the population earn less than the average. Statisticians boil down what you saw into a bit of jargon: they say that society's income distribution is 'skewed'. Economists call it inequality.

In the 1970s the parade would have looked rather different. You'd still have seen giants at the end of it, but not quite such enormous ones. And you wouldn't have spent so much of the parade gazing down at tiny people filing past. Income was much more evened out across the population. Since then, the rich have made faster gains than the rest: in the 1970s, America's top 1 per cent of earners earned less than a tenth of the nation's income. By the first decade of the twenty-first century, it earned around a fifth.

Many people worry that inequality has become too pronounced. In the last few years, the Occupy movement protested against the rapid growth of the tallest giants, the so-called '1 per cent' of top earners. In major cities protestors camped out and set up makeshift universities where people debated the reasons for increasing inequality and what could be done about it. Economics professors joined the debate. The French economist Thomas Piketty (b. 1971) published a book in 2014, *Capital in the Twenty-First Century*, which examined the rise of the rich and confirmed fears about how fast they were pulling ahead of everybody else.

How did the giants get so huge? Karl Marx said that they're the capitalists who exploit the workers to make money; Joseph Schumpeter, that they're bold people who take risks and get rich when they get lucky. Conventional economics has a less colourful story. The question is what determines wages, most people's source of income. Economics says that workers are paid what they contribute to production. Educated people have skills that make them more productive, so they earn more. In recent decades techno-logical advances intensified the effect: people trained in computer programming and engineering were able to earn well. Unskilled workers – the burger flippers and cleaners – got left behind.

Piketty argues that things aren't as simple as this. He says that the extraordinary earnings of the tallest giants aren't the result of extraordinary productivity. It's easy to calculate the productivity of someone chopping wood – count how many logs they chop each day – but how do you calculate the contribution of an executive in a huge company like Toyota? The company's income depends on the efforts of thousands around the globe, and the productivity of just one of them is hard to pin down. Piketty argues that top incomes are determined instead by companies' habits and customs, and by what they've paid their top people in the past.

There's another ingredient of inequality: people's wealth, their houses and shares, and the businesses and land that they own. Income adds to wealth, but they're not the same thing: a retired person on a small pension who owns a valuable house has little income and a lot of wealth. Society's richest amass huge wealth: Bill Gates and Warren Buffett, with their fortunes of tens of billions of dollars, are spectacular examples.

Piketty found what he called a 'historical law of capitalism' that keeps the fortunes growing. People earn money from their wealth: profits from businesses and shares, and rents on land. If your businesses, shares and land are worth $10 million and earn you $1 million a year, then the rate of return on your wealth is 10 per cent. Piketty observed that over much of history the rate of return on wealth exceeded the growth rate of the economy. If the economy grows at a rate of 3 per cent, then your wealth expands 7 per cent faster than the output of the economy. Workers' wages are paid for out of economic output and rise when the economy gets better at producing things. Because the return on wealth exceeds economic growth, wages won't increase as quickly as your $10 million fortune does. Piketty summed it up with a formula that combined the rate of return on wealth, r, with the growth of the economy, g: $r > g$. (Piketty's book was so popular that some people even started wearing T-shirts with $r > g$ printed on the front!) Piketty found that the formula had been at work in America since the 1970s. By the twenty-first century, America's wealthiest 1 per cent owned around a third of the nation's wealth.

Economists are sometimes accused of not taking a strong position on the distribution of income. Some of them say that it's better to be in a wealthy society where a few people are much richer than the rest, than in a poor one where we're all equal but live on scraps. And a lot of modern economics is about efficiency rather than distribution. In Chapter 25 we met Kenneth Arrow and Gerard Debreu, who proved the First Welfare Theorem: under certain conditions markets are efficient in the sense that no resources are wasted. The problem is that many outcomes are efficient, including very unequal ones. They also proved something else. Suppose that out of the efficient outcomes there was one that society preferred, that with an even distribution of incomes. They showed that with some nudging, markets could get you there.

To nudge markets, governments need to redistribute by taking resources from the rich and giving them to the poor. But this upsets efficiency if it affects people's economic decisions, especially about how hard to work. So to reach the ideal point, the government must shift resources around without causing people to change their behaviour. Then markets guarantee efficiency and society can pick an equal distribution. In practice, though, this is pretty much impossible to do. The only way that the government can actually redistribute is to tax the money that rich people earn and give it to the poor. Then economists worry that too much tax will affect people's behaviour: why work hard if you lose some of your earnings in taxes? Economists talk of a trade-off between fairness and efficiency. Markets start off efficient – the First Welfare Theorem shows this – but when governments meddle by redistributing income they upset efficiency. So redistribution leads to greater equality, but a slower growing economy. You can picture the problem as using a bucket to carry wealth from the rich to the poor: there'll always be some spillage when you heave it along. How should society balance the gain in fairness with the leakage in efficiency?

The British economist Anthony Atkinson (b. 1944) says the dilemma is overstated. For one thing, the First Welfare Theorem doesn't hold in practice: markets don't begin in a state of efficiency which is then upset by redistribution. Markets often start off pretty inefficient. The bucket is leaking before you pick it up. For example, markets aren't efficient when people lack important information. One case is that in which employers can't observe how well their staff are working – but higher wages might encourage people to work hard, improving efficiency. A generous minimum wage could reduce inequality and improve efficiency, says Atkinson. There are other reasons why equality and efficiency might go together. Economists sometimes say that inequality encourages people to work in the hope of getting rich. But the hope becomes unrealistic when inequality is extreme. In that case, inequality doesn't make people work hard; instead they might despair of ever catching up. A productive economy also depends on its workforce being healthy and educated, and this comes under threat when lots of people are unable to afford healthcare or to invest in their education.

If we think that extreme inequality is unfair or threatens economic efficiency, can we do anything about it? Yes, says Piketty. Inequality is partly the result of the choices that societies make. After the Second World War growth was high and governments taxed the rich. A high g (growth) and a low r (return to wealth) kept inequality down. Since the 1970s, governments have cut taxes on wealth, pushing up r. After the global financial crisis the decline in economic growth made the difference between r and g even bigger, so inequality rose. Governments then reduced spending, which hurt the poor when public services were cut. This further pushed down growth, strengthening the rising trend of inequality. If the rise in inequality comes from how we run our economy, then it's in our power to reverse it, says Piketty.

Atkinson agrees. Along with a minimum wage, he recommends the encouragement of technologies that promote equality. It's easy to think of new technology as beyond our control, but it too is the result of our choices. If the government introduced a completely automated appointments system in hospitals, receptionists would lose their jobs while the engineers who designed the system would make lots of money. Rather than spend money on developing the new system, the government could decide to train people to be very efficient receptionists. This would lead to a more equal outcome through higher employment (and make people happier when they get to talk to a human at the hospital). And what about Piketty's formula of $r > g$? Would it be possible to bring down inequality by raising economic growth above the rate of return to wealth? Piketty thinks not. He recommends bringing it down by reducing the return to wealth: he proposes a global tax on the fortunes of the world's richest people. How likely is that? For the time being, not very, given the power and influence of the world's tallest giants.

Why Be an Economist?

Think of the last time you heard an economist talking on the news, maybe spouting tricky-sounding words about share prices, interest rates, or whatever. Perhaps you trusted what the economist said, thinking to yourself: 'Well, economists must know what they're talking about. Now let's get back to watching the football.' Leave economics to the professional economists, you might have thought. At the same time, economists often come in for a bashing. Some say that they care more about their impractical theories than the things that really make a difference to people's lives, and that on the whole they're not to be trusted. (Remember how in the nineteenth century Thomas Carlyle said that economics was the 'dismal science', while Thomas de Quincey suggested that economists had fungus for brains!)

With the global economic crisis at the beginning of this century, economists came in for even more of a bashing. Even Queen Elizabeth II doubted them. During the crisis she went to the London School of Economics and asked the economists there why none of them had seen the crisis coming. Many people thought that economists had completely lost touch with reality. They dreamt up clever mathematical theories but didn't bother with how the real economy outside their brains actually worked. Even famous economics professors said the same.

Economists simplify the world, and that's fine. To explain anything, you have to leave out what's least important to reveal what's most important. But critics said that economists had gone too far. They'd forgotten how complex the world beyond their theories really was. They'd made two dangerous simplifications. They believed that markets were efficient – that they lead to the best use of society's resources – and that on the whole people were rational – that they properly make use of information to weigh up costs and benefits. During the financial crisis, markets went badly wrong and people certainly weren't acting rationally. Economics had failed, it seemed. After all this, who'd choose to be an economist? In fact, next time you see economists talking on the news, instead of accepting what they say, perhaps you'll feel more like chucking a brick at the screen.

But hold on to your brick for a second. Economics has had its successes. Think back to our story of how economists designed systems to match kidney donors with patients and auctions to sell mobile phone licences. These would have been impossible without the nifty application of economic principles. Economics does well at solving these kinds of specific problems.

Perhaps these problems seem too specialised, though. To end our story of economics we'll look at a final economic idea, one to do with protecting the planet, the ultimate resource that we depend on for survival. It's nothing more than the application of basic economic principles that we've looked at in this book. It deals with global warming, a specific problem where economics can help a lot, and one that affects every one of us, our children and grand-children too. It shows that economics isn't removed from the real world, as some people say – far from it. Economics cares very much about the world and could help to save it.

Most scientists believe that the carbon dioxide released by factories when they burn coal or oil has caused global warming – a rise in the average temperature of the land and the oceans. It's also made the climate more unstable. This will have huge costs: floods and droughts will disrupt agriculture, particularly in Africa and Asia. When the ice caps melt, the sea level will rise and many villages and towns will suffer flooding; some may become uninhabitable.

To stop global warming it's not enough for us all to agree that it's bad. That on its own won't change our behaviour. To deal with the problem we need a dose of economics. Global warming is a version of a problem that economists have studied over and over: market failure. Specifically, global warming is an externality. As we saw earlier, an externality is an unintended side effect of something, such as the fact that your neighbour's loud trumpet-playing annoys you. Your neighbour doesn't have to pay the cost, so ends up playing too much. The American economist William Nordhaus (b. 1941) considers the emission of carbon dioxide a special type of externality because it extends over space and time. It spans the globe because carbon dioxide emitted by a German factory adds to the total stock in the earth's atmosphere and it's the total that affects the climate; German emissions affect farmers in China and Brazil. It spans generations because carbon dioxide emitted today will heat the planet for many decades to come; German emissions today will affect the unborn descendants of farmers in China and Brazil. Nordhaus calls emissions of carbon dioxide a 'double externality'.

Because carbon dioxide is such an extreme form of externality, far too much is emitted. What's the 'right' amount? Suppose that the last tonne of carbon dioxide released by a factory causes damage to the world's economies in ruined crops and flooded villages that adds up to £50. By avoiding the damage, not emitting the last tonne therefore has a £50 benefit. It would cost something not to emit it, though. Perhaps the factory would have to install filters in its chimneys. If they cost £40 it would be better for society as a whole for the factory to install them and not to emit the extra tonne. How far should the factory go in reducing its emissions? Economic principles imply that it should reduce them until the benefit from the last tonne of reduction exactly balances the cost.

Suppose that an economist adds up all the costs and benefits and says that society must halve its emissions. To achieve the reduction the government could require everyone to halve their emissions. It could even ban the burning of coal. Nordhaus says that by using principles of economics, governments can achieve the reduction at lower cost: they could get people to reduce their emissions by putting a tax on carbon. The idea is to make the costs of carbon have a greater influence on people's economic decisions. The government should set the tax at the level that ensures that society produces only half as much pollution as before.

The tax-based method is cheaper because some people can reduce their emissions more easily than others. Suppose the government puts a tax on petrol. Teachers can start cycling to work. The cost to them of reducing carbon emissions is low, less than the increased price of a gallon of petrol. Double bass players, however, can only get to rehearsals by car, so the cost to them of reducing their carbon emissions is high. They'd rather pay for the expensive petrol and continue to drive. Under a tax, people and firms with low costs of reducing carbon emissions cut their carbon use more than those with high costs. The government hits its target for emissions reduction at a lower overall cost to society than if it simply said that every individual and firm had to halve their emissions.

Another economic solution is to issue 'carbon trading permits'. They're certificates that allow whoever owns one to emit a tonne of carbon dioxide. Without a certificate you aren't allowed to emit at all. To bring about a target number of tonnes of emissions the government issues that number of certificates. Firms can then buy and sell the certificates. A firm that would find it hard to cut its emissions can buy a permit from a firm that could cut back more easily. As with a tax, polluters who can cheaply reduce their emissions cut back the most. In the 1990s America used permits to reduce the pollution that causes 'acid rain' which damages forests and lakes.

We are nowhere near solving the double externality of carbon emissions. A full solution will require cooperation between many societies with different attitudes to the environment. With less difficult environmental problems like acid rain, though, economics has helped, and Nordhaus believes that with a decisive application of the most basic tool of economics – the balancing of costs and benefits – we still have time to solve the problem of global warming and avoid a planetary disaster.

Despite its flaws, then, economics is vital to humanity. The most basic economic ideas are powerful tools for solving all sorts of problems, especially specific ones. These include those such as global warming, which will directly affect the quality of people's lives for generations to come.

But economics has struggled with broader questions about how human societies as a whole work. Do societies progress better with free markets and competition, or by people getting together and cooperating? What exact role should financial markets play in the growth of the economy? These kinds of questions are much harder to answer with simple economic principles. That's part of the reason why many economists didn't see the recent economic crisis coming. And long before the crisis, economists used their theories of free markets and rationality to redesign entire societies, such as in Africa in the 1980s and in Russia in the 1990s after communism ended. The results were disastrous. Economists pushed their basic principles too far and didn't understand the broader political and social aspects of societies that their theories left out.

If you study economics at university, you mainly learn about those basic economic principles. They're powerful and useful but you should use them with care. Some people think they're not really 'science' at all. They say that underneath economists' equations is a conservative political ideal that says that free markets, competition and individual effort are what matter above all else. A few years ago, students in Britain and America got fed up with their economics teachers and walked out of their classes. They believed that economics was a distortion of reality, and they wanted it to be more about the real world that's messy and unpredictable and hard to capture in equations.

But remember, too, that over the long sweep of history that we've seen in this book, thinkers looked at the economy in many different ways and held all sorts of political beliefs. Some were diehard supporters of capitalism, some wanted to fix it, some to destroy it. What tends to get left out of basic economics courses is the ideas of rebellious thinkers like Thorstein Veblen, Karl Marx and Friedrich Hayek, and even of the more accepted ones like Adam Smith and John Maynard Keynes. All of them were interested in the biggest questions of how economies and societies develop, less in the narrow ones about how people and firms weigh up costs and benefits when they're choosing a fridge or renting new office space.

The economists we've met in these pages came up with different ideas in response to the problems of their times. In economics there isn't one 'right' answer that stays right forever, like in a maths problem. By appreciating the different responses of history's thinkers we can be inspired to come up with our own, the new ideas we need in order to face today's economic problems, whether that's extreme inequality, financial crisis or global warming. Get them right and more of us have a chance of a good life; get them wrong and many will suffer. Some will die if they aren't able to get the food and medicine they need. It's a task for all of us, not just for professional economists.

At the start of our story we met the first people to think about economics: the philosophers of ancient Greece. They were concerned with life's most fundamental questions, ones that we grapple with to this day. What does it take to live well in a human society? What do people need to be happy and fulfilled? What makes them truly thrive? That's where economics started and, after all the arguments and disagreements, it's where it must begin from again.

Index

Page numbers in bold are where definitions of terms and concepts can be found.